Thomas M. O'Brien

Child Welfare in the Legal Setting
A Critical and Interpretive Perspective

D0223638

*Pre-publication
REVIEWS,
COMMENTARIES,
EVALUATIONS . . .*

"In this original and thought-provoking book, Thomas O'Brien draws upon the insights of postmodern organizational theories to expose the underlying processes that can damage and stigmatize families in the child welfare system. The author challenges the accepted view of child welfare as a social work function, arguing that the social work role is limited by its placement in the host setting of the legal system and describing the tensions and conflicts that make enormous demands on child welfare workers and families alike. O'Brien explores questions of critical importance to child welfare advocates, including the implications of the criminalization of child abuse, the industrialization of child welfare, mandatory reporting requirements, and the priorities of a system in which referrals without substantiated abuse amount to more than 85 percent of total referrals. His critique extends to the increasing trend toward practice specialization in which techniques are emphasized over mission and values, and assembly line operations over effective problem solving. In a very helpful discussion of the court process, the author clarifies the jurisdiction and purposes of each of the five discrete court systems that are involved in the protection of children and outlines the steps involved in investigating and adjudicating an abuse allegation.

O'Brien offers a sobering critique of the labyrinth that is the child welfare system, yet offers hope that the system can be improved. His recommendations are innovative, stimulating, and in opposition to traditional thinking. This book is both challenging and hopeful in its thorough and unconventional discussion of the child welfare system and the forces that all too often lead to community and family disruption rather than enhanced well-being. Students and social workers will be challenged to think deeply about the future of child welfare and the role of social workers in protecting children from abuse and neglect."

Linnea GlenMaye, PhD
*Associate Professor and Director,
School of Social Work,
Wichita State University*

More pre-publication
REVIEWS, COMMENTARIES, EVALUATIONS . . .

"*Child Welfare in the Legal Setting* offers readers a metacritique of the child welfare profession as it appears to an experienced public child welfare professional at the beginning of the twenty-first century. Mr. O'Brien argues for a complete restructuring of child welfare as we know it.

The book characterizes the public child welfare profession as an 'industry' or 'assembly line operation' employing 'child savers' and lamenting the 'McDonaldization' of child welfare social workers. Mr. O'Brien's discussion of the respective worldviews of attorneys and social workers, and his description of juvenile court as one of the host settings in which public child welfare social workers function, offers a creative framework for discussing the similarities and differences between the clinical and legal models of intervention. Mr. O'Brien's description of the legal process as a 'court work group' provides social workers with a conceptual model for better understanding how judges, lawyers, and other legal professionals function in the courtroom.

Overall, Mr. O'Brien's book offers a contrarian view of public child welfare and challenges some of the foundational principles that govern child welfare practice as it currently exists."

L. Michael Clark, JD
Lead Deputy County Counsel,
Office of the County Counsel,
Santa Clara County, CA

The Haworth Press®
New York • London • Oxford

This book has been given by

M. Bruce Gill, '93

Child Welfare in the Legal Setting
A Critical and Interpretive Perspective

Child Welfare
in the Legal Setting
A Critical and Interpretive Perspective

Thomas M. O'Brien

The Haworth Press®
New York • London • Oxford

The Haworth Press, Inc., 10 Alice Street, Binghamton, NY 13904-1580.

PUBLISHER'S NOTE
Identities and circumstances of individuals discussed in this book have been changed to protect confidentiality.

Cover design by Lora Wiggins.

Library of Congress Cataloging-in-Publication Data

O'Brien, Thomas M.
    Child welfare in the legal setting : a critical and interpretive perspective / Thomas M. O'Brien.
        p. cm.
    Includes bibliographical references and index.
    ISBN 0-7890-0147-0 (hard : alk. paper)—ISBN 0-7890-2351-2 (soft : alk. paper)
    1. Children—Legal status, laws, etc.—United States. 2. Social work with children—Law and legislation—United States. 3. Child welfare workers—Legal status, laws, etc.—United States. I. Title.
KF3735.O27 2004
344.7303'27—dc22

                                                                                    2003025273

CONTENTS

SECTION II: COURTS, MODELS, AND RITUALS

ABOUT THE AUTHOR

Thomas M. O'Brien, MSW, MBA, DPA, LCSW, is Assistant Professor at California State University, Chico. He holds a Master of Social Work degree from Saint Louis University, a Master of Business Administration degree from San Jose University, and a Doctor of Public Administration degree from the University of Southern California. He also holds clinical practice licenses in Nevada and California. Dr. O'Brien has worked in child welfare in Wisconsin and California and taught in schools of social work in California and Nevada. His experience in child welfare spans decades and includes work on a foster care study that led to a major change in the way foster care rates are set in California. While serving as a Calfornia NASW Director, he was on the first child welfare task force influential in the formation of the structure for funding Title IV-E in California.

Preface and Acknowledgments

This work began as a conventional approach to explaining action in public child welfare; however, as the result of research and inquiry it took another direction. The beginning of this work was my professional practice with a dependency investigation unit. The daily crisis situations, their resolutions, and the ongoing levels of tension innate to this environment brought to my consciousness the desire to understand the underlying nature of child welfare services. My interest then, as now, was not only to develop an understanding of the context of practice but also to incorporate views of child welfare that could make it easier for future social workers to understand it and to be more effective in negotiating its subtleties, protecting children, and helping parents.

Operationalizing this interest began a multiyear odyssey, a long period of study and research. Part of the fruits of this adventure is this book. I have endeavored to locate child welfare practice in a broad social, philosophical, and theoretical context. The current child welfare system reflects the values of the nation and the communities of which it is a part. Given the current state of child welfare depicted in the works of such social work theorists as Richard Gelles, William Epstein, Leroy Pelton, and Duncan Lindsey, it is obvious that we as a nation are not clear on our understandings of what the child welfare system is meant to do, and the current system is clearly in trouble.

Along the way, this work has become revolutionary in that it has come to embody, as a verbal picture, both traditional conceptions of practice and a critical and interpretive perspective. The picture of child welfare that ultimately developed shows the limited nature of our collective concerns for children and families. As a critical work, it depicts professional practice as practice within a tension-laden social institutional context. These tensions result from incongruities between the philosophy, the mission, the function, and the context of child welfare. It also embodies tensions within the practice setting including those within the legal setting, practice community members, advocacy groups, and even within our own agencies.

Child abuse and neglect, in this new picture, is socially constructed within the practice environment, including local communities. As such, it is not something that is hard and fixed—that is, it is not something we can all recognize as, for example, the green of a sycamore leaf in summer. It is dependent upon a hermeneutic circular action including productive and reproductive actions involving a confluence of collective thoughts, feelings, and actions driven by social and psychological forces. This perspective suggests that the enforcement of laws surrounding child abuse and neglect has some latent consequences. This joining of law enforcement and child protection has within itself a basic tension that affects the practice context.

We invariably treat children who have been abused or neglected differently than children who have not been abused. We give them pity, place them first on counseling waiting lists, give them special treatment in school settings, etc. In this sense, we inadvertently treat them as beings that have problems or deficits, and in this sense we negatively devalue or stigmatize them as "victims."

Inherent in our approach to children and families within the child welfare system are value conflicts. These are value differences between individuals qua individuals and the collective social community. Conflicts arise between the individual person and the collective social world, that is, the community typically represented within the legal system. As an interpretive work, this book is meant to uncover and present a picture of some of these tensions involving child welfare's mission and its social function. In particular, it is meant to bring to light some of the underlying effects of child welfare interventions.

The book also concludes that some major changes would improve the child welfare system. These recommendations evolved during my metaphoric travels; they are a natural outcome of my odyssey and are actually far removed from where my trip began. For example, my trip began in an agency that was almost exclusively university-trained social workers. From the experience, my conclusion is that changes in the conception of social workers must be made to improve child welfare. Generally, the social work profession considers only university- or college-trained social workers to be professionals. In my view, agency-trained social workers are important in the child welfare system. Child welfare is simply too complex and the educational needs of social workers so great that, in addition to college or university training, agency-specific training is needed for practitioners. To some this may be viewed as heresy; to me it is a realistic view of the needs within the field and a statement that new ways to conceptualize and organize child welfare practice are needed.

My so-called heresies do not stop with this one issue. I now believe that public child welfare organizations must be opened up within their respective domains, their communities. This should not only include the use of volunteers but also involve local community control of programs. I also believe that mandatory reporting and the dual role of social workers limit this new "open child welfare" system. Here I find myself agreeing with theorists such as Richard Gelles and Leroy Pelton regarding the need for major changes in child welfare.

This book is meant to be a supplemental text in college or university classes or a general work for the education of social workers in major training centers. It does include coverage of the competencies associated with current Title IV-E requirements as they relate to court and administrative issues. Although the book is not about economics, sociology, psychology, political science, or even philosophy, its theoretical base is grounded in all of these. The book is conceptual, but an attempt has been made to write it in an understandable and, hopefully, interesting style for those initially studying child welfare. I have avoided much of the jargon of these fields and of the social work profession and tried to be as clear and as straightforward as possible, given the degree of complexity within this domain. Ambiguity in this work is, at least in part, due to the fruits of my journey into the complex labyrinth of the context of child welfare practice. In addition, some of the ambiguity is due to the nature of the child welfare system itself or the theory that is traditionally used to describe it. Vignettes present word pictures of some of the issues involved in child welfare practice. In particular, these are meant to describe scenarios that typically defy traditional descriptions. The vignettes, including the names of people and places, are constructed by the author from his many years of experience in many different settings. Any resemblance to actual people or places is coincidental. These vignettes are designed to supplement the written narrative and to promote further analysis, thought, and discussion by the reader.

It should be emphasized that this is a critical and interpretive study—an extended explanatory sketch—rather than a practice text in the traditional sense. In this sense it is also not an "analysis" of child welfare practice. It provides neither the detailed and exhaustive study of child welfare specific to a particular jurisdiction nor the precise and empirical tests typically associated with research in social work. Its objective is to provide a new way to understand the broad context of child welfare practice. The experience drawn on for this work includes both rural and urban child welfare practice and practice in multiple states. Therefore it is written on a general level. I hope to suggest new paths for understanding and balancing—dealing with—the conflicts inherent in the social structural context of child welfare. More than anything else, this work is meant to challenge assumptions about child welfare and raise questions as to new directions for child protection.

My specific debts are many: to colleagues, friends, students, and family. All of these have provided assistance in helping me construct interesting puzzles and answers that have contributed to this work. In particular, I express my thanks to colleagues, social workers, and administrators at Santa Clara County Department of Family and Children's Services, from which I am emeritus; my professors at University of Southern California, fellow faculty at San Jose State University, University of Nevada, Las Vegas, and California State University, Chico, and students at the three universities. Some who have provided assistance at particular times and, therefore, need to be recognized include Roy Thompson and John Kirlin with conceptual perspectives; Toshio Tatara, Linnea GlenMaye, Ron Farrell, and Bill Epstein with encouragement; Sue Farr for her years of consultative support; and L. Michael Clark, Keith Thompson, and Sue Farr for reading some of this material. Ultimately, however, I am responsible for the book's shortcomings, although whatever value it has should be far more widely shared.

I also want to call attention to the help and assistance provided to me by the folks at The Haworth Press. They not only have graciously provided for extensions of deadlines but also have been most courteous and helpful in my contacts with them. In particular, the editorial work and assistance has been outstanding.

Last, and in some ways most important, has been the support from my spouse, Shirley, and my three children, Kristin, Steven, and Tanya.

Chapter 1

Beginnings

INTRODUCTION

This work is designed to present a word picture of the child welfare system that accurately depicts important aspects of the system's role within American society and culture. It uses a combination of interpretive and critical perspectives in depicting child welfare. It describes practice as tension laden, a characteristic of the critical perspective (White, 1986). It is interpretive because it involves deconstructing and analyzing aspects of the child welfare system with a goal of identifying underlying issues and patterns. This is what Dean and Fenby (1989) describe as interpretive. The most basic tension inherent in the child welfare system is that of the individual qua individual versus the administrative, statistical, or collective social world. In addition, a number of other points of tension arise due to conflicting values, program objectives, and goals, etc. Interpretation provides us with an understanding of the underlying effects of programs and policies in child welfare.

THE BOOK: AN OVERVIEW

This chapter presents underlying theoretical assumptions and important concepts that set the stage for materials presented in later chapters. These concepts are central to understanding the perspectives taken in this work and particularly to its central focus of analyzing public child welfare as intervention into family life.

Section I discusses the broad context of child welfare practice. This context includes the legal system as providing the sanction for intervention into family life with the concomitant authority for such intervention. Chapter 2 presents the social institutional perspective that locates child protection within the broader range of social problems relating to child well-being. The American child welfare system, in this context, is located within an international environment. This perspective provides an understanding of child abuse and neglect as social constructs.

Chapter 3 discusses the concept of governance with its dependence on public perceptions. These perceptions are directly related to the collective sense of legitimacy people have as to government's role in intervening in family life to provide for the protection of children. The most important aspect of this legitimacy is a basic trust individuals have of the abstract systems involved in governance. Chapter 3 also introduces a basic tension inherent within the child protection system and other social control systems. This tension is the inherent difference between individual wants, needs, and expectations and collectively expressed wants, needs, and expectations for the individual. The former are unique to the individual, while the latter are essentially "abstracted norms" to which the individual is expected to adhere.

Chapter 4 examines the multiple layers of policy and governance that provide the basic thrust of the child protection system. This includes concepts related to the blending of federal, state, and local monies, laws, and policies. These are each important in understanding the complexity of the child welfare system.

Chapter 5 discusses conceptions of organizations that are germane to understanding practice within the context of a bureaucratic organizational arrangement. This chapter discusses concepts and ideas from the organizational theory literature to explain the functioning of child welfare organizations. Chapter 6 highlights the idea that professional practice in child welfare is practice within a host setting, the legal setting. Whether this host setting for practice is positive or negative is not relevant. However, what is important is the adaptation that workers must make within this setting. The legal system and the administrative system, both of which the social worker is accountable to, are the source of some underlying tension affecting practice. This chapter also shows the embedded nature of social work in family and children's services with the legal system.

Chapter 7 shows court adaptations to the stresses of handling a high volume of cases. These include the role of metaphor and stereotypes in the processing of cases.

Section II of the book examines the child welfare system itself. It emphasizes three different models for viewing child welfare. Chapter 8 examines the organization of the court system within the federalist system. This includes a discussion of the various courts along with their primary purposes and strengths and weaknesses. Chapter 9 presents the first of three models used to view the child welfare system. The first model, the concentric circles model, presents a macro- or large-scale, top-down view of the overall performance of the child welfare system. The second model, presented in Chapter 10, is the rational legal model of legal and court action. This model presents the logical legal steps involved in case situations as they proceed through adjudication, disposition, and exit from the system. This model highlights the potential steps rather than the working level action involved in all cases. This model is most often used to train social workers to work within child welfare.

Chapter 11 presents conceptual material important in understanding the third model, the ritual process model, which analyzes child welfare interventions, including court interventions, as ritualized processes. This model combines elements of anthropology, psychology, and sociology within the context of the legal system and is discussed in Chapter 12. Important in viewing action in this context is the process of affixing stigma to individuals and families. This particular model depicts the most accurate picture of the role of social workers working with families within the total context of child welfare.

Section III begins with Chapter 13, which discusses the fiduciary, ethical, and moral foundations of practice and discusses some of the implications drawn from the material in the book. In particular, it highlights the social institutional context of ethical and value-based decision making. It argues for a shift in thinking about ethical issues involved for practitioners in child welfare. The last chapter, Chapter 14, brings together the logical streams from the other chapters as it summarizes material and suggests improvements for the child welfare system. The streams it brings together include those directly discussed in the analysis and some that are more subtly presented as in vignettes.

SOME IMPORTANT CONCEPTS OR ASSUMPTIONS

Several concepts or assumptions are important to the perspective taken in this work. The heart of the analysis presented is the idea that it examines the social and cultural world and argues for social work intervention in child welfare as needing to be strength based and centered on basic concepts of structure and process. In working with this structure and process focus, the legal system, represented by the juvenile court, is the dominant agency providing sanction for this area of professional practice. Although the juvenile court is involved in only a small percentage of total referrals, it represents the social worker's right to intervene in family life and therefore acts as either threat or action in virtually all referrals into the child protective system. In addition, an important consideration in understanding practice in child welfare is that it requires many ways of knowing. The perspective taken here is largely one that views the individual as a meaning-creating being, one who lives within a world of "abstract systems" including social institutions. This perspective is meant as a complementary view to more traditional conceptions of child welfare practice.

Intervention As Structure and Process: Assumptions

Intervention into family life in public child welfare requires legitimate grounding within a system of authority. In addition, it also requires the practitioner to understand the intervention process within this system of authority. An intervention style that emphasizes a structure-and-process approach to working with clients and the larger child welfare system satisfies this requirement. From this perspective, the social worker's role is that of mediating the natural tensions between the individual qua individual and our collective social institutions. In this sense, the social worker must blend individual or subjective perceptions and interpretations of the world with the collective or positivist orientation that dominates our social institutions.

The centering concepts of "structure" and "process" provide a solid foundation for understanding and mediating tensions and disparate conceptions within the child welfare system. The idea of structure suggests a hierarchical view of social life, but it also suggests boundaries for social processes. Structure in this usage refers to the relatively stable processes or characteristics that form the organizational boundaries within which socially sanctioned processes are performed. Thus, the idea of structure is not so much meant to suggest a fixed determinate item but rather a slow-moving process that presents a picture of social life as composed of social roles, group norms, affectional ties, and patterns of conflict management (Ephross and Vassil, 1988; Turner, 1969; Schwartz, 1974).

Vignette: Structure and Process

The new child protective services (CPS) social worker, Ben, consulted with his supervisor. He had just finished interviewing a parent having a problem with substance abuse. He was excited and virtually shouted as he crossed the room:

"I got it. I finally got it. This idea of structure and process is like rolling a ball of wool for a cat. By rolling it out in a particular direction, you provide a structure that keeps the cat's attention. The rolling string constitutes a process that leads the cat along. When I saw my client today, I just worked with her within the process of the court and its expectations. I focused on this context and helped her to sort out her situation within this context. This then becomes only one of many appointments we will have and the process is how we connect them within the structure (the court)."

The administrative and legal systems provide the structure that focuses and directs social work intervention. Social work intervention in this sense is a socially sanctioned set of processes that constitutes continually emerging characteristics of structure. They involve information exchange, social comparisons, specific social reinforcements, decision making, and even support (Ephross and Vassil, 1988). The purpose of child welfare intervention is to protect children from parental or caretaker abuse and neglect. This, by the nature of the structure of the child welfare system, means that the system is meant to keep children free from the recurrence of abuse and neglect by parents or caretakers.

On a theoretical level, structure can be viewed as the roots of a tree and the processes, as the branches, leaves, or fruit, as the continually emerging manifestations of the structure. Alternately, structure can be viewed as an agency's organizational form including goals and objectives that continually emerge as a social worker meets and serves clients either through direct practice or through making referrals to other agencies. The structure is also the laws and policy that provide the context and direction of practice.

Just as laws change over time, so do agency policies. This conception of structure and process views changes in laws and policy as structure, that is, as composed of the same elements that vary only in the rate at which they change (Turner, 1974). In Turner's (1969) view, the rate at which a particular process moves determines whether it appears to an individual as a process or a structure. In this view, there is no such thing as a fixed social structure. There are only slow-moving "statistical structures." In Turner's (1974) words,

> all is in motion but some social flows move so slowly relatively to others that they seem almost as fixed and stationary as the landscape and the geographical levels under it, though these too, are, of course, forever in slow flux. (p. 44)*

Underlying this emphasis is a view of the helping process that is central to helping clients confront and resolve problems in living which have brought them into the child welfare system. This is a "growth-centered" approach to social work practice, which is grounded within the history of social work practice and has led, at least in part, to the strengths perspective. Its underlying philosophy is that of the functionalist school and includes the philosophy and social work teachings of Virginia Robinson and Jessie Taft, social psychology teachings of George Herbert Mead, and the philosophy and psychology teachings of Charles Peirce, William James, and John Dewey. These are discussed in more detail later in this chapter.

The thrust of social work practice in child welfare is described by Smalley (1967) in her work on generic social work practice. She notes that the function of social work practice is to "release human power in individuals for personal fulfillment and social good, and to

---

*Structure then, in Turner's usage, is temporal. It is relative to the rate of perceived movement of the particular processes that are being viewed. If one views relatively fast-moving processes as a football game or even a football season, one is well aware of the rate of change and the fact that one is viewing a series of acts and dramas. As one observes the governance action of a board of supervisors, it is much more difficult to see the role and performance as purely process. However, when viewed from the perspective of twenty to thirty years, the role, activities, and even routine of these boards have changed considerably. Probably the board's role as a transportation board is a good example of its taking on additional functions and activities.

release social power for the creation of the kind of society that makes social self-realization most nearly possible for all people" (p. viii).

An underlying assumption in this work is that all individuals, including parents and children, have the capacity to rise above adversity and express an unlimited potential for improving their lives. This is not to be confused with the idea that everyone is or can be an adequate parent. However, it assumes, as does Saleebey (1997), that social work practice involves "a collaborative process depending on clients and workers to be purposeful agents and not mere functionaries. It is an approach honoring the innate wisdom of the human spirit, the inherent capacity for transformation of even the most humbled and abused" (p. 1).

Vignette: Sandy, a New Worker

Sandy, a new CPS social worker, found herself confused by the complexity of the court process. She shared this with her supervisor, who suggested that the court process was, in a way, simple:

"When you go out on a referral, you have a very limited role. This is written in law. You are expected to investigate to determine if the child has been abused or neglected. If the child has not been abused, then you must close your referral. If the child has been abused, then you need to determine if the child is safe. If the child is not safe, then the child comes into custody. If the child is safe, then you need to determine if services are needed by the family. If they are not, then you close your case. If they need services, you make a referral for services and decide if they need an ongoing social worker, etc.

"This is the first part of the process. It is all written out in laws and regulations. When you need to file a petition, come back to me and we will go over the second part of this structure. You will get it naturally as you gain experience over time."

Structure in public child welfare includes a combination of steps required by agency and court protocols that are set in federal, state, and local law and policy. As a major principle of her approach to social work practice, Smalley (1967) has described the action of structure as follows: "A conscious, knowing use of structure as it evolves from and is related to function and process introduces form, which furthers the effectiveness of all the social work processes, both primary and secondary" (p. 162).

In contrast to structure, process is described as a "course of operations" that refers to "the nature of the interacting flow which results from the use of a specific method" (Smalley, 1967, p. 17). In this situation, the interacting flow is related to the interchange that occurs between the social worker (a representative of the social institutions) and individual clients (children and adults as part of families). This is the nexus or joining point of the macrolevel society: the collective social world and the individual. The relationship between the two is described by Smalley (1967), as she notes that "structure or form in each of the social work processes should arise from the process itself, and serve to channel, contain, and make that process effective toward the realization of some agency function or purpose" (p. 162).

Vignette: Sandy Again

The child welfare worker is speaking with a parent on the front porch of the family home: "I really need to interview your daughter. If you don't let me do this, I may have to either contact the police or go to court and get a judge's order. Either way, you may be called upon to let me speak to your daughter to complete my investigation. You know that we share an interest in settling this situation as easily as we can, so the best way to do it is to let me talk with your daughter now. . . ."

This is Sandy, six months later, approaching the mother of a thirteen-year-old child. By now she had learned how to use the structure of the court process. However, what she is saying is exactly what might occur. She makes no promises, no threats. If the client wants to know more about what Sandy will do, Sandy might add that she will have a conference with her supervisor before she makes any move. That is, she sees her supervisor as part of a team. The client can decide what she wants to do knowing the potential outcomes. She can choose to let Sandy in or choose not to let her in. It is her choice and she knows the potential outcomes.

If the client chooses not to cooperate with Sandy, it is unclear what will happen; however, Sandy is being very clear about her own options. She does not know whether the police would respond or the judge would make an order, etc. Sandy by now has some idea about the reality of these options. However, since the court processes, aka structure, are not in her control she cannot ethically present these as most likely outcomes to the parent. She also cannot threaten, in my view, the client with court action since it is outside of her area of control. Sandy cannot speak as to what someone else may or may not do. To suggest otherwise is to provide false information to the client, thereby negating any potential for the formation of a trusting relationship.

Epistemological: What We Know and How We Know It

To be effective in public child welfare, the practitioner must be grounded in what Hartman (1990) describes as many ways of knowing. In particular, practice in this setting requires understanding of objectivist and subjectivist perspectives of knowing. The legal system, the administration of programs, and the juvenile court are oriented toward an objectivist view of reality and knowledge accumulation and centered on a logical positivist worldview. In this view, one reality is shared by everyone. In contrast, from a subjectivist perspective, the social world is individually and subjectively determined, and each individual holds his or her own singular view of reality. Although parts of such a reality are shared, for the most part reality is attributed to the meaning individuals ascribe to experience.

The social worker must realize that individual and subjectivist worldviews stand apart from, yet are linked to, the objectivist worldview of the child welfare system. This can be described as follows: The objective world is grounded in collectivist assumptions, while the subjective world is grounded in individualistic assumptions. The collective world is the world of aggregate data, statistical systems, and positivist research methodologies. These methodologies use not only statistics but also correlations and probabilities. In this sense, it is a world composed of statistical creations.

For example, statistical research can tell us which populations of children are at risk of being abused or neglected, and these children can become the targets of intervention. However, these statistical models with their emphasis on correlation cannot tell us with 100 percent certainty that a particular child has been or will be abused or neglected. It can only tell us the probability of such an occurrence. In contrast, the subjective world is the world of the one. In this world, we can potentially determine which individual child has been or is afraid of being abused or neglected.

In the sense that one approach talks about "statistical" worlds and the other talks about "real" worlds, a basic tension exists. When we treat families that are at risk as though they have abused or may abuse or neglect their children, we in effect stigmatize them—or as Erving Goffman (1963) would say, we negatively devalue them. We can see this concretely by simply asking how many of us were raised without being abused or neglected in high-risk families. The answer is that many of us were indeed raised in these families without abuse. There is an essential conflict or tension in our statistical worldview and the individual's personal worldview. In a sense, Boston's famed Irish-American poet-reformer, Bishop John Boyle O'Reilley, may have been right in his criticism of the Charity Organization Society's emphasis on gathering statistics describing the collective problems of clients instead of helping them with their personal problems. According to Trattner (1994), O'Reilley noted scathingly that the society "scrimped and iced, In the name of a cautious, statistical Christ" (p. 99).

The approach in this work in viewing individual behavior and action is that social reality is socially constructed, held by and unique to individuals. The central idea is that each individual constructs his or her own reality and holds a corresponding underlying belief in its efficacy in describing experience. That is to say, each person has a personal reality that he or she believes is accurate in describing the world (Rogers, 1989). This reality is constructed and reconstructed through a variety of social and psychological processes and has been described by Berger and Luckmann (1967) and Strauch (1989), among others.

THE INDIVIDUAL AS CONSTRUCTING MEANING

While public child welfare includes objectivist and subjectivist approaches to the world, a key linking device is the meaning that individuals and social groups ascribe to experience. The idea that the individual is a meaning-creating being is important in understanding the behavior of individuals. What is important in motivating individuals is that which they believe or interpret as important. In this sense, what others believe is true is less important than the meaning an individual attributes to the situation. For example, people will have a distrust of everyone connected with a court process if their past experiences have led them to a worldview of courts as untrustworthy. They cannot be expected to believe either a social worker or an attorney about matters connected to a court in such a situation. Each individual constructs or attributes his or her own meaning to events that occur in life.

While individual meaning serves to mediate objective and subjective realities, a key consideration is the action of individual consciousness. Individual consciousness operates to integrate thoughts and feelings in sense of self and social identity. The result is what C. S. Peirce (1955) describes from a pragmatist view of philosophy as the individual's "triadic" (p. 267) creation of his or her reality. In the larger social context, thoughts and feelings operate in action with language to develop and maintain social realities. Donald Schon (1983) describes this three-part process as it relates to professional practice as action thery.

To Peirce, our reality is the creation of the individual and is the result of this triune or triangle of interdependent actions by individuals. He refers to these feelings, thoughts, and actions. Of their interdependence, he notes:

> Triadic relation, mediation, genuine thirdness, thirdness as such—is an essential ingredient of reality, yet does not by itself constitute reality, since this category . . . can have no concrete being without action, as a separate object on which to work its government, just as action cannot exist without the immediate being of feeling on which to act. (Peirce, 1955, p. 266)

This concept of meaning as linking individual and collective levels has also been noted by social work theorists. Specifically, meaning serves as a linking concept to ideas of the individual self as objectively knowable and individual identity as subjectively knowable and formable through narratives or "stories" (Saari, 1991, 1992). From a clinical social work perspective, "it is the meaning system that is created in the individual—that bridges the gap between the person and the environment" (Katherine Nelson, 1985, cited by Saari, 1992, p. 217). Thus we have the individual through the creation of his or her own reality as finding meaning through mediating internal or subjective and external or objective phenomena. Through an act of consciousness, he or she finds what Schutz (1967) refers to as a "unity of meaning."

If we accept this linking role of meaning for the individual, it makes sense to ask the extent to which social phenomena determine or, at least, affect the formation of individual identities and conceptions of self. This is important in the sense of the question being one of the ways, if any, collective action changes perceptions of self and/ or one's identity. That is, do social institutional structures determine our behavior or sense of identity and, if so, in what way?

The answer is that broad-ranging social phenomena do affect one's social identity. Saari (1991) presents this as tied to the role of narratives, while Giddens (1991) suggests that "self-identity is . . . interpreted reflexively by the agent" (p. 53) and Corrigan (1987) describes language as important in this process as it contributes to the differential production "of subjectivities, or social identities" (pp. 30-31). Each presents a different rationale; however, each comes to the perspective of external phenomena playing an important role in the creation of social identities.

To summarize, whatever event occurs is important only to the extent that the individual attaches meaning to it. From this perspective it seems reasonable to presume that it matters less to children if they are not the favored children of their parents, than if they truly believe their parents love them. However, if they believe their parents do not love them, they may see adequate treatment as abusive treatment. The nature of the event that occurs is important to the extent to which it has an effect on the meaning the individual attaches to it. By using thought, feeling, and action, individuals construct their social realities through the establishment of meaning and attachments. They then use this meaning with its concomitant attachments to make decisions as to the behavior they become involved in. They then reattach themselves to the meaning they originally became involved with and so on. This circular or hermeneutic action returns to the individual as a new round of thoughts, feelings, and actions and ultimately new behaviors, a new circle, etc.

ABSTRACT SYSTEMS

These ideas of structure and process and meaning are essentially abstract ways of looking at or at least attempting to explain concrete phenomena. They are abstract in that they are essentially nonvisible, and in a sense they form conceptual or virtual realities that work on noncognitive levels to structure beliefs. We can show behavior that suggests these abstract concepts to us. For example, if a social worker tells a client that "the court has ordered you to participate in a drug counseling program," we would be accurate in labeling this action as using the abstract concept of structure in working with a client. The court bounds behavior and, through its order, represents the expression of its bounded collective will in intervening in the client's life.

As we know, this idea of abstract systems is important in the knowledge base of social work; however, it is particularly important if we are to understand the child welfare system. The child welfare system is essentially an "abstract system" (Giddens, 1990, p. 80), used here in the sense that it is composed of "symbolic tokens" and is itself an "expert system," the two components of abstract systems. These concepts are important to understanding the linkages between individual behaviors and collective action within the child welfare system. They are also important in understanding the fluid nature of the formation of the social categories of abuse and neglect. Abstract systems constitute the structure within which child welfare practice is grounded.

According to Giddens (1991) abstract systems are composed of two interconnected conceptual structures mentioned earlier, symbolic tokens and expert systems. Symbolic tokens serve as intermediary devices between a concrete level of experience and an expert system. Symbolic tokens essentially extract, store, and may serve as a medium of exchange for qualities extracted from concrete experience. Money and language are good examples of these tokens. In contrast, expert systems are essentially thought structures that surround us as we live our daily lives. These include conceptual structures that range from architects' beliefs in the efficacy of certain structures to the codified laws that we are expected to follow in our daily lives.

Symbolic Tokens

Money is probably the most easily recognized symbolic token. We can understand the operation of these tokens by examining the action of money in our market system. This idea of abstract systems and their development is easily traceable to the development of our market economy and to the formation of the early social welfare system. It is traceable at least to Marx's idea of the separation of the individual "value," a quality added to the manufacturing of products by workers in the production process, and its transfer to a symbolic token, that is, to money as a medium of exchange. The quality could be extracted, through the formation of property rights, stored in money, and then used later in exchange for goods or services. Since money had the capacity to store value, it contributed to the shift from the barter system to the market economy. That is, as money came into usage, the barter system of exchange gave way to the market economy and the social welfare system developed from its failings (Trattner, 1999).

On a more general level, we can say that we have a process in which qualities embedded in a production process are separated and stored and later used in some kind of transaction. These qualities that the worker embeds in the materials through production become embedded in symbolic tokens and can be stored or used in some future transaction. Money becomes a symbolic token, or kind of storage vehicle, for the value accumulated in the product or commodity through the investment of the worker in its production. Lefebvre (1968) describes this as "the form attains its perfection when every single commodity can be evaluated by one universal equivalent: money" (p. 47). As money became an abstracted and acceptable medium for storing and exchanging value, the barter system was replaced by the market system.

Symbolic tokens are essentially the media that hold the content, or quality, that has been extracted from concrete events as, for example, social interactions. Giddens (1990) notes that these tokens can be described as a "media of interchange which can be 'passed around' without regard to the specific characteristics of individuals or groups that handle them at any particular juncture" (p. 22). He suggests that money is the most common; however, power and language are two additional symbolic tokens. Language and its application to child welfare is discussed here.

Language, as a symbolic token, is probably the easiest to understand and most easily recognized in child welfare practice. As we have seen, a symbolic token essentially provides an intermediary role in the connection between producers and consumers of a product or service. Language serves to extract content or qualities from concrete experience and essentially stores this content and allows for its future use in transactions. In this sense, it operates in ways similar to money. However, to understand this, we need to understand the relationship between language and concrete experience.

Most of us tend to equate language, that is, language as a description of experience, with experience. However, this is a limited and erroneous view. Wittgenstein suggests that although we think of language being referential of experience, it is actually an alternate system (Monk, 1990). Language is not the same as that which it describes. Certainly it has connections and interpenetrates with experience. In this sense, the use of language in describing and explaining experience constitutes a kind of language game. While language is, in a sense, independent of experience, it also is interdependent with meaning related to experience and expressed in language. Hall (1987) notes that "linguistic reference is mediated by an abstract entity, namely a meaning or sense. In ordinary experience, we 'live in' our linguistic acts and their meanings function transparently. Attention is directed toward their objects, not their meanings" (Hall, 1987, p. 171).

The application of this to child welfare is straightforward yet to some extent abstract. In child welfare, the social worker's job is to investigate alleged events of abuse or neglect. In the course of these investigations, the social worker is expected to learn what happened and the context in which it happened. In doing this job, language becomes a symbolic token. Language is used to gather information on the concrete experience, the human interaction, and the context of the interactional event(s) of alleged abuse or neglect. Language is then used to reproduce the human interaction, the event(s) in case records, and potentially in a petition to the juvenile court. Thus, we can say the social worker's job is to disembed or extract interactional experience from concrete experience using language as a symbolic token or structure for storage in case records and for potential litigation in court. This concept is elaborated on in later chapters.

Expert Systems

The second component of abstract systems, according to Giddens (1991), is the idea of expert systems. Expert systems, in his conception, are "systems of technical or professional expertise that organize large areas of the material and social environments in which we live today"

(Giddens, 1990, p. 27). This can include the knowledge of such professionals as lawyers, doctors, architects, or social workers. What we are describing is not concrete experience but, rather, an understanding of the way the world works that is typically held in thought structures or written or verbal discourse about experience.

Professional expertise embedded in our material and social environments constitutes expert systems. However, this idea of expert is best integrated in general as in "many aspects of what we do in a continuous way" (Giddens, 1990, p. 27). In this sense it can be thought of as professional thought forms, or the products of what Fleck (1970) would call "thought collectives." In this view, thought collectives are communities of persons, usually but not always experts, "mutually exchanging ideas or maintaining intellectual interaction" (p. 39). Child welfare fits what Giddens (1991) describes as an expert system. It is composed of thought structures and a legal or written abstract system based on the expertise of experts, and it includes the actions of professional social workers in its operation.

In sum, child welfare practice involves practice in a universe of abstract systems. These include symbolic tokens and expert systems. These are conceptions and thought forms interrelated with language and the expression of meaning. In this sense, the child welfare system as an abstract system involves a disembedding action which essentially separates concrete productions from anchorages in temporal and spatial dimensions and embeds them in our central social institutions, administrative case files, court documents, etc. These abstract systems constitute nonvisible hierarchies of beliefs and are typically accepted as normal (taken for granted), or serve as basic and agreed-upon assumptions. In this sense, they are an expression of the basic assumptions and even values that we express with language.

SOCIAL INSTITUTIONS AS ABSTRACT SYSTEMS

This idea of social institutions as abstract systems is important in understanding not only policy and policymaking in social welfare programs but also within the larger view of the social and cultural mosaic of the global environment in which they develop. Social institutions constitute the structure in which child welfare practice is grounded. It provides the limits and boundaries and establishes expectations, aspirations, and hopes.

While individual meaning is critical to understanding not only client behavior but also the behavior of individual professionals, it is also important to understand that the social institution provides the context of practice in child welfare. Social institutions provide "the basic structure by which human beings throughout history have created order and attempted to reduce uncertainty in exchange" (North, 1990, p. 118). In this sense, they constitute the formal relationship patterns that constitute a given society (North, 1981). As patterns of relationship, social institutions include both formal and informal structures. As it applies to social work, we find social institutions as "a stable cluster of social structures that is organized to meet the basic needs of societies" (Popple and Leighninger, 1996, p. 32). What are these social institutions or social structures? On a concrete level of action, they include rules, laws, customs, role definitions, and values, to name a few. On an informal level, they also include symbols as language and thought forms (Douglas, 1986). In short, they are abstract systems.

Social institutions constitute a form of abstract system; however, they are extremely broad and encompass major governing narratives. In this sense they also constitute the context of child welfare practice. Although practice is usually thought of in terms of an individual practitioner, this conception has limited applicability as we look at the social institutional arrangements that form the context of child welfare practice. This becomes clear in later chapters.

From a similar perspective, Khushf (1998) describes the practice of medicine. He notes that medicine in a world of managed care is no longer the solo practice of physicians. Rather, given the complex web of relationships within the social institutions dealing with the context of medicine, "institutions emerge as the practitioners of health care" (p. 118).

This shifting from the individual practitioner to the social institution as the practitioner highlights a change in the role of the solo practitioner to include the function of preserving social institutions. With this shift, the physician becomes a vehicle in maintaining the status quo of social institutions. This shifting of roles from individual practitioners to institutional providers has its parallel in child welfare practice. The social worker, doing his or her job, takes on the additional function of working to preserve the social order of the society.

Vignette: Maintaining Order Within Social Institutions

The social work student was talking with her desk mate, a social worker. "My professor today was saying that we investigate and write up material on events of abuse that then become abstracted material. We then use this material and present an abstracted picture of the abuse in the petition. Then, through the court process, the perpetrator, the victim, and everyone in court relive or reenact the abuse. This begins a process in which the court, through a ritual system, essentially moves the individual family members into new stigmatized roles."

Her experienced co-worker replied, "Yes, yes, I have heard that. It is interesting, and I think it is true, but we don't need to worry about that. All we have to do is conduct the investigations, write the petitions, and take the cases to court."

From Language to Social Categories

This conception of abstract systems as it applies to child welfare involves the establishment of social categories. These categories, such as abuse and neglect in child welfare, are constructed first in law as part of public policy (Stone, 1988) and then over and over again through collective discourse and action (Bauman, 1994). Social categories, in the broadest sense, operate in a social manner (West and Zimmerman, 1991). According to West and Zimmerman (1991, p. 20), "if [they] can be seen as members of relevant categories, then [they] are categorized] . . . that way." Aspects of this production and reproduction of social phenomena through collective discourse and sense making is described by such theorists as Garfinkel (1975) and Gadamer (1989), with a view of their being grounded by what Wittgenstein referred to as "language games." Wittgenstein, according to Bauman (1994), brought the concept of language games into sociology, while Gadamer brought the vision of "the life world as a communally produced and traditionally validated assembly of meanings" (p. 40).

From a social work perspective, this introduces us to the way social categories are determined within the larger social group. This includes the development and maintenance of narratives, the formation of social institutions, the social structure and systems of social roles and status that compose the social group and its social categories including social problems and social programs. For example, Edelman (1967, 1977, 1988) describes the interplay of language, political rhetoric, and governance and the formation of major social categories associated with the defining of social problems and social programs to solve them.

Child welfare, in the broadest sense, works with both individuals and social roles and statuses within the context of social narratives. The child welfare program is designed and built around concepts of social role and status as parent, child, caretaker, guardian, foster parent, etc. In this view, the social worker is responsible for working with the "role incumbent," that is, the individual that occupies the particular role. As social workers work with macro or large systems in the field of child welfare, they work with social categories. As social workers work with individuals, they work with those individuals that are categorized or being categorized within social categories.

We can describe the connection between social work and social categories yet another way. More than anything, and as it focuses on clinical practice, the child welfare system works to develop and maintain social categories and to match people with those categories. This has the effect of devaluing and stigmatizing them (Goffman, 1963). It does this through a reproductive process that operates continuously within the child welfare community, as an expert system, and in the larger community. It produces and reproduces social categories through collective thoughts, feelings, and actions including collective and interactive dialogues.

THE SOCIAL AND CULTURAL WORLD

Culture, from the perspective taken here, is carried by individuals, shared with language and other symbolic structures, and simultaneously viewable as a collective and individual entity. In this sense, the social group can be best understood as composed of individuals who carry their own cultures, as subjectively determined, with them. At times, these individuals' cultural similarities are visible as they are described as ethnic groups, that is, as abstract systems. What then becomes important is the question of how the individual organizes his or her social world.

Culture, in this sense, constitutes an important aspect of how our social world is organized. Of course, child welfare is part of this organized social world. Culture, while having collective elements (Schein, 1985; Hofstede, 1980), is also an individual psychological structure (Sapir from Irvine, 1994) and is based on individual meaning (Saari, 1991). Although much work in social work uses a collective unit for analyzing cultures, because of the nature of the collective versus individual tensions inherent in the child welfare system, culture must be understood at the individual level of attention. Stated simply, the juvenile court, the driving force within the child welfare system, adjudicates individual issues, not collective issues.

As we have seen, for the individual, meaning, as an act of consciousness, works to integrate collective or objective elements of the society with the subjective or narrative-based process of the social construction of meaning. Collective meanings as used here refer to "their symbolism, and their significance for the individuals interacting by means of them" (Irvine, 1994, p. 61). Symbols and symbol structures are expressed with and include language. However, although meanings can be examined collectively, an important aspect of these meanings is the idea of individual meanings. Irvine, in her reconstruction of Sapir's work, notes that "meanings are attached to behavioral forms . . . [and what is important is to know] what is behind the forms of behavior. In reference to individual meanings, then, we are driven to study culture" (Irvine, 1994, p. 61). Schon (1983) adds the idea that we use language to retrospectively explain action that an individual has already completed. This view of behavior and culture thus leads us back to the concept of language as an abstracted system.

One aspect of Schon's view of the role of language that is interesting and helpful is its role in developing and maintaining appearances of rationality in professional practice. He notes that language is used retrospectively (1983) to describe thoughts, feelings, and actions taken by professionals in crisis situations. In this sense, he is describing what Kaplan (1963) describes as "reconstructed logic." This reconstruction, through language and essentially narrative, becomes a logical, coherent, and rational depiction of a combination of intuitional, subjective, and objective thinking and actions. Through the use of reconstructive language, we present retrospectively the appearance of rationality that may or may not be exactly accurate.

The model used here to depict social and cultural organization is one that views noncognitive and cognitive material in a three-level conceptual hierarchy. From this perspective, surface level action, the top level of the model, is generally viewed as action or behavior that is viewable on a conscious level. Said another way, the model presents a stratification of levels simply to illustrate the conceptual differences; however, the levels are continuous and interpenetrate one another. That is, individual behavior including speech acts can affect changing values and ultimately may affect basic assumptions of a particular group.

Significant program assumptions or even basic governing assumptions change on a policy level as changes occur in individual persons' behaviors, and then become a part of larger system of action and change processes. In this view, the levels of action, the first level, and the level of basic assumptions are interdependent. For example, changes may involve a symbolic level of experience including political spectacle and media involvement (Edelman, 1967, 1977) or can involve a ritualization process of individual and collective reflection and action (Turner, 1969; Alexander, 1990). The model used in this work is one widely used in a variety of disciplines including social work (Netting and O'Connor, 2003; Netting, Kettner, and McMurty, 1998), organizational psychology (Schein, 1985; Senge, 1990), in sociology by Jeffrey Alexander (1990), and in anthropology by Victor Turner (1969). This adapted model is shown graphically in Table 1.1.

The deepest level of culture is composed of mental models or basic assumptions that often lie behind, or one might say metaphorically, beneath, presented behaviors or social programs. These are abstract systems and form a metaphoric cornerstone of the idea of culture that in a sense transcends any individual. The adherence to these basic assumptions become habits. For the child welfare system, these constitute the systems elements we take for granted. In this sense culture forms a foundation for the governing system.

The second level of organization is that of values, beliefs, and symbols. These lie just below the threshold of individual or collective consciousness and constitute a directing force that is typically congruent with the basic assumptions solidified within the social group. This level would include subtle and less visible cultural manifestations and material that is less immediately available to the individual

TABLE 1.1. Child Welfare Model

Levels of Action: Child Welfare	Examples
Action/behavior (Visible level of culture) Artifacts, creations, and action. This is the level of the expression of "self-interest."	Everyday discussions, negotiating on issues or problems as "self-interests," daily communication and behavior, ceremony and ritual in court, etc. This also includes the level at which "symbolic tokens" as language are used to reembed events as pictures in petitions.
Values (Visible and nonvisible level of culture) Things important to individuals, both cognitively and noncognitively. We are only at times fully aware of these values.	Stereotypes, role of the family, the mother, the father, etc., "values" as beliefs about the way things ought to or should be, etc. This would also include expert systems as they rely on practice wisdom.
Idealized values, aka mental models or basic assumptions (Nonvisible and assumptions about social world) Noncognitive and shared language and conceptual categories. This is the level below the average level of shared discourse.	Constitutional structure of governance, legal system, need for collective rules, socially constructed categories as gender, race, and ethnicity and abstract and expert systems.

in the present. Here we would find beliefs associated with adherence to codes of ethics and values as promulgated by professional organizations. Family preservation programs and child protection programs would have this as a locus of organizational control.

Vignette: Family Preservation As Assumption

The country's emphasis on family preservation, although meant as a positive change, also had the negative effect of reducing the effectiveness of the child protection function of the child welfare system. According to Richard Gelles (1996), policy had been made and funding and government regulations emphasized family preservation over child protection. A basic assumption of this public policy is arguably that family preservation is a preferred strategy for the child welfare system. Political behavior, lobbying by interest groups, government officials, etc., all contributed to changes in policies with a shifting of emphasis from child protection values to family values.

The top or uppermost level is devoted to the productions or behaviors of the understructure of the social group. It constitutes actions, activities, and even artifacts or other productions of people. It represents political activity and even media presentations that describe and explain action driven by values or beliefs held on lower levels of the organization. It includes the visible manifestations of networks as social networks and centers of power and social structures that at times marginalize people (Shils, 1982). In the child welfare system, it constitutes the actions of individual social workers, viewed collectively, as they take action in accordance with the legal system and policies of agencies. It is also the level at which "thought collectives" work in constructing and reconstructing social facts, some of which may become deeply held values or assumptions.

CONCLUSION

This chapter provided a set of concepts/ideas/assumptions that underlie the approach taken in this work to describe the child welfare system. In the view taken here, child welfare is an institutional response to a perceived problem. This work is meant to expose some of the hidden elements in the child protective system. This includes the disembedding of social interaction from their actual locations in time and place and their reembedding in language and subsequent storage in case records and information systems and their at times concomitant use in litigation in juvenile court.

The effects of the operation of this system are hidden as they lie in the stigmatizing of both victims and perpetrators. These are hidden just as the effects of its actions in hurting and at times destroying families are hidden. These hidden actions occur through the operation of what Gibbons might call abstract systems.

Reembedding these social interactions in new locations and times and taking collective actions on them constitute the formation of a kind of fetish, or obsession with the idea or concept of abuse or neglect or "fetishized" system of reembedded values. In child welfare, we would see the construction of this fetish as the substantiation and accumulation of statistics on cases of child abuse or neglect. As we add these to our national calculations, it contributes to the reification of the idea of the child welfare system as protecting or saving of children from the abuse or neglect of their parents or caretakers. However, it simply changes the abuse or neglect from that occurring within the family of origin to another kind of abuse or neglect within the institutional matrixes involved in the intervention.

In this sense, the child welfare system is ensconced within what Lefebvre (1968) might call an artificial or weblike "veil of appearances" (p. 47). It is maintained through the action of interpersonal discourse, pedagogy, and ritual and ceremony (Gusfield, 1981; Meyer and Rowan, 1977). In a sense, what has been said is that there is a distinction between that which exists in a concrete form and that which we perceive to be real. That which we perceive to be real or true, for example, the objective social world, is essentially an illusion. It is what is left to perception when the veil of appearances masks the hidden reality. The concept or idea of trust is the most important connecting point of the individual qua individual and these abstract systems.

Without trust, these artificial systems carry little if any viability for defining our world. The heart of the idea of the formation and maintenance of these expert systems is the idea of individuals trusting them. However, the abstract systems are unique to us in that they are not connected to the modernist view of reality. That which we considered real in the past, is increasingly being replaced by abstract or, perhaps one could say, artificial systems.

SECTION I:
SANCTION, AUTHORITY,
AND THE LEGAL SYSTEM

Chapter 2

The Institutional Context
of Child Welfare

GLOBAL PERSPECTIVES

Introduction

Children have been important to civilizations from the beginning of documented social life. For example, the early Greeks paid special attention to children, and major religions have shown a particular sensitivity to the care and socialization of children. However, the treatment of children has to a considerable extent been tied to the level of development of particular societies. In this sense, we see some societies using children to facilitate economic or social agendas or to further economic development. Virtually all cultures have prescribed mores, norms, and values associated with the special status of children. These normative statements for the most part deal with "shoulds." That is, they relate to the way children "should" or "ought" to be educated, socialized, trained, treated, etc.

The United States is no exception to the rest of the world with respect to its interest, concern, and treatment of children. Although the country used forced emigration of children for labor, for example, in the harvesting of tobacco crops (Krisberg, 1993; Bremmer, 1970), and the out-of-home placement of children to maintain social order (Krisberg, 1993), interest in the well-being of children has evolved into a major concern. This chapter illustrates international perspectives on the care and treatment of children. This perspective is provided as a context for viewing the American child welfare system. It is meant to help locate the philosophical foundations of American child welfare policy and practice within conceptual or virtual space.

International Perspectives: Selected Stories

When we look at the global child welfare environment, we find significant varieties of situations. Some of these are shown in the following vignettes, which were selected in order to highlight differences in the cross-continental treatment of children. In general, these vignettes show children as instruments of larger systems or forces including the alternative actions and reactions of societies toward children. In the world order, children play an important, if not always a pleasant or positive, role. Broadly viewed, child welfare begins with broad questions as to the nature of child well-being.

Pakistan: Tribal Courts

A news article reports that a tribal council ordered the rape of a teenaged girl as the result of her eleven-year-old brother's violation of a community or tribal norm. The tribal norm, or unwritten law, called for a chaperone to be present whenever a young male was with a young female. In this reported situation, the brother was seen walking alone with a young girl, a member of a higher-class tribe, the Mastoi tribe. The boy and his sister were from a lower-class tribe, the Gujar tribe. Despite pleadings by family members, the tribal council ordered the rape of the teen. According to the article, "the Mastoi girl's father rejected the pleas and demanded the gang rape" (Tanveer, 2002, p. A7). The council adopted the girl's father's position:

> The boy's sister would be gang raped to shame her whole family. . . . Soon afterward, four members of the council took turns raping the eighteen-year-old sister in a mud hut as hundreds of people stood outside laughing and cheering. (p. A7)

This situation illustrates the use of children for maintaining power relationships and social order. The family was the primary unit of the society and was determined to be collectively guilty of the young boy's transgression. Control was exercised over the family by shaming them through the rape of the daughter/sister. The theory driving the behavior is that through the use or the threat of shaming, other members of the tribe would be held in control. The maintenance of the norm, of only chaperoned contact, served as a way to continue the stratification of the tribal communities. In this sense, the rape of the girl was a means of socially controlling members of the tribe.

Cambodia: Child Stealing

A newspaper story circulated by the Associated Press describes the "official" American reaction to "child stealing" by U.S. citizens in Cambodia. Child stealing has a clear legal definition in the United States, but not all countries have such a legal category. In this instance, described by the Associated Press, the Cambodian statutes fail to define child stealing as applying to this situation. Newspaper reports describe the situation as follows: "Human rights workers have confirmed cases of Cambodian facilitators visiting poor mothers in the countryside and offering them as little as $30 for their newborn, who is then placed in an 'orphanage'" (Decherd, 2001). The article notes that American families pay thousands of dollars in fees and processing costs to orphanage operators and government ministries to "adopt" these "orphans." The American government's response to the current problem is to deny visas for eleven children "adopted" by American parents (Decherd, 2001). There is no official statement of the American position; however, the American authorities do not accept Cambodia's view of this kind of situation as acceptable. Each country has its own standards for judging child well-being.

Brazil: Street Children

In Brazil, the plight of what are referred to as street children is well known. Their numbers have been growing since the 1980s. Shopkeepers, frustrated with the thievery of these "feral" children roving Brazilian streets, paid for their "extermination." In July 1993, the extermination became public as eight sleeping children in a central square in Rio were killed by off-duty police.

"The ugly details—those who tried to flee were hunted down and dispatched with a bullet in the back—and the apparent indifference of the authorities guaranteed massive media coverage" ("Hope for the No-Hopers," 2000).

According to the article, the reasons for the murder of these street children are unclear but seem to be related to a number of internal and external factors. Specifically, Brazil is a developing country experiencing a major economic restructuring. It is also struggling politically with the allocation and use of basic resources, such as land, labor, and capital. One analysis describes the street children issue as being related to family breakdown, lack of public spending, political graft, a lack of organization among the country's charities, an emphasis on public works, and a general indifference to the plight of the children.

Underlying this situation is a paradox. Specifically, Brazil is an emerging economy, at the upper end of the middle-income category of countries and with abundant natural resources including land. It also has an industrialized economy with diversified manufacturing operations. However, even with these strengths Brazil stands out because of its distinctive contrast between the lives of the rich and poor. This disparity between the wealthy and the poor suggests two distinctly different worlds. With United Nations reports as background, this has been described by the Novartis Foundation for Sustainable Development as the following:

> The contrasts . . . between modern industrialization and colonial-feudal agricultural and ownership structures—are more extreme in Brazil than in almost any other country. . . . Nearly half of Brazil's population lives in absolute poverty [with] . . . over one million children under five [being] undernourished. Health care, sanitary facilities and food resources are inadequate for most of the population, while education is the privilege of a select few. Although Brazil is the world's eighth largest industrial nation, it ranks 62nd on the UNDP's 1998 Human Development Index (HDI). (The Novartis Foundation, 2003)

Brazil's street children appear to be victims of what one might call an institutional or structural kind of abuse. Although the country is fairly well developed, authorities have not made a political decision to deal with the needs of the children. In the absence of a policy, the children's basic needs are met through casual labor with illegal begging.

Africa: Enslavement

A news report describes children in Africa as being sold into slavery to work as labor within the global economy in the growing and harvesting of cocoa beans, the primary ingredient in chocolate. West Africa produces some 43 percent of these cocoa beans. Production is done on small farms scattered throughout the area. Laborers for these farms must be capable of hard work and be able to endure a hot work environment. The work includes clearing the land, and planting, tending, and haversting the crops. Who provides the labor?

> On some of the farms, the hot, hard work of clearing the fields and harvesting the fruit is done by boys who were sold or tricked into slavery. Most of them are between the ages of 12 and 16. Some are as young as 9. (Raghavan and Chatterjee, 2001)*

In describing this problem and some of the complexity of the issues involved, a 1998 United Nations Children's Fund (UNICEF) report notes that some Ivory Coast farmers use the child "slaves," children from the poorer African neighboring countries of Mali, Burkina Faso, Benin, and Togo, for harvesting cocoa beans.

The enslavement process used in 2001 differs little from that used in the late 1500s and early 1600s to provide labor to the American colonies. During the American colonial period children were recruited by "spirits" and then transported to the early colonies to provide labor. Children were enticed, through the offer of money or good jobs, etc., by these "spirits," aka labor contractors, to travel to the early colonies and work harvesting tobacco (Bremmer, 1970).

The enslavement process involves paying the child's parent or caretaker a token amount of money, a few dollars, and then promising to pay the child's family an annual amount, a few dollars, for the child's work. The child then is transported to a farm where he or she lives and works. This is described as a kind of indentureship program in which the children work and pay room and board until they pay off their transportation costs.

Summary of Vignettes

These vignettes provide a selected view of the institutional care and protection provided to children internationally. The people of Pa-

---

*How widespread is the trafficking in children as labor? A report by the Geneva, Switzerland-based International Labor Organization, released June 15, 2001, found that trafficking in children is widespread in West Africa. In addition, "The [American] State Department's year 2000 human rights report concluded that some 15,000 children between the ages of 9 and 12 have been sold into forced labor on cotton, coffee and cocoa plantations in northern Ivory Coast in recent years" (Raghavan and Chatterjee, 2001).

kistan are dealing with issues of social integration and social control, and the country needs economic development. Brazilians are faced with a set of values, policies, and governance conflicts that limit their abilities to provide for their children. The West African and Cambodian situations are driven by internal factors such as poverty and overpopulation and external forces such as the international community.

Each country experiences a share in an international set of tensions. These international tensions are derived in part from the rapid globalization of the economies of the world and the corresponding closeness of political boundaries and media reporting. From this international perspective an important question is the role of each country vis-à-vis others as part of defining and maintaining an acceptable normative system for protecting children and families. This asks what is the nature of abuse and neglect, and how, if at all, does it apply to the world's cultures?

Implications of These Stories

What do these stories suggest in terms of child welfare or child well-being for a country such as the United States? More than anything, these vignettes illustrate a tremendous gap in economic and social development between the United States and developing countries. In contrast to the United States, countries illustrated in these vignettes show tremendous and very basic needs that children have for food, clothing, shelter, protection, and security. The vignettes illustrate institutional level protections or the lack thereof. With perhaps the exception of Brazil, the vignettes also reflect the lack of economic development.

These vignettes also show that the values or standards of care and treatment of children vary in different countries. In this sense, the care and protection of children, that is, child well-being, is related to the basic values held within a culture. These values, to some extent, are related to the country's level of economic and social development; however, this is not entirely the situation. For example, even a country such as Brazil, with an economy that ranks eighth in the world, can have social structural problems that work adversely for children. What these narratives suggest is that child welfare, defined as child well-being, varies significantly by country and by culture. In this sense, the definition of child well-being is dependent upon values held within a country and a culture. In fact, there is little consensus as to the nature, prevalence, or even the seriousness of child abuse as a social problem on an international level (Boli-Bennett and Meyer, 1978).

The vignettes also suggest that to be understood in its fullest implications, child well-being must be looked at in the broadest possible way. That is, the issues involved in child well-being are social level issues. They transcend the family system. This is particularly true with the increasing globalization of the world's economies. We see a variety of problems or issues involved with children from the perspective of their respective countries within the world community. These vignettes also suggest some of the diversity of the American child welfare system as some refugee laws and immigration bring natives of these countries into the United States as residents. In this capacity they are involved with social institutions that provide for child well-being and those involved with child protection.

CHILD WELL-BEING AT SOCIETAL, INSTITUTIONAL, AND FAMILY LEVELS

The vignettes also suggest the need to look at children and their needs within the broadest social and cultural levels of organization. A simple three-level view of child well-being and child welfare can help in understanding its breadth and depth. This three-level view includes the level of society or culture, that of the social institutions within the society, and that of the family (see Table 2.1). Fundamental to this concept is the idea that child welfare programs and services are manifestations of values, embedded within the governing system of the nation, and reflected in public policy. Policy, in this usage, includes formal and informal arrangements involving governmental, non-profit, and profit-making concerns working both individually and collectively to address social problems. This conception of policy is adapted from Dobelstein (2003) and includes a view of policy as multidimensional and involving multiple organizational levels.

Societal or Cultural Level

In the foregoing vignettes, we have seen the effects of broad economic, social, and political forces acting on the respective societies.

TABLE 2.1. Three Levels of Child Well-Being

Level	Emphasis
Society/cultural (abstracted level)	Economic and political stability, productivity, etc. These are the result of a stable and effective governing structure.
Social institutional protections (abstract systems)	The development of social institutions that contain embedded protections based on values that provide for a safe, secure, and healthful environment for children, for example, laws against child prostitution, labor laws, etc.
Within the family (concrete level of experience)	The development of institutional or residual programs to provide protection for children/families. These would have foundations in how "deviance" within the family is handled; for example, how are "family problems" that impact children handled?

Each government's acceptance or rejection of this state of affairs for children is tied to their respective governing structure and its operation. At this level, for developing countries, efforts to handle child welfare issues are almost exclusively situated within the governing apparatus. For the most part, developing countries have governing systems or structures that are themselves in an early state of development. They do not typically have a long history of economic and political development or even stability. Protections for children in developing nations have typically not yet been established. That is, protections are not typically embedded in their governing apparatus or their founding structures.

Children in developing countries need some degree of economic, political, social, and family stability. This would include collective protections and safeties for children such as health care, adequate education, food and sustenance, etc. However, more important even than these items for children is the country's need for economic and political stability.

In contrast with developing nations, the United States has embedded within its constitutional structures protections for individuals including children and adults. More will be said about this as the governing structure of the United States is discussed.

Institutional Level

The second system level of child welfare programs involves the formation of a social institutional structure that plays a part in providing for children. Simply stated and in terms of child well-being, this involves the embedding of protections of various kinds for children within the social institutions of a society. This embedding would be in keeping with the kinds of child and family nurturing, protecting, and supporting structures that are to be considered "normal" within the dominant values of the society.

This institutional level establishes a kind of social framework that provides for the handling of family or individual child level problems. It is first and foremost a question of the kinds of abstract systems that will be involved in what kinds of ways with children's well-being. With social institutions described as composed of a social structure, that is, as an abstract system of status, roles, and social positions within a nation, this questions how social institutions are organized to provide for children's safety, security, and protections. For the United States, this has historically been at the root of social policy formation to provide for children. The question is one of the extent to which child well-being is to be considered a "normal" part of living and the extent to which child welfare issues are exceptions to "normal" living.

Another way to look at this level of child welfare is to use the concepts of residual and institutional as a vehicle to understand the American bifurcation of child well-being and child welfare. Wilensky and Lebeaux (1968) in their classic work have given us these concepts of residual or institutional approaches to social welfare. The idea of institutional level programs as being distinct yet a part of institutional social welfare programs suggests that these problems impact the total population. In contrast with child well-being, child protection programs are residual in the sense that they are perceived as the result of a breakdown in social institutions.

Child well-being programs are, in this sense, institutionalized programs. Institutional in this sense refers to the embedding of values into the major social institutions in the form of protections or programs that respond to what are perceived as ongoing and continuous needs. For example, child labor laws have been embedded within the legal structure of the nation. They are part of the Department of Labor's enforcement responsibility. In this sense, children are protected from abuse within the market system by these institutional level protections. Since the mid-1930s we have gradually institutionalized assistance programs for aged and disabled persons, that is, persons unable to work within the market system. In contrast to these federal level programs, state and local laws protect children from being exploited or even abused by related and nonrelated persons.

Alternately, child welfare, in regards to protection of children from parents or caretakers, within the United States is embedded in the social welfare institution. These policies are residual in the sense that they are meant to serve as temporary safeguards for people as they may slip through the metaphoric cracks of the larger governing apparatus. Child welfare in this sense constitutes an approach to issues or problems that are exceptional to the basic values that constitute our governance assumptions. Thus, they are conceived of as programs that provide temporary interventions. Their need is not considered as an ongoing or normal aspect of life within the governing system. For example, it is not normal to abuse your child.

Child Well-Being at the Level of the Family

The third system level of child welfare programs involves the child's experience within the family, within the society, and within social institutions. The policy and program questions that are important here are those that relate to the child's role, care, and protection within the family. Implicit in this question is that of what the parent's and family's role is within the same society and social institutions.

The comparatively highly developed American system of child welfare highlights these issues. With the passage of the Child Abuse Prevention and Treatment Act (CAPTA) in 1974, the United States set forth on the path of intervening in family life on behalf of protecting children from their parents. The net result is a child welfare system in the United States that gives priority to the child's right to protection from his or her parents over the parents' right to act in a certain way as the child's parents.

Child welfare as a residual program focuses on providing temporary interventions aimed at protecting children from abuse and neglect by their parents or caretakers. It focuses only on this limited mission and population. Other kinds of needs for child protection are generally handled by other social institutions. For example, child stealing typically is handled by law enforcement rather than by public child welfare. It is conceived as a normal part of the handling of deviance within our society—it is criminal behavior and not typically a child protection issue. However, no one situation is necessarily limited to one kind of response. For example, a child stealing situation can be handled as a criminal matter and as a child protection issue simultaneously.

American child welfare policy holds the child as an independent entity with rights to protection from his or her parents and accords virtually no status to the family entity. To be sure, it accords legal status to the child's individual legal parents, but not the family unit. Child welfare intervention is actually intervention into the parental relationship, that is, the relationship of the child and his or her parents. The family, as noted earlier, is not a recognized legal entity in terms of having rights. The American system in this respect is individual child centered, although certain policies present the illusory appearance of being family centered.

For example, family preservation programs appear focused on the family; however, within the context of the child welfare system they focus only on providing family-based services. Even in the action of providing services, authority for intervention by the social worker is limited to the bond between the parent and the child. Our development of service programs within the child welfare system that focus alternately on the child, the parent, and the family, represents a cultural ambivalence. We do not know whether to try to save families or children. Why not both?

INTERNATIONAL PERSPECTIVES ON PROTECTING CHILDREN FROM PARENTS/CARETAKERS

Given the large number of developing nations and the fewer numbers of developed nations it is probably not surprising that only a few countries have policies to intervene in family life to set and enforce social norms through a legal process with the expenditure of resources. More countries are involved in the tasks of meeting basic survival needs for their children and citizens than are able to individualize qualitative norms for child protection from parents or caretakers.

However, even in looking specifically at Western developed countries we find a mixture of child welfare programs. Specifically, the United States, Canada, and England stand alone as having child welfare programs that have what Neil Gilbert (1997) refers to as a child protective orientation. These countries have similar child welfare systems in that they have mandated reporting by workers in investigation and service delivery systems that are meant to remediate problems in parenting.

In contrast, Sweden, Denmark, and Finland have mandatory reporting systems, yet focus on providing services to families. In addition, Belgium, the Netherlands, and Germany do not have mandatory reporting and use family-focused interventions that respectively incorporate a compassionate intervention model and a nonpunitive model. These countries rely heavily on volunteers. To a considerable extent, outside of the three child protective-oriented systems, volunteers are important in the operation of their child welfare systems. The protection-oriented systems rely on "experts" to work within their systems. These experts are typically social workers.

CHILD ABUSE AND NEGLECT AS SOCIAL CATEGORIES

What should be clear from the previous material is the idea that terms such as "child abuse" and "child neglect" are not fixed and universal concepts or ideas. Although children have been important in collective life, through the centuries, descriptions of abuse and neglect of children are not universal terms. They are relatively recent creations. In addition, when they are used in different settings they have different meanings. What is considered abuse in the United States may not be abuse in Mexico or in France. Even in the United States the meaning of terms such as abuse or neglect differ according to the states being examined. For example, a four-year-old child left alone may not be considered neglected in one jurisdiction but would in another.

With this almost endless diversity in the responses to children internationally, combined with seemingly infinite differences in language and values, it should not be surprising that different peoples see child welfare and particularly "child abuse" and "child neglect" in varying ways. While we see that collective responses to children's concerns differ by country, an obvious question is the extent to which concepts as abuse and neglect are associated with particular cultures. To look at this question, we must look at what these social categories of abuse and neglect actually are.

The categories of abuse and neglect are best conceived as "social constructions." In the United States the broad definitions of these categories are set in state law, but the exact working definitions of the categories are written by those experts involved in implementing the laws. These experts comprise what Fleck (1970) would call "thought collectives." They engage in ongoing discourse about the kinds of situations that are involved in various categories of abuse. Discourse in this usage includes not only verbal discussions, but also research and fact-finding activities such as those found in professional journals.

Through these wide-ranging processes and with the occurrences of various case scenarios a general consensus develops on a working level definition of these categories. This discourse is part of the general dialogic process whereby child welfare professionals work to fit other individuals into specific social categories, that is, into various social roles. This process of the fitting of people into such categories involves a variety of social, psychological, and even agency and work-related processes beyond the scope of this work but illustrated nicely in Swift (1995).

A couple of examples will make this clear. First, Swift's (1995) work on the social/legal category of child neglect in *Manufacturing Bad Mothers* provides us with an understanding of how social discourse, the structuring of work activities and interactions of workers, administrators, and clients, results in the creation of stigmatized parents, that is, "bad mothers." She describes the actual social categorization process in child welfare as "much of child welfare work is organized around the problems of identifying and categorizing the experience of clients to determine its 'fit' with specific social categories. Through these 'cutting out' procedures families become identified as neglecting or abusive parents" (pp. 67-68).

A second example of the social establishment of problem and program categories is from a German perspective. Reinhart Wolff (1997) notes that child abuse and neglect is publicly constructed by public dialogue. Professor Wolff describes child abuse and neglect as it is conceptualized in Germany as follows:

What we now call child abuse and neglect is a modern construction. As a social problem, it has been created; it is not just there, it is a discourse structure that has a dramatic impact on child protective work. Child welfare workers also take part in publicly constructing child abuse and neglect as a social problem. One cannot easily grasp it; it is not just there even if there are, of course, violated and injured kids, disturbed parents, and families in need of services. In order to justly identify it as a "social problem," a public construction of the problem is necessary, which involves societal "fact finding" and "meaning making" (an interpretation of the facts through a complex process of public discourse). Modern cultural industries, by using new paradigms and images, create a new grammar of understanding. Modern child protection movements have become cultural industries too. (p. 217)

Since child abuse and neglect are socially defined, we should not be surprised to find endless variety in terms of definitions and solutions to child abuse and neglect problems. Also, we should not be surprised to find that clear definitions and uniform approaches to solving child welfare problems do not exist. For example, as we have seen in these vignettes, people from various countries have varying ideas as to the acceptable treatment of children. Also, the states within the United States and even work groups within various child welfare systems throughout the nation have particular definitions.

Another important point in understanding the lack of a universal nature to the conception of child abuse concerns the collection of data on the occurrence and recurrence of abuse or neglect. Data either standardizes the phenomena of abuse or neglect or, perhaps more accurately, creates the illusion of uniform phenomena. Only when the people of a nation see some behaviors as a social problem do they collect statistics as to the size of the problem. This collecting of statistics, that is, the use of a counting metaphor (Stone, 1988; Edelmann, 1977), solidifies the social category within the social system. Not surprisingly, there is an international lack in the collection of statistics dealing with abuse and neglect. Finkelhor (1983) says, "In no other country was the concern [for child protection] as great as it was in the United States, and until recently, in no other country had attempts been made to gather national statistics" (p. 5). Implicit in Finkelhor's conception of child protection is the American view of protecting children from their parents or caretakers.

THE AMERICAN CHILD WELFARE SYSTEM

The American child welfare system bifurcates child well-being and child welfare, that is, child protection. Detached from child welfare and from a global perspective as noted by the previous vignettes, child well-being is concerned with the welfare of all children. At this broad level, the welfare of children is associated with the concept of child well-being and is clearly related not only to family life but to economic and social development including the stability of the governing apparatus. In addition, as we see with Brazil, basic cultural values and their contribution to the governing process also play an important part in the formulation of child welfare interventions.

To understand the American child welfare system, it is important to understand how narrowly child welfare has come to be defined in the United States. The American approach to child welfare, with its bifurcation of child well-being and child protection, has evolved into a quasi-police function in which social workers investigate allegations of abuse and neglect by parents or caretakers while child well-being issues are handled through the market system. Where the market system is simply inadequate to deal with these nonparent/caretaker issues, we have, through legislation, set limits on the misuse of children.

The best example of legislation dealing with child well-being in the United States is the establishment of laws protecting children from hazards outside of the family. For example, child labor laws set limits on manufacturing concerns regarding the use of children as labor. However, other types of institutional abuse are also problematic. For example, teachers and/or priests abusing children present unique challenges. In the former, prosecution for criminal offenses is an alternative, while in the latter, recourse seems to be civil lawsuits to control institutional-level child abuse.

This bifurcation of child well-being and child protection presents interesting tensions and issues that parents must deal with. The following vignettes illustrate some of these questions of neglect and responsibility or the lack of responsibility.

Vignette: Children in the Marketplace

In 1995, the American Academy of Pediatrics declared that "advertising directed at children is inherently deceptive and exploits children under eight years of age. The Academy did not recommend a ban on such advertising because it seemed impractical and would infringe upon advertisers' freedom of speech." (Schlosser, 2001, p. 262)

Vignette: Children As Targets

A *Wall Street Journal* article on January 31, 2003, proclaimed that "Happy Meals Are No Longer Bringing Smiles at McDonald's: Sales Have Fallen for Three Years; Chain Mulls Adding Mom's Meal, Carrot Sticks, Higher Quality Toys." According to the article, McDonald's continues to lead the market in sales to children. The Happy Meal accounts for more than 20 percent of its revenue. The company's beefing up of sales to children through an enhancement of its toy giveaways has not been successful. The article notes "the McDonald's hold on children is weakening. 'We can do better with Happy Meals,' says Bill Lamar, McDonald's U.S. marketing chief." (Leung and Vranica, 2003, p. B1)

To understand the American child welfare system, we need to conceptualize the system itself. A traditional view of child welfare services involves classifying them as protective services, foster care, and adoptions (Downs, Costin, and McFadden, 1996). A second and, to some extent, dominant view of the classification of services from an institutional level is from Alfred Kadushin and Judith Martin (1988). Kadushin uses a three-part classification system that describes child welfare services as services provided in support of the parent's role with children. He notes these categories as "supportive, supplemental, or substitutive" (p. 26).

Kadushin and Martin's (1988) idea is that "institutional level" services can focus on each of these general categories. Thus, supporting services would include such things as counseling or even medical services for children. Supplemental services would include such services as public welfare, income supplementation programs, etc. The substitutive services categories could include either of the other two focuses of services; however, they are provided within the context of the involuntary service delivery system, that is, children's protective services. The emphasis in this work is on what Kadushin might call substitutive services, that is children's protective services. These substitutive services would comprise what Downs, Costin, and McFadden (1996) describe as the traditional services of protective services, foster care, and adoptions. These services are for the most part nonvoluntary and have much of their delivery system determined by the legal and administrative systems. It is this nonvoluntary aspect of child welfare with which this work is concerned.

THE ORGANIZATION OF CHILD WELFARE PROGRAMS

A key issue in understanding child welfare is utilizing the type of model or theoretical lens that can best provide an adequate picture of the legally determined child welfare programs and their administration. The approach taken in this work is aimed at discussing the individual and collective behavior in society, that explains how the child welfare system operates. Toward that end, society is conceptualized as a mass society (Shils, 1982), as integrated with internalized habits (Bellah, 1985) and thoughts (Douglas, 1986, 1994), as ritualized action (Turner, 1969; Bell, 1992; Gusfield, 1981, 1986), and as composed of social institutions (North, 1990). However, first and foremost it is viewed as an organizational society (Presthus, 1978) and bureaucratized (Hummel, 1982). How can these elements be put together into a working model? The basic working model of organizational culture, values, and behavior discussed in the preceding chapter provides such a conceptual frame.

CONCLUSION

We have seen to this point a macrolevel perspective for viewing public child welfare. Viewing child welfare from a global perspective provides a glimpse of an institutionally diverse environment. From this perspective we see three levels of policy and programs serving the needs of children. These include the general overall governing context in which children's needs are provided for, the development of laws and programs that embed values into social institutions, and the actual laws and programs that are a part and parcel of the child protection system. In sum, these institutional arrangements aim to protect children from institutional kinds of abuse, and the child abuse and neglect laws and policy are meant to protect children from their parents or caretakers. In the United States all three of these have come to be important to children.

Chapter 3

Governance, Legitimacy, and Trust

INTRODUCTION

Viewing child welfare as intervention into family life and using the concept of structure, what gives social workers the right to intervene in family life? That is, what is the structure that directs action? Another way to ask this is to ask how authority is grounded in society and in child welfare? What makes such interventions legitimate? So far, we have seen how the concepts of child well-being and child welfare relate to each other within different governing jurisdictions, that is, countries. This has provided us with a broad-ranging view of child welfare. In particular, we have seen how the American system of child welfare is bifurcated with child protection dealing with the "inappropriate" care and treatment of children by parents and caretakers, while social institutions provide institutional protections for children, that is, for their well-being. In the United States, for the most part, child protection is synonymous with child welfare.

This chapter examines the structure in which the child welfare system is embedded and within which social workers in the United States operate. This includes the constitutional governing system and the administrative structure in the United States and the social worker's role as mediating the relationship between the individual qua individual and social institutions. It also describes in general terms the "child welfare community," also at times referred to as the "child abuse industry," the nature of child abuse prevention, and the role of the social worker as mediating the tension between macrolevel social institutions and the individual.

THE AMERICAN SYSTEM: A FOCUS ON PARENTAL OR CARETAKER BEHAVIOR

In contrast to most other countries, the United States expends vast resources protecting children from their parents and caretakers. We hire a virtual army of professionals to investigate abuse and neglect and to provide services to children and families in the child welfare system. In contrast, other countries, particularly developing countries, focus more on community development activities to provide for the well-being of children and/or use community volunteers and family members to intervene with families.

CHILD PROTECTIVE SERVICES AS CHILD WELFARE

When we use the term *child welfare,* we are usually referring to the children's protective services (CPS) function. In this work, these terms are used interchangeably. The American child welfare system, aka the children's protective services system, has evolved from the early 1800s to the present. Beginning with the Children's Aid Society and the early child savers it has evolved into a highly complex and at times highly litigious system. The mission of the early child savers was the saving of the cities through the outplacement of the children of the poor and minorities, at that time, Italians and Irish (African Americans were not included in early protective efforts).

The early child savers placed children in foster homes in the agricultural areas of the Midwest. Today's child savers investigate allegations of abuse and neglect, remove children assessed as being in danger of abuse and neglect from their parents or caretakers, and, ultimately, through the child welfare system, return them home or place them in a permanent living situation. In today's system child abuse and neglect of children is increasingly being criminalized in the United States.

The child protection system, including police and social workers, is organized around referrals alleging violations of child abuse and neglect laws. Workers in the system track such allegations, respond to these reports, substantiate or prove the allegations, and then take action. Action can include referring a parent of a child for services, arresting a perpetrator, removing a child from his or her parent, or requiring parents to participate in remedial activities such as counseling or parent training classes. Also, professionals in the child protection system may, along with actions to protect a child, charge the parents or caretakers with violations of criminal statutes and send them to jail or prison. This is the heart of today's public child welfare system.

CHILD WELFARE AS AN INDUSTRY

The modern child welfare system involves a wide range of professionals, clients, former clients, and even "victims" in recovery. This system includes a major directing agency, the child protective agency, mandated reporters, and institutional forces for responding to allegations. The industry includes professionals, doctors, nurses, teachers, foster parents, child care workers, counselors, film developers, victims in recovery, etc. This veritable army of professionals has been accurately described by Costin, Karger, and Stoesz (1996) as the "child abuse industry," which is composed of "psychotherapists, attorneys, and other service providers" (p. 13). More concretely, graphically, and with equal accuracy, Hubner and Wolfson (1996), describe the child welfare system and its actions and activities and the legal part of this industry as follows:

> Investigators check out charges of abuse, and an army of social workers provides services. Separate sets of attorneys guard the legal rights of parents and of children; a third set guards the legal rights of the social workers. Volunteer advocates, who often know the children better than the professionals, sometimes appear in court to push the system to do what it is supposed to do. Therapists help families understand and control violence. An industry of "rehabs" work with alcohol and drug problems. Foster parents take over when a family falls apart. Children who have suffered serious psychological damage are placed in residential care facilities that routinely cost $7,000 a month. (p. vii)

The American child welfare system is expensive. In 1995, it involved estimated expenditures of at least $14.4 billion (Boots et al., 1999). In addition, it includes hidden costs associated with enforcement by police as well as court and other litigation costs. In addition, there are untallied costs associated with ensuring the well-being of other children and the protection of children from nonfamily exploiters, such as third-party abusers or neglectors. Of course this does not include human costs as the effects of children, parents, and siblings or costs of legal representation of family members.

PREVENTION

No discussion of the child welfare system in America would be complete without mentioning the concept of prevention as it applies to the abuse or neglect of children. Generally, three types of prevention—primary, secondary, and tertiary—are commonly recognized within health systems and are applicable to the prevention of child maltreatment in child welfare. These focus on either the occurrence or recurrence of child abuse or neglect (Wiehe, 1996).

In child welfare, primary prevention is meant to prevent the first occurrence of abuse or neglect to children within the particular domain of the active agency. An example of primary prevention, given by Wiehe (1996), was the use of a polio vaccination on the total population in the 1950s and 1960s to prevent polio. In child welfare, this level of prevention would be extremely difficult and very expensive.

The major problem in doing primary prevention is the lack of an exact and fixed definition of abuse or neglect. Also, humans are not predictable in terms of their behavior or action. Thus, unlike polio, the causes of child abuse and neglect are unclear and indeterminate. Researchers working with aggregate data can easily find variables that point to the risk of abuse or neglect; however, these are extremely broad-ranging variables as the children of the poor, children of single parents, children of peoples of color, or other marginalized populations. An example of a primary prevention activity might be a program providing mandatory training in parenting skills to the general and total population of parents and potential parents within the nation.

In child welfare, secondary prevention refers to preventing the recurrence of child maltreatment. Prevention on this level relates to efforts that identify individuals at risk of being repeat victims of abuse or neglect and trying to keep them from being revictimized. Generally, prevention programs designed by agency personnel to reduce child maltreatment among their client population fall in this category. These programs limit the population to those who have already been abused and seek to "prevent" subsequent actions of abuse.

In order to do secondary prevention, the recognition of the cohort is fairly clear-cut. The substantiation, the determination that abuse has occurred, of a referral essentially validates that the child has been abused or neglected. A safety assessment is expected to ensure the safety of a given child from additional abuse or neglect. Two major difficulties are involved in doing secondary prevention. The first is that since child abuse and neglect is a "variable" malady, that is, it defies standardized, and uniform definitions, it does not lend itself to easy, standardized, or uniform remediation. The causes of abuse and neglect are complex and difficult to standardize. The effect is that it is virtually impossible to develop a universal description and thus an easy and efficient way to make preventative efforts. It is not like a headache for which one can take an aspirin and have it quickly disappear. The second difficulty with secondary prevention is that it can only be done with known victims/perpetrators. It does not include those persons in the general population that may be current, future, or past victims of abuse or neglect but are unknown to agencies. Secondary prevention deals only with known situations.

In the early 1970s and 1980s, a child abuse prevention movement formed through a joining of the women's movement and child protection professionals, which became the sexual abuse prevention movement (Berrick and Gilbert, 1991). Traced to 1971, the movement, represented by the Women Against Rape Collective (WAR), fielded its first Child Assault Prevention (CAP) program at a Columbus, Ohio, Catholic elementary school (Berrick and Gilbert, 1991). From these beginnings, it spread throughout the United States. It gained a significant boost from 1980 to 1985 through funding from the National Conference on Child Abuse and Neglect. The program works to teach children in elementary schools to recognize the signs of sexual abuse and to report it to authorities. This model essentially works to prevent abuse in part of the total universe of possible victims and the recurrence of abuse for those that are or have been abused. It functions to find unreported victims or potential victims and then to facilitate their reporting.

In contrast to the other two models, tertiary prevention focuses on remediation. Secondary prevention activities discussed previously to some extent mirror tertiary prevention. The aim of tertiary prevention is to eliminate problems that already exist so the child will not experience further abuse or neglect. Providing a parent, that is, a "perpetrator" of abuse or neglect, with counseling toward a goal of eliminating the parent's problems would be tertiary prevention.

The difference between secondary and tertiary prevention relates to the extent to which the problem has become embedded within individuals or families. Situations with a deeper embedding would seem to be in greater need of therapeutic intervention than those in which the abusive behavior was more situational. These categories, while dominant in health systems, are also incipient within child abuse networks.

AMERICAN CHILD WELFARE AS INTERVENTION INTO FAMILY LIFE

Although child welfare is often thought of and described by the media and members of communities as tied to institutional level interventions, in actuality, the American system of child welfare, as a professional area of social work practice, is generally limited to intervention in family life to protect children from their parents and caretakers. In this sense, it is a major intervention into the American family. Reports are made and social workers investigate the reports. If the reports are substantiated, services are offered; if they are not substantiated, the case is closed. If services are accepted by the parent, the case is typically passed on to another social worker or another agency for service provision. At times petitions are filed in juvenile court and these become involved in a highly litigious process.* This intervention for substantiated situations of abuse or neglect can result in parents finding themselves prosecuted for child abuse or neglect and their children coming under the control of the juvenile court.

Through a working relationship between police and social workers, criminal prosecution of parents has significantly increased over the past forty years. Parents who admit their guilt to social workers may have these admissions used against them in criminal court. Even without admissions, if evidence developed in the child protection case is admissible in criminal court, the parents may be charged and convicted with criminal actions. This constitutes the criminalization of child abuse by parents or caretakers.

---

*Based on calculations from twelve reporting jurisdictions McDonald and Associates (2001) found about 190,000 petitions filed. Based on national calculations this would represent about 7 percent of total referrals. Alternately it represents approximately one-third of all substantiated referrals. What is clear is that we simply do not know how many children are referred to the juvenile court for protection.

Criminalization of child abuse has important implications for the child welfare system. It involves issues of trust and issues of effects on families. The issue becomes one of the reasonable trust the parents may have in social workers or even in other child welfare professionals after their initial experience with the child welfare system. Specifically, most social workers do not inform parents that their verbal admissions may be used against them in criminal court. Simultaneously, many child protection social workers believe that the parent "taking responsibility" for the abuse is a positive factor in terms of the child being safe. However, through the criminalization process, if the matter goes to court, the parents' taking responsibility will work against them in that they will have already admitted guilt to the "abuse" of the child.* A reasonable question then needs to be asked: Can the parents reasonably trust future social workers?

A second issue involved in the criminalization of child welfare services is that of the changes generated within family systems when parents spend money on their legal defense and/or lose earnings while they serve time in jail. The families that enter the child protective system tend to be the poor and peoples of color. Depending on the particular geographic and economic environment, some 50 to 75 percent of all child abuse reports involve child welfare clients that are Temporary Assistance to Needy Families (TANF) eligible, based on income. They have limited economic resources. Simply defending a charge in criminal court can cost thousands of dollars. The main breadwinner serving time in jail can mean a lost job, with concomitant social structural shifts within the family. These kinds of adjustments simply cause more stress for the family and essentially work against the reunification of the family.

Trust and Legitimacy in the Modern State?

Trust

Given the nature of the child welfare system as an abstract system, it is important to understand the shifting relationships between indi-

---

*Much of the child abuse treatment culture believes very strongly that an important step for a perpetrator is to admit guilt. At times, without such an admission, treatment may be terminated and at times a child may not be returned because the parent failed treatment. The problem is that "guilt" or innocence is a legal concept, not a therapeutic technique, except in a limited number of treatment models.

viduals and social institutions. As we have seen, symbolic tokens and expert systems constitute the linking systems between the concrete world of experience of individuals and the larger and removed abstract system, the social institutions. The child welfare system is an expert system and is essentially represented by the line social worker. The key factor lying with the formation and maintenance of these expert systems is the idea of individuals trusting these systems. Giddens (1991) provides an example of a man sitting in his house surrounded by expert systems. These house systems, "expert systems," have been built by various professionals. For example, architects designed the building, legal professionals plotted out the legal documents, and contractors such as plumbers, carpenters, and roofers built the house. They all have added their expertise in the building of the house. Now the man sits in his house and trusts that the roof will not fall, the water will run, the lights will work. We must conclude that he trusted their craftsmanship. Thus, we see trust is important in our individual and collective reliance on these expert systems.

If the parent feels betrayed by a social worker, can one reasonably expect him or her to trust in the intangible and confusing system? Pelton (1989, 1990, 1991, 1997) argues that this is a fundamental problem with our child welfare system. He, in this respect, is correct. He notes "something fundamentally wrong" (1989, p. 140) with the approach in child welfare. To him the workers and agency are put in an untenable position, "in which they try to gain the parents' trust and cooperation in order to help the family at the same time that they are viewed by the family as a potential threat" (1989, p. 140). The social worker is a threat to the family, at least in terms of criminal prosecution.

To understand the nature of our trust in abstract systems, we must look more deeply into governance issues. We must seek to understand what people believe about the governing structure, that is, the organizational structure of the nation, since that is what the child welfare system is embedded in.

The Legitimizing of the Governance System

What establishes the organizational structure of our society and thus the child welfare system? It is helpful to draw from anthropology and the concept of a cultural "grounding metaphor" for our culture.

This idea of a grounding metaphor is described by Mary Douglas (1986) as a concept "by which the formal structure of a crucial set of social relations is found in the physical world, or in the supernatural world, or in eternity, anywhere, so long as it is not seen as a socially contrived arrangement" (p. 48). A traditional way of viewing the establishment of this grounding metaphor is through the concept of a "founding." According to Arendt (1986), the founding of America was willful, in that it was "under the direct and conscious direction of men" (pp. 46-47). Also, it was designed after the foundings of the Greek and Roman city-states and included the use of ritual and ceremony. It also, as ritual, involved a synthesis and transformation of individual meaning or beliefs into a collectively held set of "fixed" beliefs (this process is beyond the scope of this work but is supported by such theorists as Kertzer [1988], Jung and Kerenyi [1969], Arendt [1986], Eliade [1975], and Gunnell [1987]) or "expert systems."

This idea of a grounding metaphor involves the literal building of a physical structure and a written constitution dedicated to a set of beliefs and ideologies related to the governance of a nation. More than anything, it constitutes a legitimating or grounding of the culture in a belief system, a kind of expert system. This belief system constitutes a coalescence of collective thoughts, feelings, and values that set into action the authority system, that is, the social structure of a culture or country. In short, this process involves the formation and embedding of governance norms within the governing apparatus of the nation. Thus, the constitution provides what Max Weber (1978b) would call the basic legitimate structure for governance.

The Constitution and the Bill of Rights As Embedded "Mental Models" of Our Culture

With the constitutional structure came the legitimatization of authority, along with the foundational ideology or sets of beliefs and values related to both governance, as a macrolevel structure, and processes that included individual rights identified in the Bill of Rights. This includes what Schein (1985, p. 18) would call the "basic assumptions," Alexander (1990, p. 188) would call the "ideational values," and Senge (1990, pp. 8,9) would call the "mental models" of the nation. The basic assumptions of the governing system, its system of rules, is essentially an abstract system. These establish and maintain the values and visible levels of culture. They also constitute the fundamental building blocks of the society and are essentially the institutional rules that provide a frame or structure for cultural action (Douglas, 1986). In this respect, child welfare intervention must be consonant with the values of society and with the legitimate social institutions established within this constitutional structure. In this way, the governing apparatus of the modern state is established and even trusted, or should be trusted, by the populace.

The governing apparatus, through the constitutional frame, constitutes the political institution of the society and has a complementary role with other social institutions such as the family, the economy, education, the church, and the welfare system. From a social work perspective, this organizational structure of social institutions, an abstract system, established through the Constitution, constitutes a part of what Brueggemann (2002) refers to as the megastructures that "dominate almost all of the economic, political, and social space we inhabit today" (p. 117). These dominant social institutions constitute our collective social order.

The governance worldview constitutes a top level view of our social system, while a bottom level view, that is, from the individual viewing the top of the hierarchy, constitutes a more limited perspective. This can be described metaphorically as a "forest" view versus a "tree" view of the nation. These opposing worldviews are noted by Brueggemann (2002) as differing for the individual viewing the world from his or her own perspective to one in viewing the world from a collectivist perspective. To him, this schism of individual and collectivist perspectives suggests a "polarization of the individual and organizational [levels of society that] creates a political crisis in which we are distanced from centers of power and prevented from making decisions which really matter to us" (p. 117). Nowhere is this more clear than within the operation of the child welfare system. This is an issue of trust—trust of the child welfare system and in the social worker representing that system.

Joining the Individual and the Collectivity in Child Welfare

How do these divergent pressures and tensions come together? They come together in the policymaking process and in the line level work that social workers do with clients. But how do the large-scale actions of policymakers directly impact individuals within the society and particularly in child welfare? They come together, of course, through the persons who act as legislators for the larger society. These legislators constitute a metaphoric joining point of these mediating roles and in their policymaking roles they become part of the structure that affects individuals' lives. In a very concrete way the governing elite is expected to make decisions on social problems and design programs to address the needs of individuals.

The programs and policies developed in the policymaking environment depend on countless individuals for their implementation. These individuals act as agents for the governing system and include staff, special interest groups, etc. As agents represent the elite and enact policy, problems with policies and programs become visible at times as new problems. As a result of these operational issues, new policy is developed. This continues infinitely as policymakers continue to work to solve problems (Dobelstein, 2003).

Vignette: From the Bottom

Richard Johnson couldn't believe it. He had gone to work in the morning at his regular time. At 10:00 a.m. he received a call from his wife. She was hysterical. A police officer had stopped by the house to tell her that their ten-year-old twin boys, Bobby and Robby, had been taken into protective custody at 9:00 a.m. At school they were interviewed by the police and a CPS social worker and taken into custody. Why? The boys had "ritual-like" burns/bruises on their hands and would not or could not tell the police or social worker how they got them. Richard believed it was from them playing with those "infernal" bikes. They rode and jumped to the point of bruising their bodies. No matter. Richard could not believe that the police or a CPS social worker could go to the school, interview a child, and place the child in custody all without telling the parents or having a warrant. What about the U.S. Constitution? "We have rights," he said as he called his attorney. The advice from his attorney is to "be cool." But his attorney also tells him it certainly is legal, even though he doesn't think it's right.

The "From the Bottom" vignette raises at least four questions. The first is, What gives the state the right to intervene in Richard Johnson's life? The second is, What are the limits, if any, of this right? The third is, What structures the state's intervention into his life? Last,

What is the role of the social worker from this macroscopic perspective? The first is a legal or judicial issue, the second relates to our constitutional structure, the third relates to the administrative structure including organizational culture and management, and the last relates to the professional role of social workers. The first two are examined in this chapter and the third and fourth are examined in the next two chapters.

The Authority to Intervene: Parens Patriae

The legal right to intervene in family life is the judicial doctrine of *parens patriae.* This concept, developed through judicial authority, has its origins in English common law. It is defined by Black's (1979) legal dictionary as originating "from the English common law where the King had a royal prerogative to act as guardian to persons with legal disabilities such as infants, idiots and lunatics" (p. 1003). Moreover, in the United States this authority resides in or belongs to the states (Black, 1979). It gives the state the right to intervene in family life on behalf of protecting its own interests. That is, the state is seen as having an interest in the care and treatment of children. In essence, Dobelstein (2003) would call this "judicial policy."

Historically, intervention into family life under the Elizabethan Poor Laws was by the overseer of the poor. In contrast, today's interventions are generally driven by the legal doctrine of *parens patriae.* This doctrine "describes the power of the state to act in the parent's place for the purpose of protecting a child and his or her property" (Sagatun and Edwards, 1995, p. 7). This doctrine provided the basis for the establishment of the first juvenile court, the Illinois Juvenile Court, in 1899 (Sagatun and Edwards, 1995) and continues to serve as the foundation for child protection interventions.

The concept was first applied in the United States in 1838 by a Pennsylvania court, in which the court ruled that the state had an interest in its children. The court's finding was the result of a strategic approach by privileged Americans who were concerned with the apparent connection between increased pauperism and the rise of delinquency (Krisberg, 1993). This was a child-saver group aiming to protect the cities from the poor. These politically powerful individuals, including men of wealthy, established families, prosperous merchants, and professionals, came to be labeled by historians as Conservative Reformers. They viewed themselves as God's elect and aimed to accomplish his objectives in secular life. However, their interests in the poor were rather more mundane. Krisberg (1993) notes that their "primary motivation was protection of their class privileges" (Krisberg, 1993, p. 16) and in reestablishing social order, that is, in attacking what they perceived as dangers to the status quo. "Popular democracy was anathema to them" (Krisberg, 1993, p. 16).

They were able to effectively use the legal system to authorize the placement of children in their facilities, houses of refuge. The power came through *Ex parte Crouse* in 1838. The court ruled that the doctrine of *parens patriae* applied to the involuntary commitment of children to houses of refuge. In this case, the father of a child that had been committed to a house of refuge argued that his right as a parent had been violated. The court's position and determination was that the parental right was not inalienable, and it could be set aside based on the *parens patriae* doctrine. According to the court in the *Crouse* case, "The infant has been snatched from a course [by the state] which must have ended in confirmed depravity, and not only is the restraint of her person lawful, but it would be an act of extreme cruelty to release her from it" (Hawes, 1991, p. 17).

The Constitution As Limiting Intervention

The doctrine of *parens patriae* gives the state the right to intervene in children's lives as a kind of surrogate parent, but what are the limits of this intervention? Understanding these limits is important for working in the American child welfare system. The quick answer to the question is the Constitution. The Constitution, of course, is the literary expression of the founding of the nation's governing system. It is the document that emanated from the founding process and serves to provide the governing structure for the nation.

The Constitution, through the Bill of Rights, serves to limit the state's actions of intervening into family life. In particular, the amendments to the Constitution provide rights to individuals that limit the actions of social institutions. In that it limits intervention into people's lives, the Constitution structures legal actions within the child welfare system. Social workers' interventions are limited by individual's legal rights under the constitutional structure. This means that social workers are not allowed to do certain things because of constitutional protections. To understand the work of the Constitution as limiting action within the American child welfare system, one must look at its key provisions and how they affect child welfare.

CONSTITUTIONAL RIGHTS

The Individual: The Constitutional Rights Perspective

Four constitutional protections circumscribe interventions into individuals' lives. These protections constitute essential rules that must be followed by the state in its actions of governance. These rights apply to individuals, not to families. The Constitution does not make any provision for the social institution of the family. As noted earlier, some legislators have developed "family preservation" programs, for example; however, these represent legislative policy rather than constitutional requirements.

For the social worker in child welfare, the Fourth, Fifth, Sixth, and Fourteenth Amendments to the Constitution limit intervention into individuals' lives. These limits are essentially embedded in child welfare agencies, within policies and procedures. They have come to be taken for granted and are in many instances rarely visible as constitutional protections. Social workers in child protective agencies do not typically discuss these as limiting what they do, but rather discuss policy that incorporates and operationalizes these limits. These amendments with a brief description are as follows:

Fourth Amendment

> The right of the people to be secure in their persons, houses, papers, and effects, against unreasonable searches and seizures, shall not be violated, and no Warrants shall issue, but upon probable cause, supported by Oath or affirmation, and particularly describing the place to be searched, and the persons or things to be seized.

Although search warrants are not typically required for child protection social workers to investigate allegations of abuse or neglect, this amendment provides a structure within which the social worker and police must work. This amendment sets the standard of probable cause for obtaining a warrant for the seizure of persons or things. Around the nation, there is not a standard protocol as to when a social worker must have a warrant to take a child into custody. For example, in some jurisdictions it is a standard practice to get a court order for removing a child, while in other jurisdictions if a social worker believes a child is in immediate danger he or she may take a child into custody. Also, in some jurisdictions only police officers as peace officers may take children into custody.

This warrant requirement essentially means that child protection social workers can have access to the home of a parent only with the parent's permission. They have no right to enter without a warrant. They also have no right to remove any "evidence" of a crime. Only police, as peace officers, have such powers and theirs are circumscribed by procedures and protocols associated with the procurement of a warrant. However, if a parent is unwilling to provide the social worker with access to the child, and the social worker has reasonable cause to believe the child has been or will be abused or neglected, he or she can request police to respond. At that point, dependent upon the level of concern for the well-being of the child, police may be able to gain access to the child even without a warrant.

Vignette: Police, Drugs, and Child Protection

Margaret, a CPS social worker in the after-hours program, was responding to a call from a school reporting that a seven-year-old boy had serious bruises on his arms and legs. Also, his father reportedly was potentially violent and involved with drug sales. Margaret called for police backup. The police came and stood behind Margaret as she talked to the mother and negotiated her access to the boy, including entrance to the home. As soon as Margaret entered the house, the police entered and began to look for drugs. Later Margaret told a colleague, "Those big, burly police officers didn't help at all. They just pushed me in front so when I got in they could go on a search for drugs—all to avoid getting a warrant."

The "Police, Drugs, and Child Protection" vignette illustrates unintended effects of the warrantless search. Police may gain access to a home on the basis of a child abuse investigation and while there may be able to see evidence of drug manufacture, sales, etc. The net outcome may be an arrest of the father or mother on drug possession charges. This appears to be one of several by-products of our War on Drugs described by McNamara (1997).

Fifth Amendment

> No person shall be held to answer for a capital, or otherwise in-famous crime, unless on a presentment or indictment of a Grand Jury, except in cases arising in the land or naval forces, or in the Militia, when in actual service in time of War or public danger; nor shall any person be subject for the same offence to be twice put in jeopardy of life or limb; nor shall be compelled in any criminal case to be a witness against himself, nor be deprived of life, liberty, or property, without due process of law; nor shall private property be taken for public use, without just compensa-tion.

The issue here is the individual's right to be informed of his or her rights with respect to due process within a criminal prosecution. This amendment was noted in the *Miranda vs. Arizona* case by the court in citing the right of suspects in criminal matters to be informed of their due process rights.

Two rulings in the Supreme Court emphasized juveniles' rights to legal due process. These included *Kent v. United States* in 1966 and *In re Gault* in 1967. The *Kent* case involved a juvenile that was trans-ferred to adult criminal court without an adequate hearing. According to Sagatun and Edwards (1995) the court "noted that the minor was receiving the 'worst of both worlds,' as he received inadequate due process and inadequate care and treatment" (p. 9). In the *Gault* case, the minor had been in a treatment facility for five years for a crime for which he would have spent a few months in jail had he been an adult. The Supreme Court found that "the state had assumed jurisdiction of Gerry Gault without affording him constitutional rights" (p. 9). The court ruled that a minor needed to be afforded certain constitutional rights before the state could intervene. The required noticing in-cluded

1. the notice of the charges against him or her;
2. the right to legal counsel;

3. the privilege against self-incrimination, that is, the right to remain silent; and
4. the right to confront and cross-examine witnesses.

The right to remain silent essentially means that a person cannot be compelled to be a witness against himself or herself (Sagatun and Edwards, 1995).

Although the rights outlined in the *Gault* case appear clear, considerable variation occurs in terms of how they are applied to juveniles in dependency cases. Both of the previously cited cases involved "delinquent" children, thus some jurisdictions interpret the decision as applicable only to delinquents. Thus they may treat "dependent" children with less forthrightness. For example, jurisdictions vary as to when they give parents a copy of the petition, a formal exposition of the charges or allegations before the court. Also, jurisdictions at times interpret the right to legal counsel as requiring an attorney at only certain stages of the adjudication process, while some jurisdictions use Court Appointed Special Advocates (CASAs) or guardians ad litem to advocate for parents or children.

This amendment also has been interpreted as protecting a person from being tried twice for the same offense. From the juvenile court's perspective this has a limited role. Abuse or neglect as described in most codes does not exclusively require one event. That is, it is not the same as driving without a license in that either you were or you were not. In child abuse/neglect scenarios the event would be connected to its having a detrimental effect on a child. For example, the petition might say, "the parent hit the child resulting in deep bruising." This would illustrate that the parent did something to the child that caused detriment. In such a situation, an alternate petition might be filed. The exception being some cases that may be dismissed with prejudice.

Perhaps most important, the Fifth Amendment requires reasonable and fair application of the law. According to Purpura (1997), "**Due process of law,** as stated in the Fifth Amendment, means that laws must be reasonable and applied in a fair manner while upholding individual rights" (p. 75). This suggests that social workers must be sure that clients are provided with informed consent regarding their discussions with the social worker.

An important issue in public child welfare is social workers interviewing parents, getting admissions of guilt, and then the parents later being criminally prosecuted for violations and having their "confessions" used against them. The thinking that providing parents with informed consent is not necessary rests on the view that since social workers are not peace officers, they have no right to conduct criminal investigations. Also, while they interview "alleged perpetrators," not "suspects," of abuse or neglect and since they are not peace officers, there is no need to inform clients of the potential use of their "confessions." Clearly a distinction can be made between alleged perpetrators and suspects in a legal sense, and between the social worker and a peace officer. However, given that police typically have full access to social workers' reports, ethical if not moral issues are involved in this system level action. Some jurisdictions handle this ethical/moral problem/issue by informing clients in writing of the sharing of information with the police. This amendment also allows parents not to talk with social workers.

This can be said another way. Interviews of parents or caretakers differ markedly from interrogations of suspects. Social workers typically have limited involvement with suspects of criminal laws. However, police as peace officers interview not only victims of child abuse but also suspected perpetrators and also suspects. A suspect is a person that the police believe has committed a crime. When they believe a person is a suspect, they can treat him or her under a different set of rules, that is, legal requirements.

When a person moves from the social classification of witness to the social classification of suspect, an interview becomes an interrogation for police. Court rulings related to the interrogation of suspects differ markedly from interviews of clients. Probably the most significant difference is that police are allowed not only to ask suspects leading questions but to virtually lie to suspects (Inbau, Reid, and Buckley, 1986). The important point for social workers to realize is that police interrogate suspects, while social workers interview parents, children, and sometimes relatives and witnesses.

Sixth Amendment

In all criminal prosecutions, the accused shall enjoy the right to a speedy and public trial, by an impartial jury of the State and district wherein the crime shall have been committed, which district shall have been previously ascertained by law, and to be informed of the nature and cause of the accusation; to be confronted with the witnesses against him; to have compulsory process for obtaining witnesses in his favor, and to have the Assistance of Counsel for his defense.

This amendment includes the individual's right to notice of accusations, to confront witnesses, to subpoena witnesses, and to have an attorney. As noted earlier, this is probably one of the more uneven areas of implementation of the rights of due process within the country as they relate to child welfare cases. From the criminal justice perspective, the right to counsel applies to "all the stages of the criminal justice process, from pretrial custody to the appellate process" (Purpura, 1997, p. 76). In child welfare jurisdictions, the answer to the question of its application to parents and children is that "it depends." Some jurisdictions do not regularly assign counsel to children or parents until the later stages of dependency actions, while others assign attorneys from the first hearing. The effect of this is that case situations may move through the crucial case-building stages of the judicial process without legal representation. As noted earlier, some jurisdictions attempt to offset the need for legal counsel with the use of guardians ad litem or court-appointed special advocates (CASAs); however, neither is sanctioned or skilled to represent the legal interests of either children or their parents.

As noted previously, jurisdictions vary significantly in their providing notice of allegations and hearings. Some provide such notice, others do not, and some do sometimes. For example, in some jurisdictions, parents will receive notices and a copy of the petition at the detention hearing, while at others the detention hearing is informal and parents receive such written information at a later time. The diversity of court actions is noted by Sagatun and Edwards (1995) as they describe the variation in time frames and legal representation nationally.

Vignette: What About Legal Protections?

Becky, four years old, and her brother Joey, age three, have been in foster care for two years. They came into care after their eighteen-

(continued)

(continued)

month-old sister was found dead as the result of child abuse. Both parents were involved with the child within the time frame that she died. However, the police were not able to develop enough information to charge either parent. The juvenile court had made the children dependents of the court, and the social service agency provided eighteen months of family reunification services. At the permanency planning hearing about two years into the court case, the parents were each provided with an attorney. They were now separated. The children did not have an attorney during any part of the dependency process.

Vignette: Another Approach to Due Process

Roberto was taken into custody at birth due to his mother's drug use. Three other children had also been removed due to her neglect as the result of her abuse of illegal substances. At the detention hearing, the judge ordered that Roberto and each of his parents be provided with legal counsel.

Fourteenth Amendment

Section 1. All persons born or naturalized in the United States, and subject to the jurisdiction thereof, are citizens of the United States and of the State wherein they reside. No State shall make or enforce any law which shall abridge the privileges or immunities of citizens of the United States; nor shall any State deprive any person of life, liberty, or property, without due process of law; nor deny to any person within its jurisdiction the equal protection of the laws.

This amendment simply says that no state may make or enforce its own laws that abridge these basic protections that are accorded to citizens of the United States. That is, the states are required to follow federal law with respect to due process of law and equal protection under the law.

CONCLUSION

This chapter discussed a combination of the macrolevel structure underlying, or behind if one prefers, child welfare services in the United States and the structure that provides for individual rights. The macrolevel structure includes the legislature, the executive branch, and the judiciary. This includes each of these administrative structures at each level within each state. Each level of political organization, states, regions, and counties develops its own child protection systems based on its local values.

Chapter 4

Multiple Dimensions
of Child Welfare Governance

INTRODUCTION

This chapter examines the federalist system of authority, that which operates in the child welfare system. This includes the dispersal of authority to the three governing bodies and the shifting interpretations of the governing system. It is an extension of the governing process established within the Constitution. The chapter also discusses the various levels of authority and how they blend in actual practice, including their hierarchical relationships and ambiguities, and the tensions in policy implementation that have resulted from this structure.

Before discussing these issues, it is important to address the question of why it is necessary to understand this level of governance to practice in child welfare. The concepts presented in this chapter are essentially embedded in the child welfare system, in that they are incorporated deeply within the policy structure of particular agencies as mental models or basic assumptions. Understanding this level of governance simply helps the social worker to understand the basis for policies and procedures that otherwise make little sense. In short, to be a knowledgeable and informed practitioner in child welfare, it is important to understand these governance issues. Also, for those who aspire toward administrative or supervisory positions in child welfare this knowledge is vital.

THE CONSTITUTION
AND FRAGMENTED AUTHORITY

We have already seen how the Constitution sanctions and legitimizes governance in the United States (Rohr, 1986; Arendt, 1986) and also limits government interventions. The Constitution disperses authority into three interdependent streams: administrative, legislative, and judicial. The Constitution provides a triadic and dynamic balance of power. It provides a kind of dynamic balance between the actions of abstract systems including social megastructures, and the individual qua individual with rights assured by the Bill of Rights.

Vignette: The Constitution and the Court Hearing

Bill, a social worker new to the Division of Children's Services, was attending his first settlement conference. It was a detention hearing, and it involved a young mother with a many-year history of substance abuse. The last of her five children had just been removed from her custody because police found her under the influence of an illegal substance in her apartment with her two-year-old daughter. Police had responded to an anonymous child abuse report. In this jurisdiction, police did not need a warrant to check out a child abuse/neglect allegation.

The settlement conferences were informal and held in the judge's chambers. They were designed to highlight key issues that were holding up the resolution of the matter before the court. Bill sat at a designated place at the round table. Before the meeting could begin, Ms. Walker, the public defender, stood up and proclaimed loudly, "The American Constitution guarantees each of its citizens protection from the illegal searches by big government, including the police. Taking this child into custody is just like stealing cattle. Not only is it a despicable act, but it was illegal and obviously immoral, unjust, and unfair." The judge responded, "The court recognizes your objection, Ms. Walker. Now please sit down."

THE FEDERALIST STRUCTURE

Competition, Cooperation, and Collaboration Within the Federalist Structure

We live in a federalist governing system, in which we have governance of individual states by the federal government. This is not a government of individuals by the federal government. For example, we vote in presidential elections at the local level. We elect electors, who then elect the U.S. president. We do not live in a popular democracy in which all voters vote directly for the president. Thus, our government is a government of the states rather than a government of the people. As such, it is a federation of states.

What is the nature of this federalist structure and why is it important? The structure, provided within our Constitution, involves the concept that complete power should not be invested within any particular governing body. This structure provides the foundation for the social administration of child welfare. This includes the Constitution with its Bill of Rights and the administrative arrangements that these have established. In short, this sets up a triadic system of governance. From early classes in political science, liberal arts students learn about this constitutional separation of powers within the United States. The federalist system under which the country was founded essentially divides these governing activities into legislative, executive, and judicial processes (Dobelstein, 2003). This separation of these functions into one "federated" structure leads us to refer to the structure as a federalist structure. Federated in this usage refers to a coming together of the states within the structure of the Constitution as the United States of America.

Generally, the federalist structure has remained stable, although interpretations as to the way agencies are to work together have changed over time. These changing interpretations are important to understand because agencies, such as those that characterize the child welfare system, adopt these ideological and interpretative patterns and expect social workers to perform accordingly. In recent times at least until the 1980s, this structure was viewed as competitive. Agencies were viewed as working within distinct boundaries. Each had its own mission and worked within fairly narrow parameters. Waldo (1984) describes this as "competitive federalism" (p. 121). For social workers this roughly translated into the idea that institutional arrangements involved competition between agencies. This meant that each agency provided services more or less exclusively to their own clients and boundary setting around functions was de rigueur. Generally social workers worked within their own boundaries and tried to respect the boundary systems of other practitioners.

The 1980s saw an administrative or institutional shift from a competitive model to a cooperative view of organizational interaction. Government agencies were expected to work together, cooperatively, in providing services to people. Social workers were expected to cooperate with their counterparts in other agencies in providing services to clients. Waldo (1984) describes this more recent version of federalism as "cooperative federalism" (p. 121). Under this situation, workers could cross organizational boundaries and work cooperatively for their clients' best interests. Case managers and therapists from different agencies might meet jointly with a client to improve services.

Today's world involves broad-ranging ideas such as "globalization" and "international interdependence" driven, at least in part, by "free trade" agreements. Not surprisingly, today's interpreted view of federalism is that organizational relationships as they serve clients should be collaborative. The world of which child welfare is a part includes an international community that is rapidly demanding shifts in this interpretation of federalism. The shift is to collaboration (Mathews, 1997; Newland, 2001; Farazmand, 1999). This seems to be a further shift in what Waldo observed, and if he were writing today he would probably refer to this as "collaborative federalism." In this context, it is not surprising that in today's world, de rigueur is collaboration. This is manifested in "wraparound" services and "family conferencing." The idea is that agencies, that is, organizations, work jointly through the efforts of their employees (social workers) to serve joint clients. This involves a joining of larger systems in collaborative ventures, for example, agencies, families, etc., with workers as part of the arrangements.

While the shifts in the interpretation of the federalist governance actions continue, the American Constitution remains a triadic structure of the administration and operation of programs such as the child welfare system. This three-part structure, that is, the separation of powers, is reflected in state and local governments. Each organizational level reflects a diffusion of responsibility and authority within the triadic form or structure. Thus, we have federal, state, and local courts, legislatures, and administrations.

Child Welfare Within This Triadic Structure

While we have a dispersal of authority into the three major streams of judicial, administrative, and legislative, we also have a vertical separation of levels and streams as laws, regulations, executive orders, and policies at each administrative level. We also have court opinions, findings, and case law at multiple levels. In addition, we have child welfare organizations, courts, and law enforcement also at multiple levels of organization.

Vignette: Who Has Information Systems?

Jane, a CPS social worker, was asked to sit in on an information systems meeting for her boss, the director of the department. She was asked to attend because her computer literacy and organizational skills were well known within the department. The topic for the meeting was to find ways to bring a variety of information systems together to assist social workers in their child welfare investigations. Jane was astounded to hear about the multiplicity of information systems. Criminal justice systems numbered about a dozen, her own department had some six systems for ordinary work, and other committee members had access to a number of other systems at the county, state, and federal levels. She was amazed. It had all seemed so simple. Just get access to one information system. It turns out that there were probably a couple of dozen systems, none of which "talked" with one another. *My oh my,* she thought. *How these systems people guard their turf!*

Although this discussion of administrative structures may seem abstract, it is very real to social workers working in public child welfare. In political science classes the student may find the notion of this separation of functions or power detached from daily life, but the child welfare worker works with this every day.

This separation of powers and its application to social work practice adds some unique elements to social work practice in child welfare. The social worker is expected to implement laws established through the legislative process, within the context of the administration of the local social services agency, and simultaneously be directly involved with the adjudication process of the juvenile court. In contrast with other areas of social work practice, child welfare work involves working intimately with the basic governing tension associated with differences and perceptions of difference involved in these three governing processes.

Vignette: Which Level of Law Applies?

A social worker consults with her supervisor. She is preparing to attend a hearing that afternoon. The parents, in completing eligibility documents for their son in foster care, saw the section informing them of their right to an administrative review hearing. They followed directions to appeal the services being provided to them. They wanted their child back and believed this would help. So, while the juvenile court was conducting an ongoing jurisdictional hearing, the state hearing officer was here to conduct an administrative review as to the adequacy of services the social worker had provided.

The problem for the social worker was that the parents had refused to participate with her in formulating a plan for service delivery. She had followed agency and court policy by submitting a service plan to the court, with a statement regarding the parents' failure to participate in the plan. The court had accepted the plan and was well aware of the services issues. Now, the hearing officer was in the position of conducting an administrative review that was essentially overseeing the judicial process. The worker questioned what she should do.

Vignette Clarification

Viewing the question from the social worker's position at the bottom of the constitutional hierarchy, the primary question is that of which body, the juvenile court or the administrative hearing officer, had jurisdiction. Said another way, which official body has jurisdiction over what elements in a particular situation? In general, a social worker should assume that the juvenile court either has authority over or must be involved in virtually any major decision to be made on behalf of a child under its jurisdiction. In those situations in which the court does not have such authority, for example, in situations in which the child may be adjudicated as a danger to self or others and placed in a state hospital situation, the court will typically want to be apprised of the situation. Similarly, if a child wants to leave foster care and enter the Job Corps, the court may similarly want to be involved.

Simply being respectful toward those involved is important. What would typically happen in the previous scenario is the social worker would explain the situation to the hearing officer, who would simply defer to the juvenile court.

Federalist Levels and Their Interaction

Federal Level

As we have seen, the legislative branch makes the laws, the executive branch administers the laws, and the judicial branch adjudicates the extent to which administrative action matches the legislated laws and the constitutional context. Administrative action in implementing legislative action takes the form of guidelines as policy or regulations. These regulations, while not laws, carry the weight of law. That is, they are considered to be law, unless they conflict with actual legislation. For example, when Congress enacts legislation such as the Child Abuse Prevention and Treatment Act and the president signs it and it becomes law, the federal bureaucrats write regulations that are designed to provide guidance to states in its implementation. As long as the regulations do not conflict with the law, they function for the most part just as though they are the law. Thus, as this is implemented, the distinction between regulation and legislation becomes invisible. The problem arises when a social worker gets a case situation in which these are in conflict.

State Level

Each state has its own legislation in order to implement federal law. Each state legislature must pass its own enabling legislation that is acceptable to the governor in order for him or her to sign it into law. In order to be in compliance with federal actions, the legislation must meet federal requirements. However, federal legislation is often broad enough to leave considerable room for state lawmakers to create their own public policy. This is not usually an exact duplicate of federal legislation. For this reason it is not surprising that we rarely see two state laws exactly the same. Just as at the federal level, state legislators typically implement their own laws through written regulations. These have been traditionally done by bureaucrats, but more recently have involved agency and community-based participants or stakeholders. This involvement of stakeholders is another example of collective federalism. Similar to the federal level, these regulations carry the weight of law.

For the most part, social workers work within the context of state laws and regulations. The federal law often is invisible because it is embedded within any particular state's legal system. One of the best examples of the fragmentation and decoupling of concepts from the federal statutes is the case of the Child Abuse Prevention and Treatment Act (CAPTA). While CAPTA has a definition of child abuse and neglect, each state has implemented its own version of the federal law. The result is that while federal legislation holds one definition of child abuse and neglect, each state has different definitions of child abuse and neglect. That is, each state constructs its own legal working model of the nature of child abuse and neglect.

The timing of these processes, such as legislative action and regulation writing, can vary from being very quick to being very slow. If items are considered emergency measures they typically will move on a fast track. In such cases, as we know from our own experiences with income tax issues on a national level, the passage of the law to its local level administration can be a matter of weeks or months. Alternately, for the implementation of "ordinary items" the process can take many years. Each step typically has a public response period to promulgate final regulations. At times, these public response periods will involve hearings in various parts of the nation or state. Sometimes, implementation is done without formal regulations; they are written after implementation of the law.

Judicial Policy

Judicial action takes the form of the adjudication of particular issues brought before the court. That is, "decisions by courts at various governmental levels can also enunciate social policy and give direction to governmental and societal action" (Dolgoff, Feldstein, and Skolnik, 1997, p. 120). For example, the *Gault v. Arizona* case has significantly impacted child welfare work in the United States. As we have seen, the *Gault* case shifted the child welfare system emphasis from the indeterminate sentencing system under professional decision making to the modern-day litigious system.

Prior to *Gault,* the court left considerable authority to the social worker's judgment. For example, indeterminate sentences for minors involved their being detained in custody until social workers involved in treatment centers determined that they were rehabilitated and could leave. That is, social workers were able to make clinical judgments on the extent to which the child's problems had been resolved. Custody was focused on remedying these problems. Alternately, sentences became determinate in that juveniles served specific sentences, no matter the opinion of helping professionals.

Informal Processes

A fourth element affecting the context and the structure of child welfare is that of the informal processes that are a part of society at large. Dolgoff and colleagues describe these as "public decision making and choices of societal direction . . . [being] accomplished through a spontaneous understanding of a large-scale public will" (1997, p. 129). An example of this informal governing process is a group of agency directors, social work faculty, and professional social workers joining to develop standards for the education and training of public child welfare professionals. Although not existing in a legal sense, as a practical matter they may make policy governing the education and training of social workers.

A second example is the nonenforcement of laws that discriminate against people in some jurisdictions. This often occurs when the Supreme Court overturns laws and some jurisdictions still have those laws "on the books." The laws are simply not enforceable and so they are informally ignored.

THE ADMINISTRATIVE STRUCTURE

As outlined in the preceding chapter, the third question we need to examine to understand the macrostructure within which child welfare operates is that of how the state's child welfare intervention is structured. As we have seen, the Constitution is an outward manifestation of the formative principles, values, and ideologies that constitute the grounding of the nation's system of authority. As such, it establishes the basic administrative structure for the nation including the child welfare system. This structure includes the basic rights, duties, and obligations that are associated with the governing structures and social institutions. Within this structure we have the legislature developing the program, the administration administering the program, and the judiciary making case-by-case decisions on services for individual clients.

However, several other factors have affected the administration and provision of services within child welfare. As we have seen, shifts in the interpretation of the Constitution have affected how services are administered and provided to clients. Also, external forces have affected this service delivery system. Some major economic, social, and cultural shifts have contributed to changes in the ordering and structuring of services in child welfare. In particular, major shifts from a rural, individualistic, agricultural, and competitive system at our founding to a mass society (Shils, 1982), to an organizational society (Presthus, 1978), to a bureaucratic society (Hummel, 1982), and to a postmodernist society (Brueggemann, 2002) have changed how we look at the administration and delivery of services.

Although the exact form of the organizational type may be unclear, the nation as a society must be viewed as a total entity, however imperfect this view may be. In the recent past, social workers have argued for a reductionist view of social problems. The rationale is that "an entire human service system in most communities is too complex to analyze as a whole" (Netting, Kettner, and McMurty, 1998, p. 160). Although such an approach may serve some purposes, the view taken in this work is that we must view the total system and move toward macrolevel solutions to macrolevel problems. To limit our view, however complex the system, to a partial view of the particular system simply limits our ability to understand the complex array of forces that operate on our selves, our profession, and our clients. It makes us less effective as social workers as we do not see the complete picture.

As an alternative to this partial view of the administrative system, we can expand our perceptions to the level of the "administrative state." Dwight Waldo (1984) presents us with a way to understand this organizational phenomena. In his view, American society has evolved to the point that it needs to be conceptualized and thought of as an administrative state (Waldo, 1984), that is, as a holistic entity.

Child welfare represents a national program, despite the dispersal of authority and the variations in definitions of abuse and neglect. The program is structured as a system within the context of what Waldo calls this administrative state. That is, the American "administrative state" also structures the child welfare system. In this view, American society has evolved to the point that it needs to be conceptualized and thought of as an administrative whole (Waldo, 1984). The collective social world of the United States needs to be conceived as a social organization and administrative actions need to be viewed in this manner. The child welfare system becomes one part of this larger organization.

Vignette: The Organization of Child Welfare As Metaphor

The new social worker is meeting with his supervisor. "But I don't understand! When I was in graduate school, my placements were in organizations like mental health and other counseling agencies. I worked in these agencies, people came to see me, and I counseled them. Now you are telling me that child welfare is different—that it includes not only the agency that gives me a check but the juvenile court, the educational system, the police, medical staff, child advocates, and more. I just don't understand it."

In conceptualizing the organization so broadly, the boundaries within which a social worker must work become permeable. Organizations as we traditionally think about them are bounded by physical structures and have policies and procedures that serve as guides for employee behavior and action. Child welfare agencies have policies and procedures to guide action; however, the environment within which the social worker is expected to operate is extremely broad. In fact, as an organizational type, it requires a special way of viewing organizational life.

Morgan (1996) describes organizational life as based on metaphors that lead us to see only partial views of the total phenomena. In social work, the ecological perspective, with its emphasis on transactions, is one such limiting metaphor for viewing organizational life. Instead of partial views of organizations, it is important to recognize that the child welfare system is itself an abstract system that needs to be conceptualized within the context of each particular client. In this sense, organizations are themselves described as metaphors that sustain and maintain collective life. The child welfare system in which the social worker practices is essentially a social institutional level organization.

Working on the Local Level: The Joining of Levels

Our federated structure, with various administrative, legislative, and judicial levels of organization, provides considerable complexity and can be best described as consisting of a kind of nesting relationships of public policies and laws. Each policy, including legislative, judiciary, or administrative policies with appellate levels, has a place within the abstracted set of rules that control and direct the line social worker in child welfare. These levels of legislation and regulation fit together in a virtually nonvisible web in which the social worker is expected to operate. However, in addition to the federal and state networks, the social worker must also work within the web of local agency policy and regulations and with the juvenile court and its laws, procedures, and rules.

The Hierarchy of Laws and Regulations

The administration of child welfare programs is typically involved in the actual working design and implementation of the program. In this context, the organization's administration is responsible for program-level decisions. This includes the kinds of services that will be purchased or provided for all clients within the context of the authorizing legislation.

However, the judicial system is also responsible for aspects of service provision. Specifically the juvenile court is responsible for services provided on a case by case basis. The court has a responsibility to oversee such items as reasonable efforts made by the social worker not to remove a child from a family or to return the child to the family. The agency, in contrast, is responsible for providing a set of services that the social worker, as case manager, may access to accomplish the individual goals of his or her client.

Vignette: Conflict Between Court and Agency

Beverly sat in court but couldn't believe what she had heard. The judge had just ordered the department to pay a six-month security deposit and money down for a chronically homeless client. The depart-

(continued)

(continued)

ment, with its limited budget, simply could not afford to provide housing for everyone that needed it. Now, if the judge's order held, the division could be forced to pay such funds for all homeless clients with children. She knew there would be a flock of administrative meetings as soon as she got back to the office. Her administration would say that this violated the separation of powers within the Constitution. The judiciary, in this view, had overstepped its boundaries and was now threatening to administer the child welfare programs.

One way to understand the interrelationship of these concepts is to study social work practice through the hierarchy of their power or effect. For example, in the following list we see laws, regulations, case law, and administrative procedures organized by their relative strength in compelling compliance within the child welfare setting.

Importance	Item	Significance
Most powerful	Law (written)	The law of the land
Used to determine case law	Legislators' intent in formulating law	Used by court to interpret law as part of appeal process
Second in power	Case law	The law of the land
Third in power	Regulations implementing law	Weight of law
Fourth in power	Administrative policy	Subordinate to federal regulations
Fifth in power	Administrative procedures/reviews	Carry the weight of policy

LAW AND POLICY BY APPELLATE DECISIONS

So far this discussion has focused only on the static dimensions of the legislative and administrative processes and on the operation of organizations. In addition, a dynamic aspect of the legal structure is present in public child welfare. Specifically, as each case is acted upon by the juvenile court, each side has the right to appeal decisions to a higher judicial level. The right to appeal has inherent within it specific time constraints for taking action.

Appeals must be done within the time constraints established by law. In the case of adoption cases, these various levels of appeal can take many years. Although any given court action may be decisive, permanency can be reasonably assured only after the appellate process is completed or not used. For example, for a foster/adoptive family to adopt a child who is in a juvenile court system, two legal venues are involved. The first is the juvenile court, which may take from one to a couple of years. The second court that becomes involved in some jurisdictions is the probate court. This requires a series of steps that must be taken in legal order. In total, since an appellate process can exist simultaneously with each court, a conservative estimate of the longest time for an adoption to be complete will be in terms of many years. Jurisdictions can vary considerably from this estimate.

This idea of the rights of appealing cases gives rise to the questions relating to the hierarchical nature of the legal system. In the daily operation of the court a couple of different laws or rules impact the court. The first is the rules of court for the particular jurisdiction. This compilation of court-specific rules guides the court's actions at a local level. While governing court action, at times these may not be widely distributed. The second is case law. In the legal arena, case law is essentially that which is established through the course of the appealing of cases to higher judicial levels.*

For example, in California, case law was established in 1990 by *In re Malinda S.* This Supreme Court decision established case law that allowed for the presentation of hearsay evidence in California child welfare cases. According to Sagatun and Edwards (1995) "the California Supreme Court upheld the rule that the juvenile court could properly rely upon a social study which was replete with hearsay evidence in support of its jurisdictional finding that a child was a dependent of the court" (pp. 75-76). The *Malinda S.* ruling was the result of a finding in a sexual abuse case from San Diego County in California. Since the California Supreme Court ruled on this case, it is unique to and valid throughout California. Case law can move beyond any particular state, but that subject is beyond the scope of this work.

---

*An important distinction needs to be made between case law that is established as a result of appeals and appeals that do not establish case law. Through a judicial review of appellate cases some cases are determined to be publishable. Those cases in a sense become the cases in which case law is established. Alternately, some appeal cases are rendered nonpublishable. Those cases establish issues in connection with a particular case but do not affect other cases of the same type.

In summary, the appellate process and the interrelationship of case law and legislative law, combined with ongoing administrative and legislative changes, establishes a dynamic and ever-changing legal environment in which the social worker in public child welfare practices. The implications for this in terms of practice are fairly simple and straightforward. The social worker can expect to be involved in cases that are appealed to different court systems in different jurisdictions at some time during his or her professional career. Given the trend to more highly litigated situations, social workers practicing in a complex setting will likely find themselves described as some part of an appellate process in a particular case.

LEGISLATION BY OVERSIGHT

Even with its own innate level of complexity, the legal system also involves an additional level of ambiguity. Unfortunately, the legislative process at times bogs down. The effect is that laws are enacted despite considerable confusion in their legislated programs and required actions. The net result is that at times the ambiguity that bogged legislators down in the legislative process is essentially transferred into the level of program implementation—the level at which the line-level social worker is involved. These legislative actions create extensive tensions and conflicts for social workers as they attempt to implement changes in institutional arrangements within an uncertain structure.

Americans with Disability Act (ADA) As Legislation Requiring Court Definitions

Probably one of the more common legislative approaches to these highly complex, contentious, and value-laden issues are those in which the judiciary is expected to define critical program elements. For example, Karger et al. (2003) suggests that the Americans with Disability Act was enacted with a view that the judiciary would determine how the law would be implemented. He notes that "the ADA was obviously based on good intentions. It was an open-ended act predicated on letting the courts decide on the particulars of the law" (p. 146). In this action, the legislator wrote extremely broad descriptions and definitions with the expectation that the court would essentially re-write those definitions, through appellate decisions, to make them legal.

Education for Foster Children As Ambiguous Legislation

Similarly, in public child welfare, Mark Jacobs (1986), in his analysis of the forces behind child welfare organizational operational changes, found internal program conflicts that made it difficult for workers implementing programs at the local level. The changes he analyzed were made through Public Law 93-647, the Social Services Amendments of 1974, which created Title XX, and Public Law 94-142, the Education for All Handicapped Act of 1975. These acts appeared to increase entitlements and services; however, their effect was to create a local level administrative structure that was both vague and ambiguous in what they offered and in terms of who was eligible. This particularly affected foster children who were considered under the jurisdiction of this legislation.

Jacobs (1986) found that this lack of clarity resulted in local administrative conflicts concerning the placement of a select group of special educationally qualified children. The effect of the formulation of federal law on the individual level, that is, the level of the social worker—the level of seeing and helping individuals—was to create a complex local level replete with organizational conflict. These situations, while involving individual children, required extensive work by line level practitioners to resolve disputes. The net result on an organizational level was a considerable amount of ambiguity regarding who was responsible for what aspect of the implementation of the law. Social workers felt considerable frustration as they were called upon to implement aspects of the law that they had no authority to enact.

Vignette: Ambiguity at the Local Level

Shirley, a CPS social worker, placed Jamie, age eight, in a foster home in Somewhere County. She did this following usual court and agency protocols. Two days later, she received a call from the foster

(continued)

(continued)

mom, who told her the school district wouldn't provide an educational program for Jamie. Upon calling the district, Shirley learned that under new special educational requirements the placement of a child within a school district required prior "legal noticing" and prior approval of the school district. This was the first that she had heard of this. Inquiring among other social workers and supervisors and court personnel, she found none that knew about this new law. In checking further with the school district administrators, she learned that while noticing was a requirement, the district didn't have a protocol for receiving the notice or acting on it. In addition, since the noticing procedure wasn't followed, the child would not be served in the school system. The solution was to begin an advocacy process to get services to the child. She talked with the foster parents and formulated an appeal of the decision. Meanwhile, the child had no school placement.

Since there is a lack of uniformity among school districts, another organization within the federalist structure, the situation in the "Ambiguity at the Local Level" vignette was faced in each district. In addition, since it was not dealt with on an organizational level, each social worker with each case had to repeat Shirley's advocacy process. Since there was no communication with the administrators of the child welfare agency (the regulations were educational regulations, not welfare regulations) this kind of ambiguity is not visible to them. Thus, no official protocols were established to handle these issues. That is, the social service workers, since they did not recognize the issue as an "official" concern pertinent to their program, did not develop or release protocols dealing with the provision of such noticing involving confidential material. The net result for the social worker is simply much confusion and frustration as he or she attempts to meet the multiple demands of many different sections of the federal and state levels of government and the general community.

CAPTA As Overly Broad

The Child Abuse Prevention and Treatment Act represents yet another piece of federal legislation that actually resulted in an incongruity between a broadly defined problem and the local level of administration's capacity to act. The legislation included an overly broad definition of child abuse and neglect, which essentially set up a reporting system for many actions that did not constitute abuse or neglect within individual states. The exact definitions of abuse and neglect are determined by the states, and they do not match the federal reporting guidelines. The result is that local level administrations such as counties and states are reimbursed for taking referrals that do not constitute legally defined abuse or neglect within their respective domains. That is, the federal statute casts a wide net to bring in suspected cases of child abuse and neglect and the actual child protection system then limits those it acts on. Referrals, in this sense, are taken on situations that do not constitute abuse or neglect by local statutes and on which there may appear to be slight grounds for protective action.

Child Abuse Legislation Without Statistical Support

Berrick and Gilbert (1991) note that at the time Congress set up a "child abuse" reporting system for sexual abuse, no body of information substantiated the dimensions of the problem. Nonetheless, child abuse was included within the statutes for reporting abuse and neglect. The inclusion of child abuse as a reportable behavior was, according to them, the result of a convergence of forces relating to the feminist movement and issues connected with rape.

In summary, from this top-down perspective, the social worker's job involves three interconnected elements. These include meeting administrative requirements that are spelled out in legislation and through executive orders at federal, state, and local levels, as relevant to their agencies. For the most part, these legislative and executive processes mesh fairly well with one another. They also must meet the administrative requirements as determined by the judiciary. The court is the final arbiter for all children who are reported as being at risk of or victims of abuse or neglect within a community. For those children adjudicated as needing protection, the court is truly the final arbiter of the plan for the child. The social worker makes recommendations, and the judge of the juvenile court makes findings and orders, that is, decisions on individual cases. The judge's actions are based on such items as federal law, state law, and case law. This idea of multiple jurisdictions and multiple levels of policy create a constant source of tension for social workers.

Vignette: Contested Placement

Susan P., a placement social worker, has just received a telephone call. She had planned to move Michelle, in two days, from one foster home to another one closer to Michelle's mother's home. This is a home that Michelle "found" for herself. Michelle is fourteen years old and her current foster parents have given the agency legal notice that she has to be moved. The home Michelle found is about a block away from her paternal aunt. The home is also fairly close to her mother's home and should facilitate reunification planning. Also, it is believed that Michelle can spend considerable time with the paternal aunt. However, just yesterday her mother and the paternal aunt had a disagreement. The aunt still believes she can work with the mom and so the placement is still a "go." Now the mother's attorney has called and is demanding a full juvenile court hearing prior to the move. In his opinion, the hearing is required because Susan is planning to place Michelle "out of county." The new foster home is across the street from the county line and technically is out of county. Susan must now look to emergency care, the children's shelter, for Michelle since she cannot legally place her in the new home without a court order.

The "Contested Placement" vignette shows how the complexity may catch a social worker quickly within a legal web. The issue is the placement of children outside local jurisdictions. The problem and policy action can be traced to the mid-1800s. The first major foster placement effort, the Children's Aid Society, ended amid protests and legislation prohibiting the placement of children outside of New York State. The society had, through the use of their "orphan trains," been placing children in the West. The West was what we know today as the Midwest—the states of Wisconsin, Illinois, Minnesota, Missouri, etc. The society did not provide post-placement services and allegedly misrepresented the legal status of children.

In any event, legislation in many states was aimed at stopping the placement of children across state lines. With the advent of the federal foster care program, we have a prohibition of such placements (sometimes the prohibitions and due process requirements involve county jurisdictions) without the provision of due process rights for everyone concerned. Thus, Susan, the social worker must hold off on placing Michelle, despite the need for her to leave her current placement. Michelle must move to a temporary care program, await a hearing in two weeks with possible trial, and Susan must write a lengthy report.

CONCLUSION

This idea of the governing structure is that a complex, three-dimensional hierarchical array of policy and governance exists within our child welfare system. This structure involves policy and its implementation "action at the federal, state, and local levels by executive, legislative, judicial, bureaucratic, and nongovernmental individuals and organizations within the context of the constitution" (Dolgoff et al., 1997, p. 121). Legislation passed on the federal level becomes law, typically, when signed by the president. It may be subsequently reviewed as to its congruence with the U.S. Constitution through the filing of a court action. After passage, it moves to the state legislatures for action. State legislators decide upon their own implementation of the federal legislation. Upon passage, this legislation goes to the governor and becomes law upon his or her signing. If a set amount of time passes without signing, it is vetoed.

To be implemented, each piece of legislation, now a part of the law, must be written in the form of regulations. Regulations are written at each level of governance including federal, state, county, city, etc. Child welfare social workers practice within this network of federal, state, and county laws and regulations. This structure guides and directs child welfare practice for nonvoluntary clients.

This policymaking and implementation is also hierarchical and specialized in the decisions that any particular unit is able to make. For example, within the federalist model, the federal government is not able to impose programs on the local level. That is, it does not have jurisdiction over local government. However, it can offer financial or other types of incentives to induce local jurisdictions to adopt programs. Tied to those incentives are also program expectations. This is the so-called carrot-and-stick approach. The financial incentive serves as the metaphoric carrot, or favorable inducement for local government to develop programs. In contrast to the incentive, the metaphoric stick is the threat of losing money if the programs are not continued effectively by the local administration. In order to take advantage of incentives, local jurisdictions must comply with federal program guidelines.

For example, programs funded by the federal government, including child welfare programs, are expected to comply with federal civil rights laws. If federal funds are not involved, there would not be an economic compliance requirement. The federal government holds the same kinds of expectations for other nongovernmental organizations with whom it does business. For example, if administrators of a nonprofit residential treatment center agree to take children through the public child welfare system, which is funded in part by federal funds, they are expected to comply with all federal laws, including laws prohibiting discrimination, staffing requirements, and use of funds.

Chapter 5

The Organizational Context of Practice

INTRODUCTION

To this point we have located child welfare, that is, child protection, in the United States within the context of the governing structure. The Constitution provides authority for and limits to child welfare intervention into family life. We have also looked at the dispersion of authority that is an important aspect of our constitutional framework. This chapter turns to the organizational context for child welfare practice. The context as described here is meant to include the environment in which the line level social worker practices, including the agency that employs the social worker and administers child welfare programs. In the broadest sense, this context includes the federalist structure. However, it also includes at the local level the context of the community and the employing agency.

A contention in this work is that child welfare work is contextually social work within a social institutional frame or, alternately, social work in a host setting. However, child welfare is currently conceptualized and treated within the literature as social work agency based practice. For this reason, it is important to understand the nature of agencies as organizations and their effect on child welfare interventions. This chapter is focused toward that end.

THE COMMUNITY AS A CONTEXT
FOR CHILD WELFARE

The Community As Organization

The community provides the social context for child welfare practice. The concept of community in the simplest view is a group of externally identifiable individuals who share a personal or collective interest, value, ideology, or have other connecting linkages. The most dramatic effect a local community has on practice in child welfare is through its values and norms for child protection. Although these values and norms manifest in a variety of work activities and dialogues, probably the most visible is through stories in the mass media about abused or neglected children and the agency's actions or inactions toward the event. For example, a story about a twelve-month-old child shaken to death by a father, while under child protection supervision, will in many communities result in a large community reaction. In others, it may merit a few stories in the newspaper and a kind of "ho hum" reaction. The exact reaction can tell us much about the values of the community (that is, who is quoted, what they say, what happens after the story breaks).

The Child Welfare Industry Revisited

While these mass media events can tell us much about community norms and values regarding child abuse and neglect, the workaday world of the social worker also produces, reproduces, holds, and communicates a set of norms and values. In the daily course of working in child welfare, the social worker cooperates with a wide range of other professionals who work with clients of the child welfare system. These professionals typically provide services that may be required under law, public policy, or simply for humanitarian purposes. They are usually contracted for and paid for by government or in some cases nonprofit organizations. These private agencies and providers may be proprietary, nonprofit, or, alternately, other mixed types of agencies. Taken together within a given community these constitute an "industry" that is supported by the child welfare system. The norms and values of the members of this industry help to define child abuse and neglect and are important in determining the administrative direction of the agency.

Although the formal child welfare programs within any one state differ from those in another, they share the concept of a "child welfare industry" that is deeply enmeshed with the administration and provision of services to clients. We have already seen views of the child welfare industry from Hubner and Wolfson (1996) and Costin, Karger, and Stoesz (1995). These particular industry participants share a commonality of values, beliefs, and norms or standards as to what is child abuse and neglect and what is expected from the child protective agency.

THE INDUSTRIALIZATION OF CHILD WELFARE

Industrialization of Service Delivery in Historic Perspective

The organization and administration of child welfare in the United States is embedded in the culture of the country. It cannot be seen as independent of its culture. To understand the organizations that administer child welfare programs we must look at the structure of other organizations within the culture. In general, organizational arrangements, as already alluded to, have evolved from a bureaucratic to a postmodern type of arrangement. On the organizational level, at which work is done, organizational types have evolved from assembly line operations to highly "McDonaldized" kinds of organizations. This shifting and transformation within the workplace are discussed here as they apply to child welfare.

The first major impact on service delivery systems was the assembly line operation. This evolved with the formation of auto assembly lines in the early 1900s and subsequently with the scientific management theory led by Frederick Taylor, an industrial psychologist. The development of assembly line operations represent what Wilensky and Lebeaux (1968) refer to as the early impact of industrialization in America. They describe the auto assembly plant as "featuring a conveyor system that grips the worker bodily to the line" (p. 60). James D. Thompson (1967) refers to this organizational form as using a "long-linked" technology (p. 16). From an organizational perspective, this approach is based on the concept of the serial interdependence of activities. That is, each step in the production process must follow mechanically in a particular order for the production to be completed. Each step or activity is dependent upon the completion of the one preceding it. For example, the engine in an automobile must be installed on the frame for it to be tested, etc. In terms of individuals, the assumption is that for treatment to begin and presumably be effective, the person must go through a sequence of steps or work stations. Typically this begins with "intake."

The industrialization process leads to the specialization and the growth in the service industries of a nation. Industrialization in this usage is a process of social, economic, and political change generated by technological innovations in the production of goods and services. In short, it is a general social process driven by rising economic activity. With increased industrialization has come an increase in productivity and income. Accompanying this has been an increase in the use of labor, particularly the poor and less educated within the labor market. For example, the introduction of assembly line production of automobiles allowed employers to take advantage of available labor. That labor, meaning the plant workers, since they were "attached" to the assembly line and the jobs were simple and mechanistic, did not require extensive education and training. It was a good fit for the stage of economic development in the "roaring twenties."

Industrialization leads to specialization and specialization serves as a prerequisite for professionalism. Wilensky and Lebeaux (1968) note that professionalism is "the result of the underlying industrialization process" (p. 285). In this sense, the industrialization process is manifested through the specialization of production activities. Work activities must be broken down into increasingly discrete and specific tasks to improve the production process. Each worker, then, completes the same set of activities time and time again. Thus, an intake worker spends her day doing intakes. This assembly line operation involves what Wilensky and Lebeaux (1968, pp. 299-300) refer to as "functional specificity."

This functional specificity in child welfare is manifested and driven at least in part by the administrative process of creating ever more specialized activities. This becomes necessary with increased demands for accountability through the accumulation of numbers, the counting of items produced, tasks accomplished, etc., and is fed, in part by a continuing lack of university-trained social workers. Typically, the specialized activities, with their related tasks, are grouped together by function. For example, in California, the emergency response program includes a range of activities and tasks (services) that effectively constitute a program. It also constitutes a funding category for the administrative jurisdiction. It has also become a function within the child welfare system. Social workers who are assigned to the emergency response program essentially do intake for the child welfare system. Their jobs involve a range of activities organized around the concept of responding to "referrals" and making a determination as to whether they are substantiated or not. After completing these activities and related tasks, they either close their referral or change the referral into a "case" and transfer it to another program and a new social worker. This functionally specific action is part and parcel of the nature of the child welfare system. It is an assembly line process. It involves long linked technology, that is, a range of activities that are done in a serially interdependent order.

This industrialization including the specialization of functions and their organization around management efficiencies also has created secondary goals that can replace the stated goals and missions of organizations. Hagedorn (1995), for example, describes the organization of child welfare in Milwaukee, Wisconsin, from a management perspective as it has come to be a case processing system. He notes:

> The "case," that is, a parent or child, is passed between departments, within the social service bureaucracy, each concerned with their specific focus, with no one having the overall responsibility of assessing the needs of the entire family. Each transfer between departments, of course, entails more paperwork. And while the paperwork is being done, the client is often left in limbo, waiting on the next worker to take his or her turn. (p. 42)

The Social Welfare Assembly Line

Generally, social service organizations in the United States have become a kind of assembly line operation. This can be seen through the operation of a typical voluntary mental health program. A client first is screened by an intake worker. Here an assessment is done with a particular coding for the problem to be worked on. The client is then referred to the specialist for that particular problem, a "treatment" worker. The client then receives treatment and exits the system. If the agency staff is up to date on ways of evaluating the success of their program, the client might receive a follow-up telephone call, much as clients of auto dealerships and hospitals do, asking for an evaluation of their services. If the agency staff is behind in such evaluations, the client will not have further contact with the agency. In total he or she might have from two to a dozen or so visits. If the client has another problem, he or she must go through the same steps again. That is, the client is seen by the same or another intake social worker, who codes the malady and then passes the client on to the same or another treatment social worker. Each problem constitutes a new referral and the sequential steps. Problem identification must precede treatment.

A child protection agency parallels this construction and repair process, although it differs due to the involuntary nature of its service delivery system. In this context, an emergency response worker meets with the child/family and conducts an investigation, usually called an assessment in the professional literature. After completing the investigation and concluding that the allegations are substantiated, the child is taken into custody or the parent is referred for a specialized service.

The emergency response social workers are doing the intake function. Their job is to do intake on referrals. That, in a large agency, is all they typically do within this functionally organized organization. The label "referral" applies to the initial report prior to the completion of an investigation. Upon completion of the investigation, the referral is either closed or processed into a "case." In this work, "referral" and "case" are generally used as interchangeable although in real organizational life they are significantly different. For a child taken into custody, another specialist takes over the case and the parents are referred to an advocate.

The second specialist works to establish the right to provide treatment to the family, that is, he or she works to establish court jurisdiction. This, however it is referred to, constitutes this worker's specialized function, his or her job. This is what he or she does, in a large agency, day after day after day.

After jurisdiction is established, another social worker becomes involved in working with the client, in making referrals, overseeing the treatment process, and making determinations as to the success of the interventions. This worker does case management and refers to other systems for treatment. Similar to the other social workers, this is his or her repetitive job.

Each professional social worker performs part of the total intervention. However, none sees the total process or its success or failure. Thus, individual workers do not learn the extent to which their interventions were successful or not successful with clients. Swift (1995) describes this partializing process as each worker has only a small part in creating the final product. Furthermore, because workers are separated from the conceptualization of the final product and its purposes, they are not positioned to see or evaluate the whole of the work process. (p. 53)

This is similar to what we do with our automobiles. For example, we may take our car to a mechanic because of an overheating problem. We make an appointment and bring the vehicle into the shop at the appointed time. The mechanic diagnoses the extent of the problem. Depending on the outcome, another mechanic may be called in to repair or replace a radiator or a hose, a head gasket, or even possibly to rebuild an engine. At each step, the automobile's owner decides how to proceed and weighs the costs of each intervention. By the time repairs are completed, the car may have been through three to six work stations, depending on the services chosen by the owner.

From the perspective of the child protective agency and this industrialized organizational structure, it is interesting to consider clients' rights to services. For example, Kutchins (1998), in an extensive analysis, concludes that clients have a legal right to services; however, they do not have a legal right to effective services.

From Industrialization to McDonaldization

An important question, given Wilensky and Lebeaux's 1968 book, is how much change there has been in the shape, function, and understanding of industrialization and organizations over time. As an organization, the child welfare system mirrors the environment of which it is a part. As such it takes its lead from the organizational set of its environment.

For example, agencies in child welfare tend to be highly localized within their environments and as such they mirror industrialized systems. They represent what Ramos (1981) would describe as an organization that emphasizes instrumentally rational economic activity over substantive or value-based rationality (Ramos, 1981). That is, the emphasis is on the means, techniques, and management processes rather than on the accomplishment of missions. These organizations also emphasize bureaucratic values including technical compliance, i.e., paper flows and specialization of activities toward the establishment and maintenance of efficiency, uniformity, and consistency in bureaucratic activities (Hummel, 1982). More than anything, they increasingly are dominated by cultures given to efficiency and conformity and with an emphasis on values associated with revenues.

A larger and more expansive view of our culture as a kind of modern day bureaucracy is described by what Ritzer (1996) calls the McDonaldization of Society. He stresses how, as a society, we have adopted the basic principles upon which McDonald's was built. Writing similarly, Schlosser (2001) presents convincing evidence that our views of organizations have become severely limited. To him, the cultural values of the fast food industry have come to permeate our national and daily lives. Both of these authors suggest that this new organizational form has replaced society as bureaucratic to become a new kind of organizational form, a kind of modernized bureaucrat society.

If this is true, what is the new form? Since the industrialization of American society, economic life is being replaced by a process called globalization. This is an era in which the factors of production, the production process, and the systems of distribution have become detached from nation-states and reattached to the global environment. Probably one of the better descriptions of this new global world is that of the idea of a transnational society (from Raymond Aron, a French sociologist, according to Sklair, 1991). Behind this idea of a transnational society is the concept (or abstraction) that the nation-state is now related to other nation-states as a series of "transnational practices" (Sklair, 1991, pp. 2-5). Thus, the nation-state becomes a subsystem of the larger global system. An organization in this view is spread throughout the global environment. Production, headquarters, marketing assembly, etc., may be in multiple locations and even on different continents.

Although local organizations may not have global connections, it appears that some of the uncoupling of production, administration, marketing, etc., has permeated our local communities. Schlosser's (2001) and Ritzer's (1996) views seem to be accurate in depicting the child welfare work environment. That is, the process of McDonaldizing society has begun with industry but rapidly has permeated social institutions. Ritzer (1996) notes that it

> affects not only the restaurant business, but also education, work, health care . . . the family, and virtually every other aspect of society. McDonaldization has shown every sign of being an

inexorable process by sweeping through seemingly impervious institutions and parts of the world. (p. 1)

It is driven by what Ritzer calls providing consumers, workers, and managers with four dimensions of experience. These include "efficiency, calculability, predictability and control" (p. 9).

What, if anything, does this mean for local agencies as social service agencies? In short, it means that social service agencies and child welfare agencies, in particular, operate as institutionalized assembly lines that provide fast piecemeal and packaged services in a serialized fashion to clients who have virtually no choices. Clients enter the service center (voluntarily or through court mandate), and select or are told the services they are to receive. Then these standardized services are given to them, they are expected to exit quickly, and to come back only when they need or are ready to select new menu items. This quick in, quick out style system is efficient in producing limited services in what may be called "service bits." For example, those who want or need parenting classes get the same parenting classes. If people need something special, they are outside the service delivery system.

This is in contrast with services that Thompson (1967) would describe as "intensive" services. These later services would include collaborative and client service delivery systems that wrap themselves around client systems. That is, rather than emphasizing serial order and standardized and uniform service delivery, this more complex service delivery system would provide holistic, diverse, unique-to-the-client services within the client's domain. Workstations would be out and the client's home setting would become de rigueur.

Other than an ideological focus, if not an organizational focus, on collaboration, child welfare organizations seem to continue to mirror the mechanical view of organizations. In particular and at least in part, they are driven by the income maintenance system of which they are typically a part. These "mechanized organizations" are organized around tight bureaucratic controls that emphasize routines, reliability, and predictability in operations (Morgan, 1996; Hummel, 1982). They also limit the development of human capacities, and can easily produce behavior that, although rational to individuals within the organization, is irrational to those outside of it (Morgan, 1996).

These mechanized organizations emphasize sameness, uniformity, and standardization versus diversity and uniqueness. An underlying assumption of these organizations is that the individual worker is replaceable. That is, one social worker is as good as another. If someone leaves the organization, the manager just hires another person, trains him or her in the same procedures and he or she will do just as well as the other person. The issue to the agency is purely one of economics. However, herein lies the advantage for the agency. By turning over more highly paid senior workers and by leaving caseloads uncovered, agency directors can not only nullify the cost issues but can come out ahead on budgets.

Summary of Industrialization

The effect then of this functional specialization is that clients, parents, children, and families have multiple social workers each of whom has a very narrow function to perform. With this, as Hagedorn (1995) notes, comes multiple case transfers. Some outstanding examples include those described by Gelles (1996) and Pelzer (1997). However, virtually any agency can produce similar kinds of case transfers between workers. Here children and individual adults become cases that are transferred between specialized units of social workers. In this sense, the child welfare system is a case processing system (Hagedorn, 1995). Hagedorn (1995) argues that these administratively directed steps are largely designed to give the bureaucracy control rather than to provide quality services to the family. While the agency operates within its bureaucratic context, the interactions and dialogic processes involved in setting up and handling cases has the effect of creating and maintaining social categories that ultimately stigmatize individuals by devaluing them within the larger society.

THE EFFECTS OF INDUSTRIALIZATION: ALIENATION, TRAINED INCAPACITY, AND CASE PRODUCTION

What are the effects of this industrialization, this mechanical production process? They are at least threefold. First, it leads to an alienation of both workers and clients. Second, it leads to a kind of psychological disengaging of workers from the larger mission of the agency, that which Veblen might call a "trained incapacity." Kenneth Burke (1984) notes that "by trained incapacity he meant that state of affairs whereby one's very abilities can function as blindness" (p. 7). The third effect is the creation and maintenance of social classification systems that ensure the continuation of the system as it is currently functioning.

Alienation: Worker and Client Feeling Detached from Abstract System

The idea of alienation, as it is used here, refers to a detached perception or feeling in response to working in a hierarchical structure in which the social worker has very little or no control over the processes of serving clients. Social workers in such structures, through their lack of participation, become socially conditioned to the one-way communication down the bureaucratic hierarchy that is pervasive in such organizations.

This separation of the worker from control of the production process, the agency's implementation of the helping process, is endemic to the mechanized or bureaucratic type of organizational structure, aka functional specific organization type. This kind of organizational structure dates from at least the "scientific management" movement and Frederick Taylor's emphasis on time and motion studies. It emphasizes a micro style of organizing work in specialized pieces, first into activities and then into discrete tasks. It is tied to concepts as "time and motion" studies and are in current usage in public child welfare agencies. Swift (1995) agrees with Braverman (1974) in his view that scientific management, referred to as "Taylorism," effectively separates the conceptualization of work from the actual work itself. This separation, according to Swift (1995), results in a separation of the line worker from the outcome of her or his work activities. In Swift's words, this separation of

> the conceptualization of work, carried out by the upper levels of management, from its execution by workers [results in managers perceiving an efficient operation and the need for more specialization and thus there comes] further divisions of labour, so that each worker has only a small part in creating the final product. Furthermore, because workers are separated from the conceptualization of the final product and its purposes, they are not positioned to see or evaluate the whole of the work process. (p. 53)

For the most part, workers experiencing feelings of alienation learn to adapt by attempting to create organizational change, simply blaming the system for poor management, policies, or support, or essentially taking the blame (Brueggemann, 2002). When these ways of adapting are unsuccessful, they leave the agency.

In addition to the lack of worker control over the work process, what other processes lead to this alienation? For the most part the dominant features driving alienation are the processes of industrialization itself. The industrialization process is widespread in that it is attached to our institutional arrangements. These institutional arrangements or abstract systems essentially are tied to the concept of instrumental or economic rationality manifested in the market economy. The problem with the instrumentally rational organization structure is that it is devoid of meaning for the worker and it psychologically numbs the worker. A number of theorists, including Brueggemann (2002), Bender (1978), Hummel (1982), and Ramos (1981), assert that instrumental rationality and a market orientation dominate our lives and limit the meanings we experience not only at work but within our communities.

This collective attachment to the market system as a megastructure of modern society emphasizes efficiency over other values. What is important to us collectively is calculability in the form of the numbers, that is, of production activities. The effect of this emphasis is the loss of the "opportunity for authentic close personal relationships with others outside the home" (Brueggemann, 2002, p. 122). On an individual level within an organization the alternatives workers typically have include psychologically distancing themselves from the "dissonance," immersing themselves in doing paperwork, computer data entry, or other ministerial aspects of the assigned job, or, if they can bear the tension, working for environmental change (Brueggemann, 2002, p. 240).

Of this "functional specificity" and the detaching of the worker from the total production process, Wilensky and Lebeaux (1968) suggest that the effect is the removing of the "joy out of the work" (p. 60) from the worker. This is done by removing uniqueness, diversity, and mental attention from the job. The effect is a "mechanically controlled workplace, repetitiveness, minimum skill [required], predetermination of tools and techniques, minute subdivision of product, [and] surface mental attention" (p. 60).

This alienation applies to social workers and also to clients. Workers feel disenfranchised, and clients feel even more separate. Whether it is a child victim telling her story to a new worker for the fifth time or a parent not having telephone calls returned, the feelings are of disengagement. Clients have a hard time trusting in the abstract system of child welfare as they experience a seemingly endless chain of social workers doing assessments, providing services, etc.

Vignette: The Alienation of a Client

The new supervisor ended his phone conversation with the father of a child just taken into custody. The supervisor was about to go to a case assignment meeting at which yesterday's intakes would be assigned to court workers. The father was upset because he had been at the school yesterday when his son was taken into custody. Since then, the father said he had talked with five social workers that had been assigned to his case and no one would help him. Before the supervisor went to the morning case assignment meeting he thought about the father's situation.

"The people he saw as social workers might have been an emergency response social worker who, with police, took the child in custody; a shelter admissions worker who admitted the child to the shelter; a diversion worker who considers diverting children from the shelter; a shelter worker who requested information from him about the child; a CPS supervisor who answered his questions about who the social worker would be, and now he is talking to me, the supervisor that will assign another worker to do an investigation. Hmm, five workers?" The agency, in its official way of counting, would count only the emergency response social worker.

Trained Incapacity: Bounded Cognitive Capacities

Another effect of this organizational structuring of child welfare is the production in social workers of limited worldviews or perspectives of client situations. The effect of the long-term employment of social workers in this detached state of specialized activities and disconnected actions and outcomes is an internalizing of external boundaries to work activities in the form of mental models that limit perception and understanding. The increasing simplification of the work activity can result in a "closing down" or "limiting" of one's worldview. Wilensky and Lebeaux (1978) describe this as the development of a "mental stupor" observed and reported by Adam Smith in his classic story of the pinmakers:

> One drew out the wire, another straightened it, a third cut it, a fourth pointed it, a fifth ground it at the top, two or three others did the necessary operations to make the head. All of this resulted in marvelous economies, but, as Adam Smith saw at that early date, work simplification could also result in a kind of mental stupor for the worker. (p. 59)

This process of setting up systems that result in disempowering social workers, and creating a mental stupor is done by the specializing of activities and tasks and emphasizing technique over substance. For example, an emphasis and priority to compliance with instrumental or technical tasks in a highly specialized job may result in 100 percent compliance with work techniques as data entry or cataloging forms, but it also can lead to clients not being seen when they are available. This contributes to what Robert Merton (1957) described as "unplanned consequences."

For example, the development of sophisticated computer technology in child welfare that requires extensive data entry will shift the social worker's attention, subtly and sometimes not so subtly, from clients to computers. It should not then be surprising when social workers inadvertently overlook seemingly obvious details in case situations. After all, they were concentrating on getting the data right for entering the case material in the computer system.

A second perspective for understanding this is from Kenneth Burke (1984) who describes the concept from Thorstein Veblen as that of "trained incapacity" and from John Dewey as "occupational psychosis" (Burke, 1984, p. 38). Here the concept is that the job limits the boundaries within which the worker learns to pay attention. The effect is that the workers learn to direct their attention to phenomena that are expected to occur on a regular basis. By emphasizing these regularly occurring phenomena, the worker at times misses irregularly occurring phenomena. The outcome of this job structuring is a high degree of compliance with agency technical procedures that lead to the worker developing a bounded perceptual system.

How does this apply to child welfare? Gelles in his book *The Book of David* (1996) argues effectively that the emphasis in the family preservation program has resulted in children not being adequately protected. In his intensive analysis of the David case, he noted the lack of perspective taken by individual workers and the system itself in making decisions with the end result being the death of a child. A central point that he makes is that family preservation as being administered was not effective at protecting children. Although Gelles did not examine organizational behavior, some of the workers described in his work functioned within very narrow constructs, that is, within a bounded perceptual system of their jobs, much as Smith (1952) and Veblen (1977) had observed.

Similarly, Marc Parent in his book *Turning Stones* (1996) shows the routine nature of the CPS social worker's job. He does an excellent job of portraying the system's virtually "mechanical" way of handling some of the most devastating of human situations. This mechanical processing of cases builds in, i.e., socializes, social workers into limited perceptual boundaries or limits. This internalizing of external boundaries becomes most visible when there are "handoffs" or "transfers" of cases.

Although Parent (1996) did not examine organizational behavior, he did portray the organizational effects of the death of a child. As he described the situation, the concern within the agency seemed to be more with whether the social worker had followed the correct procedures rather than understanding the circumstances that led to the death. Paradoxically, the child died despite the social worker following administrative procedures. The problem for the organization as a whole is that individual workers learn not to exercise discretion, including creativity or even common sense, in systems that treat them much like assembly line workers in a soft drink processing plant. Senge (1990) describes this as follows:

> When asked what they do for a living, most people describe the tasks they perform every day, not the *purpose* of the greater enterprise in which they take part. Most see themselves within a "system" in which they have little or no influence. They "do their job," put in their time, and try to cope with the forces outside of their control. Consequently, they tend to see their responsibilities as limited to the boundaries of their position. (p. 18)

Vignette: Processing a Case

It is 8:30 a.m. Charlie, a social worker for Modern County gets a "new immediate response" referral. He carefully notes the case number, the children's names, and the parents' names. He writes on a separate notepad the missing information that he will need to (1) close the referral, (2) pass the referral on to another worker as a case, or (3) make it a case. He has two lists of information, both necessary to process the case. For example, he notes a discrepancy between the mother's name on the referral and the "case name" he has been given. The referral calls the mother "Sanchez" while the case uses the name "Jackson." He makes a note to be sure to clarify this as it could be a big problem in processing the case. (As he sits at his desk, he remembers a previous case in which the mom wanted to use her new husband's name on the case record, but there was no way he could get the case name changed from what was originally a part of the record.) Based on the referral information, he thinks he can have this referral cleared and the processing done by noon if the mother is home. He knows that his supervisor will be around later today asking when he will clear the referral. If he is not able to see the mom this morning, he believes that he can drive by the house, leave his business card, and close it out first thing in the morning.

Case Production: Producing and Reproducing Social Categories

The third effect of the organization of the child welfare system is its operation in the production and reproduction of the social categories of abuse and neglect. This producing and reproducing action of the system relates to its action with respect to the social categories of abuse and neglect. It is continual production and reproduction of these social categories that highlight the child welfare system as what Giddens (1991) might call an abstract system. Swift (1995) describes this production and reproduction process as including routine agency processes such as opening and closing cases, gathering and recording and using client histories, as singular and collective efforts to categorize clients within the social categories described within the jurisdictions' laws. To her, the construction of the actual cases of neglect (and presumably abuse)

> arises and becomes visible through the processes of a specific context, the child welfare agency or department. This organiza-

tion carries with it historical meanings drawn from both legal and professional discourses and is organized around bureaucratic principles. The organization of child welfare not only express these generalizing processes but must continually be geared to them, for example, through funding mechanisms. Child neglect as an abstract concept is one that implies legal, professional, and organizational mandates. That is, invocation of the term through mandated sources provides the grounds for substantial and ongoing courses of action to occur. However, the legal and professional mandates frequently prescribe somewhat different courses of action and therefore produce contradictions for workers. . . . The bureaucratic features of the setting provide for the production and administration of social categories such as neglect to become visible. (p. 62)

In this view, the case processing and approval processes and dialogic processes involving members of the child welfare community, including the child welfare agency, the court work group, and the child welfare worker combine to define in operational terms the categories of abuse and neglect. This occurs within the context of organizations designed around the perceived management needs of administrators.

Vignette: A Multidisciplinary Team Staffing

The new social work supervisor was attending her first multidisciplinary team (MDT) staffing. The group, about a dozen in number, represented the child welfare environment. It included a public health nurse, a probation officer, a police officer, another child welfare supervisor, a child advocate, a teacher, a pediatrician, a psychologist, and a presenting social worker with her supervisor. The other CPS supervisor had told her, "Remember that collaboration means we find a consensus with this group." Her own supervisor had told her, "This group represents the child welfare community and, given the difficulty in determining who exactly fits in the category of abuse and neglect, we need to work to make sure that we cover all bases."

Now she heard a case being presented. As she listened, it was very clear that the members of the team believed the two children needed child protective intervention. The problem was that based on what she

(continued)

(continued)

heard, she didn't believe the court, with its work group-established norms and values, would see this as fitting any of the legal categories. Then through a dialogue with the team, she was able to work out a solution. A social worker would be assigned, team members would provide additional information, and jointly the social worker and the team members would do the best they could in meeting the needs of the children and family, within one of the categories of abuse or neglect.

Case Creation As Tension Reduction

One of the ways to look at this process of case creation and the shifting and changing of the content of social categories over time is the idea of collaborative dialogic and action processes involving social workers and child industry members. Over time, this works as a kind of tension reduction process. First, we need to understand that typically, as we have seen above, what is reportable as abuse and neglect does not necessarily fit the legal categories of abuse and neglect. Second, the legal standard requiring mandated reporting is typically a weaker standard than that of detaining a child.

Thus, what is reportable is not necessarily that which can be petitioned in a particular court. However, for filing a petition, an exacting criteria must be met and there must be a clear-cut fit with one of the categories of child abuse within the jurisdiction. However, the exact definitions of these categories are determined by state law, collective interpretations, and each individual on a subjective basis.

The social workers correlate their internal visions of the category with what they know the court work group will see as an "objective" fit with the particular category. Any dialogue the social workers have with other individuals can lead to changes in the social workers' views of the nature of the categories. If action is taken on this new definition and it becomes established as normatively accurate, it can lead to change in the court work group definitions for the social categories. In this manner, through dialogue and action in a hermeneutic, circular pattern, tensions between community members and social workers are reduced. In this sense, the social worker serves as a mediating influence with the larger community in defining abuse and neglect with the community including the child abuse industry.

Vignette: A Missing Fit with Social Categories of Abuse and Neglect

A program manager called a meeting of child welfare supervisors and selected social workers. She had been notified that the local newspaper would publish a story in the following day's newspaper that was critical of the division in its handling of a recent case. The case involved allegations of abuse of children by what was called a religious cult. The case had been investigated, and it was determined that the religious cult was actually a recognized religion. Therefore, it was not believed that there were grounds for pursuing the matter further. Now, the father of a four-year-old girl is alleging that the child has been exposed to the ritual killing of animals. The problem from the division's perspective is that legitimate religious ceremonies cannot by themselves be seen as detrimental to the welfare of children. However, some religious behavior could generate a very negative reaction within the community. Now, faced with this eminent problem, this group was challenged with making sure that the worker looked not at the religious behavior but at the detriment, if any, to the child. It was determined that the question that needed to be addressed was whether the child experienced detriment resulting from the care and supervision of the parent. The religion and its ritual were outside the purview of the division; however, the parent's actions were not. The social categories of abuse and neglect treat of the detriment to the child by the parent or caretaker, not the actions of recognized religious institutions.

THE SOCIAL WORKER'S ROLE AS MEDIATING LEVELS OF ORGANIZATION

The last question raised in Chapter 4 is that of what the social worker's role is from the perspective of the larger organizational structure, i.e., the megastructures of our society. Stated simply, part of the social worker's job is the mediation of the forces driving the tensions between organizational levels. There is a steady tug or pull from some, or all, of these forces on virtually every case situation a social worker is involved in. These levels of forces are as follows:

- Administration
- Judicial work group
- Prosecuting attorney
- Police

- Agency policies/procedures
- Child abuse industry
- Education

Social workers are expected to intervene at the metaphoric intersection of what C. Wright Mills (1959) referred to as "private troubles" and "public issues." Private troubles are those related to the individual and are typically within the individual's range of immediate relations and personal awareness (Dolgoff et al., 1997). These private troubles become public issues when they transcend the individual's local environment and inner life and interpenetrate the larger structure of social and historic life (Dolgoff et al., 1997).

For example, a father, confronted by a "backtalking" teenage son, has a private trouble in determining how to handle and direct the child. Depending upon the father's response to this private trouble it can continue to be a private problem or, alternately, it can become a public issue. A response that raises it to the level of a public issue would be to strike the teen in such a way as it causes injury and results in a referral alleging abuse by the father.

Social workers in child welfare are expected to work with these personal troubles that have or may become public issues. In this sense, social workers have the right to intervene in individual or family life for purely personal troubles that either have become or may become public issues. Those that have become public issues are those that fit in the categories of abuse or neglect established in law, while those that may become public issues are "at risk" of coming within those social categories.

A referral of the father for possible abuse would seem to be an "at-risk" situation. Social workers in this sense have a dual charge. They are expected to investigate allegations on behalf of the public and to take appropriate action on behalf of public issues, and they are expected to help people with their private troubles. As part of this charge, the social worker has the right and obligation to conduct an investigation to determine if a personal trouble has become a public issue.

Although these roles are many and complex, the simplest way to describe this mediating role is that social workers are expected to investigate and intervene in people's lives on behalf of the larger society. Simultaneously, they are expected to protect children by sometimes removing them from families, to change families so children are safe, and to identify and change social injustices within the child welfare system. Here the social worker is called on to mediate the actions of macrolevel forces and microlevel forces. This includes the idea that social workers in some settings are expected to perform mediating roles (Schwartz, 1974).

Social Worker As Dealing with Forces

Although the social worker has been characterized as performing a mediating role, another way of conceptualizing this is the social worker as a "mediating force." A "force" as used here is a quality imputed to an individual. It can also be viewed as a quality imputed to an individual in a social role that includes the ability to generate change. The social worker's role then can be conceptualized as a force that mediates other forces. This puts the social worker in the center of a constellation of forces that place pressures on individuals to conform to the norms of the larger society no matter how irrelevant they may be. For example, the social worker might need to deal with a wide range of family and community members complaining about the appropriateness or inappropriateness of the father's handling of his backtalking son. This way of looking at the social worker's role has what researchers refer to as "face validity" in that it describes the feelings social workers have in terms of being at the center of countervailing forces or tensions.

One of these three functions of the mediating role must be considered particularly important. Most important, from the perspective of social work practice, is the action of a third force function. Schwartz's (1974) description of a third force function is of one in which at times "the practitioner is required neither to 'change the people' nor to 'change the system,' but to change the ways in which they deal with each other" (p. 360). This, for example, may involve the social worker helping mandated reporters of abuse and neglect and the subjects of reports to change something about how they relate to each other.

Vignette: Ritalin for Whose Need?

Antoine Garcia was the subject of a child neglect report made by his elementary school. They reported he was in special education and had an individualized educational plan (IEP) which required that he take Ritalin on a daily basis. When he had his Ritalin, he functioned quite well in school. The problem was that his mom did not often give him his Ritalin. His mother related to the social worker how she did not see the problems with Antoine that the school said he had. She believed the school was picking on Antoine unfairly. The social worker, Julia Gonzales, worked with the parents and the school to improve how they worked together. The mom agreed to give Antoine his medication in the morning before school and the school agreed to assign a Spanish-speaking aid to answer the mom's questions about Antoine and his progress.

A central point in this book is that the social work role with non-voluntary clients is itself a mediating role between large-scale systems and the individual client (system). In this role, the social worker's job involves serving as an intermediary vehicle for the establishment, change, negotiation, and enforcement of the norms and values of the collective population in their application to particular individuals. The child protection system is viewed as enforcing norms as values. In this sense, the social worker in child welfare deals with conflicting values (Kaminsky and Cosmano, 1990).

CONCLUSION

This chapter examined the organization of child welfare from the perspective of organizational theory. The organization of most child welfare organizations is around bureaucratic values that emphasize serial processing of cases with uniform and standardized service delivery processes. Although this appears to meet administrative needs, it is limited in its capacity for making employees feel a part of the service delivery system. The result is employees who learn to limit their performance, feel alienated, and do their jobs in a mechanistic manner. The organization, through its actions as an "abstract system," produces and reproduces the phenomena of abuse and neglect.

Chapter 6

The Legal System As Host Setting: Context and History

INTRODUCTION

The central assumption in this chapter is that social work practice in child welfare is practice within a host setting. It is a "host setting" (Johnson, 1995, p. 18) in that the legal system, as represented by the juvenile court, essentially drives this intervention into involuntary clients' lives. In order to understand child welfare practice in the twenty-first century, it is important to understand the kinds of embedded mental models, basic assumptions, values, and behavior that drives this setting. This chapter discusses the concept of practice in a host setting with its underlying meanings. In addition, it begins an analysis of the history, values, and worldviews of practitioners in the legal environment and contrasts them with social work worldviews. This discussion is continued in Chapter 7.

PRACTICE IN A HOST SETTING

A central thesis of this book is that social work practice in child welfare is practice in a host setting. Although several authors suggest that social work practice in child welfare is practice in a setting that is dominated by the social work profession (Kadushin and Martin, 1988; Swift, 1995), actual practice suggests otherwise. In addition, at least three arguments support the position in this work that child welfare is practice in a host setting, that is, a legal setting. The first is the long-standing involvement of the medical profession in child welfare issues. This has been noteworthy since the work of Dr. Kempe with the "battered child syndrome"; however, it has continued to this day with pediatricians and nurses actively involved in communities across the nation. No multidisciplinary team conference or death review committee is complete without medical personnel, particularly pediatricians, as part of the team.

Second, child welfare, at least within the boundaries of social work, has been historically tied to the administration of income maintenance programs for the poor. Even early social workers, the "friendly visitors" of the Charity Organization Societies, were involved in the coordination of financial assistance. However, this distinction has become more pronounced since the 1969 to 1974 separation of income maintenance and services caseloads. Although this separation in line workers' function occurred, the administration of the programs stayed conjoined.

Today we have income maintenance programs as the dominant administrative programs, in terms of numbers of staff and dollars in revenue handled. The income maintenance programs are substantially different than social service programs in the sense that they are designed around standardized, uniform standards to ensure equity and homogeneity in the distribution of funds to the poor. In contrast, social workers in child welfare must work with nonstandardized, qualitatively different and diverse peoples. Social workers must individualize children, parents, and their families. In this sense, these organizational structures are not designed for social service delivery. The administrative emphasis in income maintenance is on the accomplishment of specific case handling tasks, while social work's emphasis is on working with clients to solve problems.

The third consideration is that the key point of decision making on nonvoluntary child welfare cases is the juvenile court. In the American child welfare system major decisions on cases are made by the juvenile court. This, dependent upon the jurisdiction, can involve material included in assessments, the statement of goals of therapeutic interventions, and the particular kinds of treatment and training that might be required of parents. Social workers as the experts in this setting make recommendations to the court, and the court considers these recommendations as it makes its orders. Alternately, if a case is settled at intake, that is, not referred to the juvenile court, potential of involving the court is prominent in negotiating the outcome. That is, the threat of coercive action by the social worker is driven by the potential for juvenile court involvement. This chapter and Chapter 7 focus on the primary setting for child welfare practice as that of the legal system.

What Does a Host Setting for Practice Require?

Since social work in child welfare occurs in a host setting, several things are particularly important. First and foremost is the idea that social workers must adapt to the dominant norms and values within that setting (Johnson, 1995). If they violate the norms or values of the setting, they become powerless in helping clients. Second, although social workers must adapt to this environment, they must maintain their separate professional identity; otherwise they will take on the persona of the setting. The net result for the particular jurisdiction is fewer social workers and more attorney-like professionals. To ensure social workers keep this identity, agency managers often set up unique structures for social workers to maintain attachments to their peers. For example, a desk, phone, and workstation are at times maintained in the social worker's "home" agency for the social worker.

Social Workers in a Host Setting

Given the extensive boundaries of the total child welfare industry, social workers are in a minority as they staff positions. Also as we have seen, the dominant system that drives the case by case intervention into the family system is the legal system, that is, the juvenile court system. Since the *Gault v. Arizona* court decision, children and their parents have been increasingly afforded their constitutional rights. This is not to say that parents, children, and social workers do not experience differences with their respective counsel; rather, it is to say that the major case-related decisions are made by the juvenile court.

To understand the issues and factors involved in practicing social work in a host legal setting, we must look to basic values and assumptions of the legal profession, which dominate the setting. This chapter uses the relationship between social workers and attorneys to discuss the legal profession's basic values and behaviors. This focus is used to explain similarities and differences, particularly with respect to interests, perceptions, concepts, and value orientations as an introduction to the dominant values of the setting. It also examines stereotypes that operate, and have historically been identified, as factors impinging on the working relationship of attorneys and social workers. It uses the three-part model introduced in Chapter 1 to examine these contrasting ideologies, values, and interests with styles of working. It concludes with a discussion of some of the central concepts important to professional social work practice in child welfare.

Probably the most important concept is that social workers have limited authority for independent action. They are charged with the responsibility to respond to allegations of abuse or neglect, to make assessments of the degree of risk to the child, and to take appropriate action to ensure the child is safe. In some jurisdictions social workers may take a child into temporary custody; however, the more usual arrangement is that the police may be involved in the custody process. This is at least in part related to the police role in investigating allegations of criminal conduct. After a child is taken into custody, legal decisions are made, particularly within the context of the juvenile court law for the particular jurisdiction. This effectively limits the role of the social worker. Pizzini (1994) summarizes this relationship between the social worker and the court when she says:

> Thus the juvenile court judge, not the social workers, makes the final determination regarding whether or not the CPS agency will be involved in the lives of families against their will. This fact is often overlooked by critics of the CPS system. (Pizzini, 1994, p. 37)

TENSIONS: SOCIAL WORKERS IN COURT SETTINGS

Several sources of tension can be identified for social workers within the court setting. Given the dominant view that child welfare is a social work function, some social workers develop the idea that they make decisions on cases rather than recommendations. While the social worker's central role with the court system is to make recommendations, the court's role is to be the adjudicator of matters. From a legal perspective, the court makes a judicial decision on particular petitions, i.e., cases. In this context, the social worker conducts investigations and assessments and makes recommendations for the court to consider. However, under law, the judiciary has the responsibility to make the significant legal decisions. The social worker's report and testimony is only one part of what the judge is required to consider.

A second area of tension that at times arises is the conflict between the administrative function of the child welfare agency and the judicial function of the court. As we have seen, at times, the social worker is caught in the middle between a juvenile court judge and a department director that have ongoing disagreements about their respective roles. The judge, for example, may view the needs of a particular client in a way that is contrary to the department's policy on funding programs for clients. For example, housing for homeless parents is typically not funded by child welfare agencies. However, at times, the judge may believe that with adequate housing the child would not need to be removed from the family. Also, the McDonaldization phenomenon, that is, the standardization of service delivery programs, at times runs counter to the judge's view that service programs ought to be tailored for the specific needs of individualized clients.

A third host setting point of tension involves conflicts in basic worldviews between social workers and legal professionals. This tension involves underlying values and ideological conflict between attorneys and social workers. These issues are discussed in Chapter 7.

Vignette: Setting the Stage at Court

Two voices sounded down the hall as Ms. Rogers, a social worker new to child welfare, came out of the courtroom. She didn't recognize the voices but could tell they were attorneys. One was saying to the other, "Those bleeding-heart social workers make me angry. They have no conception of what the real life of raising children is like. They foist their views of proper parental care onto parents and then present it to the court as fact. But, today, in court, I got the social worker.

"I thought of that cartoon we saw yesterday. Remember, the one in which the parents came home, found their children gone, the house a shambles, and writing on the mirror that said, 'social workers have been here'? And the father's comment as he oversees the mess is, 'Dear, we have termites!'

"Well, I thought of that today as we were waiting for a detention hearing. The social worker had taken this child into custody with no grounds. Of course, they do that all the time! But still it isn't right. So, when the court asked me if I had any comment on behalf of the par-

(continued)

(continued)

ents, I told the judge that parents ought to be safe from social workers. That the social worker in this case had acted improperly. She had taken the child into custody without a warrant, and without a reasonable cause to believe the child was in immediate danger of abuse or neglect. Of course it didn't matter, but I felt better . . ."

The voice trailed away as the persons moved down the hallway.

Ms. Rogers, as a new social worker, was shocked at such "nonprofessional" behavior on the part of the parents' attorney. She shared her opinion with other social workers and found they all agreed that was typical attorney attitude and behavior.

Attorneys and Social Workers

Whether this behavior is typical of attorneys or even whether all social workers believe this about attorneys is not of concern to us. Of concern to us in understanding child welfare practice in this host environment is what it tells us of the nature of the juvenile court setting as a setting for social work practice. Of the varied professions that participate in juvenile court processes, attorneys and social workers are the most numerous.

Why is the conflict between attorneys and social workers so difficult? Probably the most important element driving this conflict is the fact that the court is a natural setting for attorneys and a host setting for social workers. The presiding judges are typically attorneys and that makes the legal profession the dominant profession. Social workers must adapt to the dominant norms and values within that setting (Johnson, 1995). Although social workers must adapt to this environment, they must maintain their separate professional identity (Johnson, 1995).

Although the conflict is between two professional groups, the effect on other persons is considerable. For example, Lau (1983) has identified their effect as being threefold. First, the disharmony among professionals serving the same clientele can potentially harm the client and negatively impact the people who work in such an environment. For example, for new social workers the thought of working with other professionals who hold such poor attitudes could be daunting. Similarly, for practicing attorneys working with social workers, poor attitudes also create a very negative working environment. With each professional group sharing such attitudes, any disagreement can quickly escalate into open conflict to the detriment of not only the professionals but also their shared client and the client's family.

Second, if professionals do not trust one another's motivations and actions, the resulting duplication and repetition in service provision can be problematic for clients. This can be seen most clearly in the multiple interviewing of child witnesses/victims when professionals do not trust one another. This applies to attorneys and social workers and also to other professionals such as police. For example, an attorney who does not trust the social worker to make proper referrals may attempt to duplicate such referrals with the effect of confusing the client. Alternatively, attorneys may employ their own social workers because of a lack of trust in social workers employed in CPS settings.

Third, the cost and damage done within the community is similarly damaging to society. Here, people in the community pick up the attitudes, tensions, and biases of each group. The problem occurs when these biases are acted out in the child abuse response system. If professionals act on these biases, difficulties that are unrelated to child abuse issues may arise. For example, parents who are exposed to pejorative behavior, such as blaming or name calling, on the part of their attorney certainly cannot be expected to trust their social worker. The result for the social worker is perhaps at best that he or she has a resistant client.

Given these effects an important set of questions is how can we explain this phenomena and then how can we counsel new social workers so they may avoid this emotional quagmire and successfully advocate and negotiate on behalf of their clients. Through following a certain set of processes, for the most part, these problematic situations can become positive attributes of practice. The historic connections between these professions and some troublesome stereotypes operate with social workers and attorneys to explain some actual differences in working style between the professions.

Historic Context: Affinity and Conflict

Historically the working relationship between social workers and attorneys has not only been amicable but also mutually supportive. They typically worked closely together on behalf of clients. This relationship of practitioners across professional lines has varied over time. In particular it has emphasized a cooperative relationship in social work's early founding period, with an informal separation as social work moved away from an emphasis on reform and toward psychoanalytic theory, and then to a degree of polarization as legal rights became the issue in the 1960s.

HISTORY OF THE SOCIAL WORK PROFESSION

The Founding of Social Work: A Period of Cooperation

The early founding period of social work, as we have seen, emphasized "society saving" activities (Pfohl, 1977). Here, social workers worked with and for attorneys as they jointly responded to the problems of the day. For the most part, these were problems of poverty, vagrancy, and homelessness. However, they were driven by concerns for maintaining the social order of the larger society. To understand the dominance of the basic underlying values within this host setting, it is important to realize that the law is used as synonymous with the larger idea of social order, corrections, criminal justice, prisons, jails, and even lawyers.

The beginning of the foster care movement most clearly demonstrates this "society saving" component. As we have seen, this "child saving" movement was intended as a society saving activity (Pfohl, 1977). This movement is typically associated with Charles Loring Brace and the Children's Aid Society. With the now famous orphan trains, the emphasis was on saving the streets of New York from the "dangerous classes" by sending them to farms in the Midwest (Brace, 1973).

Similarly, social reformers and lawyers of the refuge movement of the 1820s and 1830s shared the goal of maintaining the social order. Here, as we have seen, the "conservative reformers" used the legal system, and the *parens patriae* doctrine, as the vehicle to remove children from their parents. They did this through case law and legislation (Trattner, 1976). In particular, through *Commonwealth v. M'Keagy* in 1831 and *Ex parte Crouse* in 1838, they were able to avoid dealing with due process issues and to assert this doctrine as applicable to children (Krisberg, 1993; Hawes, 1991). These houses of refuge became the vehicle for removing threats to social order, mostly children of new immigrants, from the community (Krisberg, 1993).

The social worker's historic role as an instrument of social order is supported through the development of its core methodology within the profession. Historically, the helping process was built on the relationship of the social worker and the client. A friendly relationship developed despite a disparity in social status between the worker and the client. The social worker was also expected to investigate the clients' appeals for assistance and to determine the worthy and unworthy among them and then to "provide the needy with the proper amount of moral exhortation" (Trattner, 1994, p. 96).

Continuing into the early part of the twentieth century until about the mid-1930s, social work and the legal system were closely connected. Social workers were involved in family courts, prisons, legal aid offices, and even private law firms. Also, social workers were involved in community activities directed at getting laws in place, improving enforcement of laws, and bettering conditions for communities.

However, social workers played even more significant parts within the court system in cases involving child delinquency, abuse, and neglect. As part of the progressive era, which included the creation of the juvenile court in 1899, social workers played increasingly important roles. With the avowed purpose of not stigmatizing child offenders and providing a plan of "reeducation rather than retribution" (Trattner, 1994, p. 126), social workers essentially functioned as the "advocate for the child, family and state simultaneously" (Barker and Branson, 1993, p. 3).

The legal framework for court action in this era was the Chancery system. This theory-based set of rules relied on the judge making judgments of "equity" and "fairness" as opposed to a rule of law (Black, 1979). It abolished the use of criminal procedures in courts, with the result being a nonadversarial proceeding (Trattner, 1976). This period emphasized collective issues rather than an individual rights perspective.

Much of the work of social workers in these settings was the precursor to work in child welfare today. This work typically involved "investigating and reporting to the legal authorities the conditions to which children and the disadvantaged were subjected" (Barker and Branson, 1993, p. 3). Within the context of their jobs, many social workers spent as much time in court testifying as they did working with clients (Barker and Branson, 1993). These words about waiting in court have a familiar ring to twenty-first-century social workers in child welfare.

In this cooperative period, lawyers were instrumental in the early development of social work. For example, the Children's Aid Society, Charles Loring Brace's organization, which is commonly held as one of the first organizational bases of social work practice (Trattner, 1994), was founded and led by a lawyer, Robert Weeks DeForest (Barker and Branson, 1993). Mr. DeForest was also involved in early social work education and is credited as the founder of the Columbia University School of Social Work (Barker and Branson, 1993).

In addition to DeForest, such noteworthy lawyers as Florence Kelley and Sophonisba Breckinridge were instrumental in the early development of social work. Both had ties to Jane Addams and Hull House in Chicago. Kelley was instrumental in the founding of the United States Children's Bureau and is often identified as a founder of the social work profession, while Breckinridge was instrumental in bringing social work education into the university system and led the movement to include legal courses in the social work curriculum (Barker and Branson, 1993). This period also saw an intensive intellectual climate that gave rise to pragmatist philosophy and the "functionalist school of social work." These became the early roots of the strengths perspective as they were expressed through the process approach of Jessie Taft and Virginia Robinson (Smalley, 1967; Early and GlenMaye, 2000).

While lawyers were instrumental in the development of social work, more evidence supports the position that social work initially was closely tied to the legal system. For example, Barker and Branson (1993) argue that social work developed in the early twentieth century largely to fulfill legal functions. Activities of social workers, from this perspective, included investigating families "to determine if parents were abusing their children or otherwise not meeting their children's developmental needs" (Barker and Branson, 1993, p. 2). Ancillary parts of the social worker's roles included reporting findings of these investigations and testifying as necessary in courts of law. Social workers also worked as probation officers in prisons, courts, and with youth gangs within communities.

Separation: Social Work Turns to Psychoanalysis

Although social work education began as agency-based training, it began to shift to universities in the early 1900s. With this shift, the profession experienced a period of uncertainty regarding its ideological roots. In the initial phase of this transition, social work found a home, albeit temporarily, under the umbrella of sociology (Trattner, 1976). This emphasis built on the "reform" emphasis of the early settlement house movement. The emphasis was on collective theory and action. Trattner (1994) refers to this as the emphasis on the "causes" associated with community problems.

Several factors combined in the early 1900s to generate a major shift from this macrofocus to a clinical focus for social work. World War I saw the settlement house movement lose prestige within the profession as such luminaries as Jane Addams fought for peace. Although she won the Nobel Prize, her prestige in the profession suffered. Second, the country needed and was willing to pay social workers to counsel victims of war-related problems. This represented the beginning of a dominance of one-on-one counseling within the profession.

Third, a shift of private fund-raising from individual solicitations by agencies to solicitations and disbursements by federated structures resulted in a drying up of funding for community action. For the most part these community chests began to dominate the solicitation and disbursement of private funds. This shifting of disbursements to community chests (the precursors of today's united funds agencies) led to political concerns regarding the kinds of intervention for which the funds would be used. This led to a drop in the distribution of funds to settlement houses, as their focus on social reform was not popular (Trattner, 1976). The effect was reduced innovation and independence for settlement houses. With it came a decline in social workers working at the community level.

Last, but not least, was the shifting ideological status within the profession itself. In 1915, John Flexner, in a paper delivered at the National Conference of Charities, charged that social work was not a profession because it had "no unique method" (Trattner, 1976, p. 258). This was answered by Mary Richmond's 500-page book, *Social Diagnosis,* published in 1918.

With her classic work Mary Richmond tied social work to its early roots within the charity organization societies, but used a methodological style adapted to some extent from the legal profession. Her efforts are associated with the deficits model in social work (Early and GlenMaye, 2000), and with the clinical style of individual intervention, referred to as the diagnostic model (Smalley, 1967). In her work, Richmond expressed her thanks to several legal professionals for their help in formulating her conceptual framework (Fogelson, 1970). Her work constituted a theoretical formulation that tied social work to its roots in the Elizabethan Poor Laws with emphasis on the legal rights of the poor. This, of course, closely allied social workers with attorneys with their shared emphasis on legal rights.

With the Great Depression and New Deal period of 1929 to 1941, social work completed its shift from a legal and community orientation to a psychoanalytic and individually oriented profession. Due to Mary Richmond's book, combined with Freud's popularity, social work moved to providing psychological counseling for the poor, in essence, "blaming the victim" for the problem of poverty (Trattner, 1994). With this shift, caseworkers grew in prestige and status as the shift of emphasis in social work from the cause of social problems to the function of helping the victims of such problems became complete. This also marked the beginning of what Costin, Karger, and Stoesz (1996) described as the "Flight from Authority." Social workers increasingly moved away from working with nonvoluntary clients.

Courses in schools of social work shifted from sociology and legal offerings to courses in psychology. Field placements in legal settings were typically replaced by placements in mental health settings (Barker and Branson, 1993). Although social workers, in their literature and at their symposiums, called for closer relationships with legal professionals, few practical steps were taken (Sloan, 1967). With social work turning to "clinical" practice, prisons, juvenile courts, and probation systems turned to other disciplines to meet their needs (Handler, 1976). Although some social workers continued doing social reform work, these increasingly were persons educated outside of schools of social work (Trattner, 1994; Wilensky and Lebeaux, 1968).

This period also saw tremendous growth of social work as a profession and a concomitant growth in areas of practice. The number of social workers grew in response to the increasing urbanization and industrialization within the country (Wilensky and Lebeaux, 1968).

From 1910 to 1950, the number of social workers grew from 5,000 to 75,000 (Wilensky and Lebeaux, 1968). Although the growth of the population of social workers was significant, industrial and urban growth was even greater. During the same time period the number of newer professions as engineers, scientists, etc., grew some eighty times to 741,000 by 1950 (Wilensky and Lebeaux, 1968).

Along with this rapid growth came an expansion of social work into group practice, community organization, and research. It also brought the formation of joint membership organizations including, among others, the American Association of Group Workers (1946) and the Social Work Research Group (1949). With the formation of the National Association of Social Workers in 1955, these organizations merged. This newly formed professional organization was not based on populations such as probation, corrections, or even child welfare (Trattner, 1999). The emphasis was on such factors as practice interests and methods as casework and group work. It is important to note that the formation of organizations followed two paths. These included organizations directed toward better organizing systems and organizations of practitioners (Costin, Karger, and Stoesz, 1996; Trattner, 1999).

With this also came a loss of interest in legal issues on the part of social workers. From about 1929 until about 1940, the professionals became silent on the issue of law and social work. A number of perceptive articles appeared in the 1940s and then little or nothing was written until about the 1960s to the 1970s (Fogelson, 1970). The War on Poverty with the programs developed under the Office of Economic Opportunity (OEO) introduced another shift in the social work profession. With OEO programs came a new focus for social work. However, this focus was time limited and social workers soon found themselves involved with the profession's emphasis as one of facilitating the making of good referrals for service rather than working directly in such systems.

The Modern Era: Legal Rights, Tension, Conflict, and Collaboration

As we have seen with the Supreme Court decision *In re Gault,* the emphasis on service provision to juveniles shifted from the progressive era emphasis on best interests of the child to an emphasis on children's rights. With the Gault decision, the legal rights of children took precedence over interests, needs, or even treatment. The effect was to replace social workers with lawyers as advocates for children and families in most courts. Now, instead of social workers representing the child, the parents, and the family, the representation in court shifted to attorneys, who were assigned to each litigant in a manner to prevent conflicts of interests. The effect was to increase the litigious nature of proceedings in the juvenile court.

With the shift from the progressive emphasis on the best interest of the child to the emphasis on the degree of legal due process, social worker roles became supportive of lawyers' roles with respect to establishing jurisdiction of the court over a child or a parent/caretaker. In particular, with the profession's indifference to this client population, dependent children, and with an increasing legal presence in court, it is not surprising that individuals without university training as social workers increasingly did investigations of potential abuse.

CONCLUSION

This chapter has discussed the idea of child welfare as practice in a host setting. It identified three different sources of tension. These related to the social worker's perception of his or her role vis-à-vis the court, conflict between agency and court functions, and conflicts in legal and social work worldviews. It also discussed the context of host setting practice for social workers within a setting that is essentially a legal setting. Social workers have had a successful history of working closely with legal professionals. This chapter sets the stage for the next chapter, which deals with phenomena related to worldviews, reasoning, and approaches to practice.

Chapter 7

Images and Realities of the Legal System: Metaphor, Myths, and Stereotypes

INTRODUCTION

This chapter continues the discussion of the concept of social work in a host setting, that is, the legal system, that was begun in the preceding chapter. This chapter emphasizes the more subtle aspects of the relationships between social workers and attorneys. These take the form of metaphors, myths, and even stereotypes. These constitute the underlying and, for most purposes, the most important aspects of these working relationships. This chapter examines the issues that affect practice for both attorneys and social workers.

STEREOTYPES: THEIR NATURE AND ACTION

One of the more interesting phenomena in the literature regarding the interfacing of the social work and the legal professions is the emphasis on the role of stereotypes. For example, such writers on forensic social work as Barker and Branson (1993), Russel (1988), Schroeder (1995), Steele (1972), Whitmer (1983), and Brendan et al. (1986) discuss to some extent the role, existence, and action of various stereotypes. Before discussing some of their ideas, we must understand the relationship of stereotypes to the process of reasoning (aka inquiry) and how stereotypes affect action.

Just what are stereotypes? They can be viewed in different ways; however, a reasonable definition is "a set of widely held shared generalizations about the psychological characteristics of a group or class of people" (Reber, 1985, p. 730). Thus a stereotype holds within it what we may call prejudices about individuals based on their membership in a particular group. Although we would prefer not to deal with such prejudices, we must examine them to sort out issues involved in the relationship of attorneys and social workers.

Stereotypes play an active part in our interpreting experience. For example, Farrell (1991) notes that they serve as a set of schemata which provide a way to organize material for interpretation. As schemata "they are simple, coherent, and relatively enduring structures" (Farrell, 1991, p. 532) and serve as a set of guides for action (Reber, 1985). As guides to action and as cognitive structures they can also be conceptualized as metaphors. In this usage, as metaphors, they are a part of internalized structures that guide individual perceptions and actions (Lakoff and Johnson, 1980). In short, stereotypes impact feelings, thoughts, and action, even though they may have little logical relationship to any actual individual or group experience. When someone holds a stereotype about another person, it is far easier for him or her to hold to it and act upon it than to give it up and find a new rationale for thoughts or action.

How do stereotypes guide or affect action in a court setting? They provide a shorthand view of individuals and their behavior. This includes such stereotypes as "crime stereotypes," "victim stereotypes" and even "social worker" and "attorney" stereotypes (see Box 7.1). These simple models provide a quick and efficient way to identify and act on the normative patterns important within the court process. Farrell and Holmes (1991) credit the identification of these phenomena to Sudnow (1965) and Emerson (1983) and note that "these definitions evolve their distinctive quality and are reaffirmed continuously through everyday interaction of court actors as they deal with alleged offenders" (Farrell and Holmes, 1991, p. 532). This affirmation and reaffirmation through the interaction of court actors affirms their role in producing and reproducing social categories as part of the court adjudication process.

Stereotypes also play an important part in explaining action in court settings. For example, stereotypes of persons of minority races and the poor were reported by Swigert and Farrell (1977) to be powerful in explaining sentencing behavior by judges in homicide cases. That is, they work to create efficiency in the handling of cases, by providing shorthand guidance for action. If the plaintiff fit a particular racial stereotype, that is, a particular social category, the court was more likely than not to make a particular finding and order.

BOX 7.1. Stereotypes

By Social Workers of Attorneys

- They are aggressive.
- They have no feelings.
- They are self-serving, crooked, conniving, and conceited.
- They are greedy.
- They are rigid, technical tricksters.
- They wrongly identify with clients' "wants" instead of "needs."
- They focus on winning at any cost.

By Attorneys of Social Workers

- They are women and belong home raising children.
- They are bleeding-heart liberals and idealistic do-gooders.
- They are flighty, obstructionist, starry-eyed, and naive.
- They are ineffectual, overidentified with, and overprotective of clients.
- They are whimsical and emotional rather than objective.
- They are all heart and no head.

The Actions of Metaphor (Stereotypes) in Juvenile Court

Three important considerations must be examined to understand the operation of these stereotypes or specialized metaphors in a juvenile court setting. These considerations include their action in contributing to the efficiency of court operations, their effect on the treatment of exceptional cases, and their connection to descriptive language as part of the litigation process. Farrell (1991) notes that stereotypes are useful in simplifying the world and increasing the efficiency of the court. They provide this same function in juvenile court. They also contribute to the court's operation in environments with constraints of time and resources. They do this through assisting in the differentiation of routine cases from exceptional cases. In this way, exceptional cases can gain a disproportionate share of resources, including time, thereby increasing the efficiency of the court. One might hypothesize that the busier the court, the more likely stereotypes are a part of the adjudication process.

As matters move through the juvenile court processes, particular stereotypes and metaphors become attached to the petitions, to the social study, and ultimately to court action. These metaphors become vehicles that contribute to feelings on the part of social workers, attorneys, judges, children, and parents, etc. The strong emotional attachment, to some extent, then controls or influences the litigation of particular cases. This is seen during the process in which cases move to resolution. Often a settlement may come through a small change in the language in a petition. In these cases, the negotiation was able to remove the inflammable emotional attachments to the particular metaphors or stereotypes thus leading to common agreement. Of course, at times, no language change is negotiated and trials ensue. The choice of metaphors in writing petitions and the emotional attachments to them makes them important considerations in the movement of cases through the juvenile court. Social workers, dependent on forming and maintaining good working relationships with clients, need some control over the writing of petitions.

The Worldviews of Social Workers and Attorneys

Stereotypes, aka metaphors, raise questions regarding the grounding of the conceptual systems of members of the legal and social work professions. In particular, a major concern is how we understand the similarities and differences between the two professions if we work only on the level of stereotypes as metaphors. If we accept the view that any particular individual's personal reality is a social construction developed through an interaction of biopsychosocial factors and personal narratives (Saari, 1991), we would find that individual thought processes include both mythic and metaphoric content (Berger and Luckmann, 1967; Strauch, 1989). That is, each person experiences a personal reality that is unique to that individual. Because the personal reality is bounded by the limits of language and its capacity to describe the world used in its description, the question then regarding stereotypes is how do they fit in this perspective?

The point is that seemingly rational thought is at times not rational and is, in fact, rather primitive. In this perspective, although we may collectively strive for logical processes of thought, that is, rational thought, we may experience another kind of thought. This "experienced" thought is often considered irrational or even primitive. Otto

Rank (1932) describes this primitive thought well as a "subjective 'explanation' of mythical phenomena by psycho-biological happenings . . . which, in contrast to our logical process of thought, is called 'unconscious' by Freud, 'autistic' by Bleuler, 'symbolic' by Jung, 'prelogical' by Levy-Bruhl, and 'mythical' by Cassier" (p. 120).

How does this primitive thought relate to social work practice in public child welfare? The clearest answer to this is that it serves to extend the action of rational thought by defining and explaining situations beyond the ken of rational thought. It works in the formulation of the collective realities that attorneys and social workers build regarding one another and their respective clients through close interaction as part of the court work group. Through the action of rational thought and interactions irrational thought structures are developed. In such circumstances, a stereotype functions as a set of prejudicial notions regarding a person or persons that works to define individuals as members of a group that are outside of one's own direct experience. That is, when you cannot explain something rationally, mythic or nonrational thought in the sense of being erroneous or ungrounded thought and beliefs prevail. However, although inaccurate, these conceptions exist and are important to understanding the prejudices that underlie each profession.

Also, like myths, stereotypes are to some extent based upon accurate views. The problem is that no one individual embodies all the characteristics that are contained in collective views of his or her group or profession. Stereotyping is the action of attributing collective views to individuals.

Some Functions of Stereotypes

Even though we may argue that the use of stereotypes creates fuzzy logic, it does work to some extent to describe relations between social workers and attorneys. In this sense, however erroneous, they do explain some behavior. They also show the extent to which relationships between attorneys and social workers have broken down within the litigious court environment. They are also helpful in showing broad dimensions of underlying values issues that are involved with each profession. Certainly as real life communication between individuals breaks down, stereotypes can be expected to come into operation.

Alternately, stereotypes can be examined and worked through as individuals develop working relationships as individual persons with other individuals.

UNDERSTANDING CONFLICT BETWEEN SOCIAL WORKERS AND ATTORNEYS

While attorneys are used to illustrate conflict with social workers, social workers also hold stereotypes regarding attorneys. The difference is in the substitution of attorney cartoons and jokes for the social worker jokes.

Worldviews

The weltanschauung (worldview) of attorneys and social workers provide an underlying source of tension for members of these professions. For attorneys, the basic collection of beliefs about life and the universe is one that views human facts in terms of their particular relevance to situations and holds them as accurate in depicting events that have been alleged. Attorneys typically are schooled in and rely on what Mueller describes as a "timeless scientific model" (Mueller and Murphy, 1965, p. 99). This is a clear-cut model of behavior and begins and ends with fairly black-and-white assumptions. Mueller describes this, using the metaphor of a door, as "the client is either inside or outside the legal framework . . . [but] seldom in between" (Mueller and Murphy, 1965, p. 99).

In short, the legal worldview of attorneys centers on the idea that the world is comprised of objectively determinable facts and that these do accurately depict events as they happen or happened. This depicting of events relates to the logical progression of cause and effect. The determination of the "facts" takes place in a court setting in which the court ascribes meaning to these events according to the written word. Thus the court applies the rule of law in determining if a violation of a codified norm has occurred. This is a positivist perspective.

Attorneys distinguish the idea of a demonstrably provable fact from personal opinion. The former requires the development of a body of evidence that is admissible in court and attains a particular level or standard of proof. The latter, personal opinion, is simply what any particular person subjectively believes to be true.

Language to attorneys, as to positivist researchers, tends to be viewed as a valid representation for the real world. In this view, language serves as a referent for concrete experience. Thus, language is given a primacy in terms of its capacity to accurately depict the world of individual or collective experience. Human experience can be described with language and, of course, this means that the totality of human experience can be written in language.

In contrast, the clinical social worker worldview is value based and typically includes a composite of thoughts, feelings, and actions. In contrast to attorneys, social workers' reasoning is more circular and involves the use of intuition and self-reflection (Brueggemann, 1996). Language is seen as a tool that people use to communicate feelings and thoughts. It also embodies meaning (Saari, 1991) with a reciprocity between language and culture (von Bertalanffy, 1968; Saari, 1991).

Because feelings and thoughts can vary over time and even place, their expression may also vary. In order to truly understand the world in which people live, an adequate assessment must be completed. One element in completing that assessment, necessary to understanding the causal dynamics operating, is the objectively provable fact. However, the fact is determined from inside the client's mental structure. In this sense, facts are subjectively determined. Also, "in this context the facts of objective reality have no relevancy except in the assessment of individual potential or limitations at a point in time at a given place" (Cook and Cook, 1963, p. 413). This is a subjective view of an objective reality.

Language, to a social worker, is more likely to be considered an entity with symbolic significance rather than something of literal importance. Language is typically seen as only one way of depicting reality. It is more apt to be seen by a social worker as commensurate with Wittgenstein's view of language as "language games" (Wittgenstein, 1966, p. 8; Monk, 1990, p. 331). In this sense, language is a system, albeit an "abstract system," separate from but interdependent with concrete experience. Wittgenstein makes this point in *Zettel* (1970) when he compares it with concrete activities such as cooking and washing. He states that "the use of language is in a certain sense autonomous, as cooking and washing are not" (p. 59e). Language is limited in its referential component within this complex and subjectively determined social world.

Table 7.1 presents a graphic depiction of items important in understanding similarities and differences between attorneys and social workers.

TABLE 7.1. Similarities and Differences Between Social Workers and Attorneys

Factors	Social Workers	Attorneys
Professional worldview and assumptions about the nature of being (ontology)	Reality as a composite of thought, feelings, and action, with language as an intermediate vehicle used to describe a reality rather than as a referent of reality itself.	Reality is dominated by thought, with a positivist approach to research, and language as a referent of reality, which is external and uniform for everyone.
Ways of knowing (epistemology)	Knowing is behavioral, emotional, and cognitive with a "gut" feeling. That is, intuition is an important way of knowing.	Since language represents the real world, knowledge through the senses is determined to be valid. To be knowledge it must be measurable and verifiable.
The nature of the world and future of knowing	Parts of the world are not knowable because they are subjectively determined. The best we can know are the quantitative pieces.	The world/universe is all-knowable. We simply must research and prove or disprove various hypotheses to arrive at collective human understanding.
Ways of thinking	Intuitive with a clearly complex array of factors. Social workers thrive on gray area issues and problems.	Orderly, with language emphasizing black-and-white issues.
Units of attention	Individuals and family	Individual client
Approach to case situations	From general to specific data	From specific to general data
Locus of control	Agency and profession	Profession and court
Training emphasis	Acceptance and understanding	Assertiveness and order

Source: Adapted and expanded from Brendan et al. (1986).

Adversarial System

The focal point of the conflict between lawyers and social workers is most often the court's adversarial process (Steele, 1972). This conflict is the result of misunderstandings by social workers and attorneys as to their proper roles within the complex abstracted structure of child welfare. For social workers, the difficulty is in the role of the legal system, the assumptions around which it is organized, and what it does. Attorneys assume that human conflict is inevitable and that the court's function is to resolve such conflict quickly and fairly. They also assume that the court's judgment is final and will be accepted and obeyed. Thus, if everyone does as expected, the conflict is ended.

However, the court system is limited in its capacity to effectively deal with the entirety of humans' problems. Its historic roots are "a mutation of the historic method of settling disputes by mutual combat" (Steele, 1972, p. 109). Particularly important in understanding this limitation is the idea that "the adversarial process is not designed to deal with human emotions, and this fact must be universally appreciated" (Steele, 1972, p. 108). The court, through the adversarial process, focuses on settling conflicts by discovering the facts, placing the blame, and affixing responsibility within the context or rule of applicable law. To be effective in resolving said conflicts, the individual participants must buy into the court as the proper body for affixing blame and resolving their conflicts.

Training and Education

Given the court's mission, it is not unexpected that the attorney's training emphasis is on an aggressive search for truth and order *within* the adversarial system. This term "within" needs to be highlighted because it suggests some clear limits involved in the training of attorneys. The centerpiece for the practice of law is that of advocacy for a particular client or for his or her interest. This is in contrast to the social worker's training emphasis on interdisciplinary studies and a practical application of strategies and methods aimed at helping people solve problems.

In contrast, lawyers are typically committed to problem resolution through adversarial procedures and are enjoined from even appearing to represent conflicting interests. Here the emphasis is on law, logic, and the adversarial process. In contrast to the eclectic and highly value-based training of the social worker, this is highly focused and centered on the adversarial process. Lau (1983) describes these two very well when she notes that

> Law, with its emphasis on the Socratic case method, the development of logic, and the proliferation of the adversary method, bears little resemblance to the social work emphasis on dignity and worth of the individual, the development of worker self-awareness, and the client's right to self-determination. (pp. 24-25)

In contrast, social work education emphasizes such softer qualities as the understanding and acceptance of individual differences and uniqueness. The education for social workers is typically broad ranging, multidisciplinary, and focused on values such as self-determination, human dignity, and ethical decision making. This is particularly true of generalist practice that may typically emphasize such approaches as the strengths perspective or existential perspectives as solution-focused therapy. This education also encourages self-knowledge, self-reflection, and intuitive action. The emphasis is on social work intervention as problem solving through the use of a mediating model with families with conflicting interests (Weil, 1982).

While the basic logic in use differs among professional groups (Kaplan, 1963) such as social workers and attorneys, their initial approach to cases also differs considerably. Attorneys typically begin with a specific analysis of the circumstances and generally move toward more general features of cases. For example, an attorney for a child protective agency might begin, "What did the mother do?" and then move to more general questions such as "What kinds of extenuating circumstances were there?" Alternately, social workers begin with ambiguity and move toward specifics. Social workers' mental movement is from general to specific, while attorneys' movement (which, of course, includes the court's focus) is from specific to general. Needless to say, major problems can occur in communication if both parties have not completed their respective case assessments.

Levels of Values

A set of underlying assumptions or mental models and values serves to differentiate the logical styles of attorneys and social workers. Attorneys begin with an underlying assumption that the law applies equally to all and that the client will be accepted for service (Mueller and Murphy, 1965, p. 100). The assumption is that everyone needs the same service and therefore the provision of service should be standardized. Here the social worker is seen as a supplier of standard services. The attorney's focus is best suited for tangible or concrete services, such as the provision of a shelter for a homeless mother and her child. Less of a fit is the more complex and less concrete needs of a homeless mom and her child, who have been kicked out of three previous shelters because of a chronic head lice problem.

In the case of counseling services being provided, "the lawyer thinks of the process in terms of his own activities of advice-giving, conciliation, mediation, or arbitration" (Sloan, 1967, p. 89). What the attorney does not understand is that of the central place that relationship plays as part of the therapeutic process in social work (Sloan, 1967).

In contrast, for the social worker, the provision of a service is driven by the assessment, which takes place within a working relationship. Through the completion of a thorough assessment of the individual's strengths and weaknesses, service needs and capacities are identified. At times this means rejecting the case for service or even referring it to another service provider. The central aim is to win the war, although not necessarily the battle. From the social worker's perspective, "the lawyer is viewed as advocating for outcomes including services that the client may request, but which may not be relevant to his or her problems" (Sloan, 1967, p. 88), or, in the case of some clients, most likely teenagers, advocating for what they want, even though it is not what they truly need.

The "Timing" of Action

Timing represents a perspective that differs for attorneys and social workers (Mueller and Murphy, 1965). Specifically, the social worker is more apt to work within the structure presented by the client, what might be called "client time," while the attorney is more focused on the legal considerations, aka "court time." Here the social worker may be working with the client in order to build on strengths, which often takes considerable time, particularly with some problems. Change, from this perspective, involves an unfolding process that occurs through a number of contacts that occur over time and involve the client's increasing awareness of important issues in his or her life. Alternately, the legal position is that things must be done within the constraints of the legal system. In this view, the client's changes must occur within the time constraints established within the legal system. For example, a parent's overcoming chronic substance abuse problems may take a couple of years in actual "client time," while the legal process provides for only twelve months. These must be brought together in some way in order to provide adequate service to clients within the court setting.

"Units of Attention": Individual versus the Family

The difference in thinking styles becomes apparent as we examine differences in working styles with clients. Here, for attorneys, with a clear-cut, black-and-white worldview, thought processes become highly focused as they represent their individual client. They view the client, as the legal system is structured, from within the lens of the individual client. In contrast, the social worker is expected to take into consideration more than an individual client. For example, by training, values, and perspective, it is virtually impossible to exclude from the social worker's mind, thoughts regarding the child's family. The "unit of attention," that is, the focus of one's attention, may be a child, but that child must be viewed within the perspective of the family. This factor introduced during the progressive era continues to be reinforced in professional education: the total system must be considered. The result may be a wide range of conflicting perspectives between social workers and attorneys.

Given the parameters established within the court system, attorneys seldom operate with a conflict of interest. Their client is typically an individual. If there were a possible conflict, the court would typically assign another attorney to represent the individual affected by the potential conflict. In contrast, the social worker is trained to work with families or at least with individuals that are part of families. Even when agencies bifurcate responsibilities by assigning multiple children in a family to multiple social workers, the social workers' assessment tools still view the child within the family context. This is not to say that they cannot or do not limit their assessments to their particular child but, rather, the lens they use in viewing the client is more broad. Even in more clear-cut situations, such as in severe child abuse cases, the social worker must be concerned for the family. Weil (1982) describes the social worker as playing a variety of roles as family advocate, child protective investigator, parent worker, and foster care worker:

> Sometimes these roles are separate, but often a social worker is expected to work to support families as units and at the same time carry child protective investigation responsibilities. The best interests of parents may not be congruent with the best interests of children, yet the social worker has a professional and ethical responsibility to parents as well as children. (p. 394)

This concern, while important for the protection of the child, would also be important from the perspective of the child's need for his or her family.

Action Level

Although the adversarial process provides the framework for resolving conflict between social workers and attorneys, language differences serve as a flag bearer in such situations. Language, in this usage, includes the professional jargon that each learns in his or her respective educational programs. This includes the legalese of attorneys and the social workese of social workers. Terms such as "prima facia," "jurisdictional," "evidentiary rules," "recusal," "discovery," and "dispo" constitute just a small piece of the legalese important to a court setting. Similarly, the meaning of such terms as "assessments," "generalist practice," "concentration," "transference," "units of attention," "countertransference," "bonding," "attachment," and "referrals" are mysterious to those outside of social work. The language differences work together with other factors to contribute to some degree of discomfort in relationships between attorneys and social workers. At times, this discomfort may rise to the level of outright fear, at least a "fear of the unknown" that may accompany such transactions (Mueller and Murphy, 1965, p. 99).

The Definition of Facts

If the adversarial process is the focus of tension, and language contributes to its development, the most misunderstood aspect of the entire process is that of the alternate perceptions and importance of "facts" within the court process. The underlying differences between attorneys and social workers described earlier leads to alternate, but not irreconcilable, view of facts. Since the court is the dominant determiner of social reality in the public child welfare system, and the law is a socially and logically constructed and highly rational edifice, facts are particularly important in its operation. Of course, as noted, the focus of attorneys is on facts.

The establishment of the facts of a particular matter constitutes the grist of court proceedings—the heart and soul of the jurisdictional process. The significant point is that the attorney's worldview includes a focus on "facts" and their relationship to particular scenarios as they affect and have consequences for the person or parties they represent (Brendan et al., 1986). In fact, psychiatry and social work's legacy to the legal system is the development of specific rules whereby facts are determined. For example, according to Mueller and Murphy (1965), before psychiatry's insights into motivation, the legal system would attribute intent based on particular laws rather than the actual reasons for the behavior. For example, the carrying of a concealed weapon would be interpreted as implying an intent to do harm, no matter what the actual reason for the action.

The well-known statement that ignorance of the law is no excuse often pertains to the intent that is presumed to be part of the law violation. So, if a fisherman is caught with a fish of illegal size, he is presumed guilty even if he believed he was fishing in a jurisdiction in which the size of the fish would be legal. The legal approach is that "if a person knows what he is doing, it makes no difference if he is not aware that he was acting contrary to the law" (Mueller and Murphy, 1965, p. 101).

In contrast to attorneys, social workers view "human facts" as intersubjectively determined and to some extent driven by feelings and relationship issues. Here the individual is seen as adjusting and adapting to relationships based on subjectively interpreted facts. Thus, one's reality may be more relative to circumstances and perceptions. From this perspective, the truth can at times be as relative as that which a particular person believes to be true. The " 'truth' is not necessarily the same to a person when he is calm as when he is angry or fearful" (Mueller and Murphy, 1965, p. 101). Two individuals may even hold competing truths to be singularly true and they both may be correct. Mueller and Murphy (1965) suggest that in some situations it is the "intensity of feelings—not facts—[that] becomes the truth according to the social worker or psychiatrist" (p. 101).

The focus of professional training in social work is typically on working with individuals and their perceptions and interpretations of events. The social worker then, through the application of a set of techniques based upon a basic value system, works to improve the adaptation of the individual and the collective group. In this sense, the social worker's focus is on the worldview presented by the client as it impacts or affects his or her interpersonal adjustment. It comes to incorporate and operate within the dominant worldview of public law by training and experience in settings such as child welfare.

SOCIAL WORK IN PUBLIC CHILD WELFARE

Given all the differences with attorneys, how are social workers to work effectively in legal settings such as public child welfare? The important distinction that must be drawn is that despite differences, the two professions share a cooperative history, a common concern for their respective clients, and a desire to empower clients through their rights of self-determination and due process. Social workers' basic belief in the empowerment of clients fits well in an environment in which individuals are accorded legal rights. From this perspective, the court, with its litigation of matters, including the affording of individuals due process rights, provides a context for the social worker to work with involuntary clients. In this respect, the individual's right to self-determination, held as so important by social workers, is bounded by court processes. Recognizing and using this boundary as suggested by Rooney (1988, 1992), can help the social worker to work effectively with mandated clients.

CONCLUSION

Currently, public child welfare functions as a host setting for social work practitioners. As such, it is incumbent upon social workers to understand the dominant ideologies in this setting and adapt to them, while maintaining their own professional value stance. This chapter analyzed these ideological and conceptual differences between the professions. It also identified areas of knowledge and expertise important to social workers in practicing in such a setting.

SECTION II:
COURTS, MODELS, AND RITUALS

1

Chapter 8

The Courts

INTRODUCTION

What should be clear at this point is that although each social worker in a child protective agency is assigned to specific referrals and cases, the action on these referrals takes place in a highly bounded service delivery system. That is, the action taken by social workers is highly structured or constrained by an abstract set of rules, norms, or laws. Laws provide the boundaries that limit who the social worker can see and even set the parameters of the transaction with a client. For example, while laws may allow for the interviewing of a child at school without the parents' permission, they also may require that the child has a person of his or her own choosing to be his or her advocate during the interview.

Also, the rules associated with investigations allow a focus only on obtaining information relevant to the allegations in the report. Thus, social workers are not authorized to obtain information that typically they would expect to obtain from traditional assessments. The legal system structures their access to information. They are able, at the point of investigations, to investigate only whether the allegations in the report are *substantiated* or *unsubstantiated.*

Nonvoluntary interventions by officials such as police, social workers, and judges are tightly constrained, while voluntary interventions are dependent upon the adult to provide direction including permission. Courts, in general, deal with both voluntary and nonvoluntary actions. For example, the request for a divorce is a voluntary approach to a court requesting intervention into one's personal life. From this perspective, a variety of courts deal with a wide assortment of problems and issues. In this sense, multiple courts are involved in the processing of a variety of referrals and cases. These often play a part in the practice of nonvoluntary child welfare, although they are outside the child protective agency's mission of protecting children from the actions or inactions of parents or caretakers. This chapter provides an overview of both sets of courts including their major functions and their relationships to child welfare agencies.

THE VARIETIES OF COURTS

These institutionalized courts are structured, that is, organized, much in keeping with the free marketplace doctrine that permeates our McDonaldized society. This includes their being highly specialized, typically with values attributed to administrative efficiency, standardization, and equity. For the most part these courts are organized around specific functions. It is important to note that various legal jurisdictions form and shape their own categories of courts. This chapter presents a broad general view of the courts organized by function. Numerous improvement projects are underway. In general, such projects are working to bring these functions closer to people's lives. Thus, any one court may at any point in time provide more or less of the functions outlined in this work. However, going into detail about these shifts is beyond the scope of this book. Thus, in many geographic areas we have highly specialized courts that serve narrow functions. The court systems that deal with children, youth, and families include the family court, probate court, and civil court.

A word must be said in advance about the probate court. As a separate entity, it is recognizable only in some jurisdictions. Black's (1979) legal dictionary describes it as "a court having general powers over probate of wills, administration of estates, and in some States, empowered to appoint guardians or approve the adoption of minors. Court with similar functions is called Surrogate or Orphan's Court in certain states" (p. 1082). In this work, it is treated as a separate entity, that is, one that operates within its own jurisdiction. For the most part this fits the procedures that operate within this court as it applies to practice in child welfare. At times, the juvenile court is able to "convene" itself as a probate court to hear matters involving children under its jurisdiction. Although this presents the picture of it being a part of the juvenile court, in terms of function and time requirements, etc., this is illusory.

This specialized organization of courts by function effectively divides the family appearing before it into functional parts. Each court provides its own functional service to families and individuals involved in its litigation. For example, to get a divorce, one would go directly to family court; however, if the issue was the care of an aging parent, one might take the matter to the probate court.

In each court, for the most part, involvement would be limited to the function of the court and the legal matter before the court. The court would not be involved in the function of another court. Issues before the probate court would not typically be examined by the family court. These court actions are in contrast to issues of abuse or neglect, which are handled exclusively within the juvenile court. The juvenile court constitutes a fourth court, after the family, probate, and civil courts, that treats issues with children and families. The juvenile court combines with the adult criminal court to complete the basic court structure that, at times, complicates child protection intervention into family life.

The voluntary courts are dependent upon the "consumer of services," the client, finding her or his way to the services provided. Because of the complexity of modern life and people's relative inexperience with the organization of the court systems, the child welfare system workers receive calls and some referrals that rightly belong in alternate court domains. This means that social workers should understand the rudiments of these alternate systems.

An important point needs to be made about the evolving nature of the entire court system. In recognition of the need to join some of these separate issues and the difficulties inherent in treating them as separate entities, the courts are involved with multiple projects to improve the quality of their proceedings. In general, many of these projects involve bringing disparate functions together, typically under the juvenile court's jurisdiction. Other approaches to the administration of justice are being considered or piloted, including the development of specialized "drug courts" and "unitary courts" for families and children's issues and, also, ways to divert children and families from the court system and into mediation programs, etc. These projects hold encouragement for improving the operation of courts.

The five courts involved in family and child life can be conceptualized as differing in terms of their primary social function; the social assumptions upon which they operate; the expectations regarding the investigations that may appear before them; the particular aspects of individuals' lives over which they have jurisdiction; and their respective "gatekeepers." The idea of "gatekeepers" relates to those social institutional roles that limit and/or control access to the respective courts. These various courts can make referrals for the protection of children to the juvenile court.

Table 8.1 compares and contrasts these factors in the five courts. The focus in this chapter and this exhibit is on matters that are important to the protection and well-being of children and to the enforcement of criminal laws regarding the abuse or neglect of children. As noted earlier in this work, the material presented is from a social work perspective. Thus, it lacks a degree of legal specificity; however, it also incorporates social and psychological perspectives.

Vignette: Guardianship Doesn't Mean the Same Thing to Everybody

Jean, a CPS social worker, received a call from Mrs. S, regarding placing her new foster child, Sallie, in school. Mrs. S reported to the social worker that she had been to the school and when asked if she was the legal guardian, she said no, that she was the foster parent. Because they heard her say that she was not the guardian, they wouldn't accept her as having the right to sign the child into the school. Jean knew from past experience that the juvenile court judge would not sign the child into the school. Her view was that she did not have the power to sign this kind of document for a child. Similarly, the school personnel, as soon as they learned the child was living in a foster home, would not accept the legal or biological parent's signature; besides, the parent was not even willing to talk to the social worker. This was further complicated in that Jean's department supervisor wouldn't let Jean sign on behalf of the child in the school.

Jean had to deal with this often. She had concluded that in this geographical area, each school made its own interpretation as to what constituted guardianship for a child. Had the foster parent simply said yes, they would have accepted her as the legal guardian. Jean picked up the phone to call the principal.

CHILD WELFARE COURTS: NONVOLUNTARY INTERVENTIONS

The nonvoluntary, social control arm of social institutions come into play with the juvenile court for children and the criminal court for adults. The juvenile court handles delinquency acts by children,

TABLE 8.1. Five Types of Courts

Court	Primary Societal Function of the Court	Social Assumptions About Parents or Caretakers	Agency Responsible for Investigating Circumstances	"Gatekeepers" Access to the Court Through	Jurisdiction the Court Can Assume: What It Can Order
Juvenile court	Protection of the child and preservation of the family	Parents are not protecting or caring properly for the child.	Child protective agency	Child protective social worker	Detain child; remove child from parent(s); termination of parental rights
Family or domestic relations court	Reallocation of property, income, and parental rights; mediate the separation of parents	Parents are competent to make decisions regarding the welfare of their children.	Parent(s) and/or their agent(s)	Parent(s)	Child support, child custody, and property settlements
Probate court	Settlement of estate, establishment of guardianship, emancipation of minors, and involuntary hospitalizations	Families are competent to handle their own affairs regarding children. Society has a responsibility for persons who are a danger to themselves or others.	Parent(s), family members, conservators, parents' agent, and social workers in mental health and child protection.	Family, conservator, investigator, and/or parent or child's agent, and child protection social worker	Guardianship of person or property and suspension of civil rights and involuntary incarceration/hospitalization
Criminal court	First to protect society and second to punish norm violators	Social control is necessary for the survival of civilization. Norm violators need to be punished.	Police for child abuse cases	Prosecuting attorney and/or grand jury	Incarceration, probation, restitution, etc.
Civil court	Compensation for losses and class action lawsuits	Victims have a right to restitution and systems are improved through litigation.	Victim or victim's agent	Victim or victim's agent	Compensation and systems change

Note: Types of courts are dependent on local jurisdiction decisions.

dependency situations involving the abuse or neglect by parents or caretakers, and cases involving "status offenders," if the particular jurisdiction provides for these teens in any way. The latter group, on a national level, is inadequately provided for in terms of supportive programs.

Juvenile Court

The juvenile court handles matters involving delinquent, dependent, and status offender children. Dependent children are loosely defined as children who are viewed as victims of abuse or neglect by parents or caretakers. In contrast, delinquent children are those that are under the age of emancipation and have violated criminal statutes. In some situations, dependent upon jurisdiction and charges, juveniles charged with criminal activity are charged as adults and those hearings are in criminal court. The juvenile court typically makes the decision to transfer jurisdiction on these children to the criminal court.

Status offenders are children who present behaviors that would be legal if they were eighteen years of age (the legal age of emancipation in the jurisdiction) or older; however, since they are under eighteen years old their behavior constitutes a violation of law. They are guilty of status offenses. For example, a child who runs away from home is breaking a law. If the child were legally an adult, this behavior would not be considered a law violation. These children are also generally referred to as "beyond control," "runaways," and sometimes as "throwaway" children.*

Some jurisdictions have social intervention programs, but most provide nothing in the form of intervention for these children. This work simply touches on them as a social problem. In some areas,

---

*A special note should be made about "throwaway" children. In general, adequate services for this population have never been in place or adequately funded. In reaction to problems parents had "controlling" their teenaged children, a backlash movement came into being. The "tough love" movement focused on helping parents limit their involvement with their "beyond control" children. Thus, many parents essentially set a limit for their children. For example, "if you want to live in this family, you have to . . . ." Many youth responded negatively to this limit and chose instead to blame their parents for their living on the streets. Over time, the parental side of this issue has been lost as many of these children today are seen, by professionals, as "throwaway" children. Actually, they present problems between children and their parents.

gangs of these modern-day American street children roam communities during the night hours. Only sporadically do stories of these large packs of children make the news media. It is a hidden problem.

Specifically the juvenile court, as it applies to the protection of children from child abuse and neglect, becomes involved in what can be termed dependency issues. The determination of the dependency status for a child follows a four-step process. The first is the receipt of a referral. The second is the investigating of the allegations by a social worker and a determination as to whether the child has been abused, neglected, or exploited as defined by state law. The third involves the social worker, or designee, filing a petition with the juvenile court alleging the abuse, neglect, or exploitation as defined in state law. The fourth involves the court in the adjudication of the petition. Adjudicate is defined as "To settle in the exercise of judicial authority . . . [to] adjudge [or implying] a judicial determination of a fact, and the entry of a judgment" (Black, 1979, p. 39). If the petition is determined by the court to be factually accurate and the child is within the social classification described in the appropriate section of the state code, the child may be made a dependent child by the court.

Since the protection to the juvenile court involves the idea of the protection of the child from the parent or caretaker, a child who is the victim of third-party abuse, neglect, or exploitation would not typically be found to need such protection. However, if the parents did something to cause the child to be a victim of a third party, this may constitute neglect by the parents and they may be culpable for not providing adequate care and supervision.

For children within its jurisdiction, the juvenile court may determine a number of issues. These would include where the child lives, visitations by parents and relatives, attending special educational programs, emergency medical authorizations, and even travel requests. In some jurisdictions, the court may exercise the authority of the probate court, which could include terminating parental rights and the adoption of the child.

From a macrolevel perspective, the juvenile court is responsible for overseeing and protecting children who are in need of such protection. The strength of this particular court, in terms of its capacity to take action within the community, lies in its authoritative position and its access to child welfare social workers. Unlike the family court, the juvenile court has social workers that serve as an authoritative extension of itself. This provides the court with an intervention capacity. The court can make a particular visitation or supervision order and the social worker, as its agent, is responsible for carrying it out. In this respect, the juvenile court is most analogous to the criminal court, which can order the police to take a specific set of actions, such as placing a suspect in custody. This ability makes the juvenile court unique within the structure of the various courts dealing with child well-being issues.

Criminal Court

Another court that is particularly germane to the practice of public child welfare social work is that of the criminal court. The criminal court handles the matters in which adults are charged with violating community laws. The purpose and focus of this court is twofold: protecting society and punishing norm violators. It is organized around the underlying assumption that society needs protection from persons who violate societal laws. This idea of norm violators as individuals manifesting deviant behavior, as we saw earlier, is applied to the child protection system. That is, the child protection system is criminalized. Police involvement centers on arrests and the criminal court is the body before which the prosecuting attorney files charges of law violations and gets convictions. Swift (1995) notes that in neglect cases the "only helping tool society has provided itself is to find parents guilty" (p. 87). What she does not say, but which must be added, is that the parent(s), upon conviction, normally can expect to have a criminal record and serve probation or jail or prison time, thus shifting many families into an economic crisis.

The police are the major enforcement arm for the criminal court. They do the investigation on criminal matters and then refer the case to the prosecuting attorney. The prosecuting attorney makes the decision to file or not file charges and the nature of the charges. The police may make a recommendation regarding charges; however, the prosecutor makes the filing decision. At times, the prosecuting attorney will use a grand jury for the purposes of furthering the prosecution through an indictment of alleged perpetrators. The use of grand juries is often criticized as unfair to defendants because of its rules of operation.

In many child welfare cases, there is crossover between child protection activities and police activities. How does this happen? Several forces drive this collaborative action. First, reporting laws typically are implicit with their focus on pursuing criminal charges against perpetrators of abuse or neglect. Child abuse reporting statutes require cross-reporting of referrals that may involve criminal conduct to the police. Thus, police review these referrals to determine if any seem to involve prosecutable offenses.

Second, police have as their major duty the enforcement of the laws of the state. Thus, most child protection jurisdictions call them to coinvestigate child abuse allegations. Police officers are usually designated under legal codes as peace officers. Being a part of this social category involves specialized employment and training. It typically comes with more personal risk, better pay, and better fringe benefits than what child protection social workers receive. Peace officers are required to be involved in criminal cases. In some jurisdictions police officers as "peace officers" are required to take a child into custody.

A third way in which police become involved with child protection cases is through their joint connection to referrals. If they are involved on the criminal justice side of a situation, they typically gain access to confidential records maintained by child protective agencies. This is typically through legitimately established discussions with social workers, copying records, or in some situations through orders of the juvenile court judge.

The decisions and control that the criminal court has in criminal cases involve a range of items including child welfare worker involvement and victims' rights issues as well as the punishment of convicted offenders. In situations in which children are dependents of the juvenile court, the social worker may receive a request for the child to testify against the parent or caretaker, or the criminal court judge may ask how the "victim" is doing as part of the sentencing consideration of a perpetrator. In these situations, following federal law, the criminal court may require an assessment to determine the extent of the victim's suffering as part of the sentencing process. This may be handled by verbal requests for information or may be more formal requests for written materials.

Vignette: Revictimizing the Victim

Harriet, a CPS social worker, received a call from a probation officer. A maternal grandfather on her caseload had been convicted of sexually molesting three granddaughters. Also, his own daughter, the girls' mother, indicated that he had sexually abused her as a child. The grandfather, with the maternal grandmother, appeared to be the main socially and economically stabilizing part of the family for these children for years. When it was discovered that he had, in a serial manner, been grooming the females as sexual abuse targets, that theory changed. Now, the probation officer was asking Harriet for information as to how the child victims were doing. What could she say?

Ombudsperson

Increasingly child welfare agencies are responding to complaints from the community and clients about shoddy and biased treatment of clients by social workers. One agency response to this problem is the use of an ombudsperson. Although not a court function, this is an important organizational function. Typically, the ombudsperson, a trained and knowledgeable clinician, interviews all parties involved in a complaint including the social worker and his or her supervisor. The ombudsperson may have a dual role. This includes the role of investigating the handling of cases and recommending actions to correct problem situations for individual clients. The second aspect of his or her role is to recommend administrative or system-wide changes that improve the child welfare program.

Vignette: The Ombudsperson

Sarah, the recently appointed ombudsperson for Somewhere County, hung up the phone. She had just spent forty minutes talking with a client. She made an appointment with the client to discuss her concerns in detail. This was the second complaint she had concerning the same social worker in the two months she had been on the job. This one was much like the others: the social worker was disrespectful and had lied to the parents, the child, and to the court. Past discussions with the social worker and her supervisor had not gone to her satisfaction. Now Sarah wondered if finally something might come out of her efforts.

VOLUNTARY CHILD AND FAMILY COURTS

So far, we have looked at courts that can be described loosely as nonvoluntary courts and systems. These social entities have staff associated with their actions. The court, without such resources, has limited resources to enforce its orders. Rather, as power is structured in our society, the enforcement of court orders is through executive lines of authority. This includes actions by police and child protection social workers. The following courts are typically dependent upon citizens to bring normal life problems before them for adjudication. They make orders; however, the parents must comply and bring the matter back to court if an enforcement issue develops. The exceptions are when other executive arms of government are involved with the social problem, such as in domestic violence issues.

Family or Domestic Relations Court

The court most people in the community are familiar with is the family court. This is the court that makes headlines as celebrities and common folk go through divorces with messy property and income settlements and child custody fights. For example, this is the court that gave O. J. Simpson custody of his children after he was legally cleared of the murder of their mother.

The essential purpose of this court is that of presiding over domestic relations issues brought before it by parents or adults. Social workers are not typically a part of the family court in that they do not conduct investigations or provide supervision by the order of the family court. At times clinical social workers may be involved as family court staff, mediating custody disputes or doing custody evaluations. Alternately, they may work as independent practitioners doing similar evaluations, or as "visitation supervisors" or as "special masters" for the family court. This kind of social work differs from work involving the juvenile court in that it is not an authoritative function and is not related to protection issues.

The primary function of this court is the allocation of property and income along with the determination of the proper custody for a child. This court is organized around the assumption that the parents are competent to make decisions for the child and to adequately supervise and protect the child (Edwards, 1987). Unlike the juvenile court, where the social worker is responsible for investigating allegations of abuse and neglect, in this court the parents are responsible for developing information that leads to the adjudication of cases. The parents, of course, may obtain an agent such as an attorney(s), investigator(s), or even a therapist to develop information that can be brought before the family court. The typical kinds of decisions that family courts make include custody of the child, visitation by custodial and noncustodial parents, child support, etc.

Connections to Juvenile Court

Since the family court is dependent upon the parent(s) taking action to access it, it is limited in its capacity to protect children. At times, divorces in process and visitation and custody issues evolve into allegations of abuse or neglect. In some such situations, children's protective social workers are called upon to investigate allegations of abuse, often sexual abuse.

Although some theorists and experts suggest that these child abuse claims involve false allegations by an upset parent (usually the mother), the real scenario is much less clear-cut. The fact is that the children are caught in situations that are emotionally confusing for them. In particular, although each parent may express a desire to care for the child, the child feels the separations in process and gets caught in a metaphoric hailstorm of feelings. Like "status offender" situations, these often do not have any good or easy solutions. For the most part, laws dealing with family issues do little to help these problematic divorce situations. The juvenile court is not a good alternative for resolving these conflicts; however, some do enter the court. A combination of the juvenile court and the family court is needed.

How these divorces and custody disputes enter the juvenile court determine to some extent how they move into and through the child welfare system. In some situations, the social worker is able to accurately assess the issues in the family and provide services that can assist the family court in resolving the central issues. The effect in such situations is to keep the child out of the child welfare system. Unfortunately, the limited amount of time available for social workers involved in handling referrals is not adequate to handle these often extremely difficult predicaments. The answer, albeit not a good one, is to shift them mechanically into a "case" status because it is "easy" and "we can sort out the details later." Because of an administrative emphasis on turning over referrals quickly, a child may be needlessly removed from his or her family.

Filing a petition in juvenile court involves alleged abuse and neglect by one or both parents. This effectively moves the family conflict from the family court arena to the juvenile court domain. However, as the parents are charged with abuse or neglect of the child and they anticipate a loss of their parental role, they become even more upset at the treatment they are receiving and react predictably to the perceived threat to their freedom (Wicklund, 1974). Entering the child protective system in this way can result in the accumulation of a history of abuse and neglect, which increases the likelihood that another referral will move the child and family into the dependency system.

Probate Court

A second court that is particularly germane to child welfare is that of the probate court, which settles estate and property issues and, importantly, guardianship issues relating to children. An underlying assumption around which the probate court is organized is that families and parents are competent to handle affairs that relate to their children. The typical kind of case handled in probate court with respect to child welfare situations is the establishment of guardianship when the parent is not able to provide for the child.

A typical child welfare scenario would involve a parent who is in jail and unable to provide financially for his or her child. The parent's parents, the child's grandparents, are at times resources for the children, but they may lack financial resources. An option through probate court is for the grandparents to become guardians for the child and raise the child, with financial support from the public sector while the parent is in prison. This "kinship care" assumes the grandparents can do it with their own income or that the income maintenance/foster care system will provide financial support to the grandparents without juvenile court involvement. Similarly, if a parent has severe emotional problems, mental health issues, drug abuse problems, etc., the probate court may be a legal resource so that someone may raise the child without the involvement of the juvenile court.

Vignette: Guardianship versus Dependency

Tess, a CPS social worker, has received a referral on a ten-year-old girl, Virginia, living with her grandmother, while her mother is in jail on drug charges. At the time of the home visit, Tess sees the grandmother, and talks with the mother over the telephone. The grandmother needs money in order to properly care for Virginia. There are two alternatives available in Tess's jurisdiction: dependency action or the establishment of a guardianship. She discusses both with the mother and grandmother. They decide on guardianship, as it will be less restrictive to their current relationship. Also, Tess knows that in juvenile court she would have to prove "detriment" to Virginia in the grandmother's care, and that is not likely given the care and attention currently provided.

In contrast to the juvenile court's standard of detriment, the family court operates according to the legal standard of the "best interests" of the child. This standard of proof is much easier to prove. Guardianship also leaves the grandmother and mother in charge of the legal relationships involving Virginia, which in Tess's view is the preferred scenario.

Although guardianships are often seen as being done by relatives, they are also handled through an attorney petitioning the court on behalf of a child to establish a nonrelative guardianship. These situations often involve very limited third party investigations and as a result can become problematic. For example, in some jurisdictions, guardianships can be established without parents knowing about it and can result in family conflicts becoming worse and ultimately some children living in the streets. Although they are runaways, these children are often labeled in professional discourse as throwaway children, and their parents are shifted to a social category of abusive or neglectful parent. Many of them are simply status offenders.

Vignette: Guardianship As Exasperating Problems

A fourteen-year-old girl was involved in emotional conflict with her parents. The conflict centered on control issues, not uncommon to this age group. Her boyfriend was having his own problems of control at

(continued)

(continued)

home with his parents. His parents saw the girl, Mary, as a stabilizing influence on their son, Mike. In response to the pleadings of the two teens, Mike's parents proceeded to get guardianship of Mary. This was done without Mary's parents being legally noticed. (Legal notice was not required in this state at this time.) About a year later Mary was taken into custody in another state after she had been "abandoned" by her guardians because of much conflict.

Probate courts may also be involved in making decisions on the emancipation of minors and on some aspects of minor marriages requiring court permission. In these cases, typically, state law would specify certain criteria that the minor would need to meet in order to be proclaimed legally emancipated. Legally emancipated in this context simply means the minor has the same legal rights as an adult. In particular this includes the right to enter into a legally binding contract within the larger community. Here, much as in family court, the case and required evidence is brought to the court by the to-be "legally freed" minor or his or her representative. The court does not typically have social workers, police, or other staff to do investigations.

Another domain that the probate court becomes involved in is that of establishing a conservatorship relationship between a person and the larger society. Specifically, the judge may find that a person is a danger to himself or herself or others and comes within the mental health statutes of the state. Upon finding this, the judge can appoint a conservator. The conservator has the power to set, in abeyance, an individual's exercise of his or her civil rights. In this sense, the probate court is more comprehensive in its authoritative operation than is the juvenile court.

The probate court typically comes into play in situations in which mentally disordered dependent children need a degree of protection that the juvenile court is unable to provide. A typical example would be a child's need for confinement in a "locked facility." Conservators have more power than the juvenile court in the sense that they can make decisions that would limit a child's freedom, even to the point of suspending her or his rights under the Constitution. For example, a dependent child cannot be placed in a locked facility without going through an alternate judicial process. For dependent children, this judicial process involves the establishment of a conservator. Of course, delinquent children are a different situation. Delinquent here is defined as children who have violated the written laws of the state.

For developmentally disabled children, alternate court processes may be involved in establishing jurisdiction and in making conservator level decisions for children. For example, in California the regional center system provides the legal vehicle for establishing a conservator relationship for children who are found to be "a danger to self or others" and "developmentally disabled." However, within some systems, parents are accorded the right to make some of these decisions.

ANCILLARY COURTS AND LEGAL ISSUES

One area of virtual hysteria that shakes child welfare organizations and child welfare workers is associated with social worker liability. For example, cases in which social workers were found liable in New Jersey may cause concern for social workers in California and vice versa. Similarly, what happens if your agency director expects you to do something unethical or even illegal and you do it and problems occur? Alternately, what if you do not do it and get fired? These important questions are beyond the scope of this work; however, this section touches on the court that may be involved in some of these issues.

**Vignette: Interstate Compact
on the Placement of Children (ICPC)**

Gloria, a social worker, reads the latest issue of *Tymme* magazine. The story tells about a child welfare worker who placed a child from Illinois in a foster home in the state of Florida but didn't do the ICPC paperwork on a timely basis. Subsequently, the child is beaten by the Florida foster parents and the Illinois social worker was fired.

Civil Court

None of these nonvoluntary courts are normal fare for line level child protective social workers, and civil courts are particularly not a usual system for social workers. However, administrators do become involved with these and the court does affect the jobs of many social workers. For social work administrators, involvement comes when someone sues the agency. Line level social workers become involved in this in an indirect manner on behalf of children in the child welfare system. There are several situations in which line level social workers may become involved.

Organizational Level Civil Court Actions

Administrators become involved in class action lawsuits aimed at changing the child welfare system and in lawsuits that allege improper treatment of individuals. There were approximately forty states involved in class action lawsuits in 1996. These numbers have been fairly constant over the past ten to fifteen years. These lawsuits range from those against local jurisdictions for violating state licensing regulations, that is, having more children in a facility than it is licensed for, to lawsuits alleging a failure to provide adequate reunification services, etc.

Many of these lawsuits continue for years. The legal processes involved in these become extremely technical from a legal perspective. The general problem that underlies these class action, change-oriented lawsuits is one of agencies having a mandate to provide a specific menu of services and not having the financial resources to provide this level of services. Through legal means, child advocates attempt to force agencies to provide services that the federal government has mandated but not funded. Advocates are rightfully concerned that agencies comply with laws. Similarly, agency directors are justified in their concern that they are mandated to provide services that are not properly funded. The result is litigation. These legal actions have on occasion been effective in creating major changes in child welfare systems.

Vignette: Civil Suit: Missouri Out of Federal Compliance

On January 21, 2003, the <www.cnn.com> Web site carried a story that a federal judge had ruled that Missouri's system for making foster care payments violated federal law because it was not based on actual costs. The judge gave Missouri two months to develop an alternative rate setting system for residential centers.

Child Protective Agency Social Worker Involvement
with Civil Courts

In addition to organizational level lawsuits, the civil court hears a range of cases in which social workers may have limited contact. These are largely of four types. These include situations in which parents believe they have been treated unfairly or have been deprived of their civil rights. These cases typically involve extensive written material being provided by parents and the naming of one or more individual social workers, supervisors, and/or administrators. For the most part these civil suits are determined to be without merit and usually do not progress far in the legal system. In many jurisdictions, these lawsuits are typically assigned to litigation experts for action. Since they involve a set of laws and issues that are very specialized, the use of experts is believed to reduce costs and the risk of losses to the organization.

These situations seem to present the greatest potential for being positively impacted by the ombudsperson program used by some agencies. By intervening and assisting the organization to establish and maintain lines of communication with disgruntled clients, one can reasonably expect some improvement in the program, particularly as viewed by clients.

A second set of situations includes those in which a child is part of a suit against another person or even an organization. These may involve such scenarios as a lawsuit filed on behalf of a child because of injury or death of a parent as the result of an accident involving a drunk driver, a medical malpractice suit based on past actions by a doctor toward the child or even the child's parent, etc. These civil lawsuits are often initiated by adults working on behalf of the child. This can be a foster parent, child advocate, an adult friend of the child, an attorney, etc. The social worker's involvement is typically minimal. However, at times some legal work may be required to protect the child from losing funds to the public welfare system or other parts of our social institutional structure, the megastructures in which we live.

A third and particularly unusual case may involve a suit by a child and her agent against the perpetrator of abuse and neglect. Although highly unusual, in child protective work they do occur. For example, a child, or his or her advocate, may file a lawsuit against a stepparent who sexually molested him or her. The lawsuit would typically ask for monetary damages. This kind of civil court action is more likely to occur within the general population when our social institutions have failed to protect the child.

Vignette: Collecting Damages for Sexual Abuse

Jocelyn, a twenty-year-old woman, sued her stepfather for monetary damages stemming from emotional problems she experienced following sexual molestation by the stepfather over a ten-year time period. The court ruled in her favor and transferred two properties to Jocelyn.

LITIGATION: SOCIAL WORK LIABILITY, FORENSIC RESPONSIBILITY, AND AGENCY ACTION

Given the tensions and stresses in the child welfare field, it is not surprising that social workers, including administrators, are concerned with actual or potential civil litigation against them. Generally, agency administrators support social workers in legal actions as long as the social worker has worked within the administrative policy of the agency. For this support, administrators expect loyalty that at times may be unreasonable, and at times may even require illegal actions, as intimated in the Wenatchee situation described in a following vignette. The concept of the fiduciary relationship provides some guidance in sorting out these tensions and the parameters available to social workers. This is discussed in Chapter 13.

Another situation that may involve civil court action involves illegal or unethical behavior by social workers or administrators. Ignoring individual idiosyncrasies, this is apt to happen around cases or situations that have a contagious emotional quality, for example, when social workers are simply expected to do more than they can, or when individuals become emotionally involved or simply act out of their own desires or self-interest. This can include an administrator becoming emotionally entangled and treating a social worker unfairly, resulting in a "wrongful termination" lawsuit.

In general, three types of situations can increase liability through the administrators getting caught up in contagious energies and taking unusual actions. These include situations involving allegations of abuse or neglect with persons well connected to the governing structure of the community, situations involving staff that administrators have personal biases against, and situations involving high media attention. The first two present challenges to simply let established protocols work within the agency. In such situations, administrators must typically respond to higher administrators but must also not become involved in the line workers' actions. Similarly, the line worker is challenged to work within his or her domain of expertise. Agencies are required to treat all clients with respect and fairness.

Vignette: The Curling Champion

Kris, a child protection social worker in a far northern state, was covering the weekend shift at the children's shelter admissions office. The police brought in two young children. The officers told Kris that they were the son and daughter of Ed Mills, the leader of the famous Mills Curling Rink. Ed Mills' ex-wife, the children's mother, had been stopped for driving under the influence, was arrested, and no one was available to take the children. The police had tried to contact the father, but he was not immediately available. He was expected to be available in the next hour. Agency protocol typically involved keeping children in custody until an assessment of the situation could be completed. If that was done in this case, surely the media would become involved.

Contagious group processes within agencies are ripe for social workers and administrators to become caught up in them. This is particularly easy in cases that involve the potential for, or actual, high media exposure. In particular, these include situations that at first sight provide the potential for a particularly egregious kind of abuse or neglect. Administrators can quickly become concerned that the agency is not doing everything it is supposed to do. In fact, they can become so concerned that they may directly or inadvertently set in operation the special handling of these situations. Such special handling can lead to major organizational problems, including the changing of administrative and management staff.

Words such as "ritual abuse," "sex rings," and "cults," inflame these processes and are typically a sure sign of a need for administrators to take nonhysteric and carefully planned action. These words can inflame an organization's normal administrative processes and lead to a certain chaotic or "witch hunt" mentality. At times, this contagious quality takes the form of doing more than they would do otherwise. For example, the agency workers may respond by precipitously removing children from a family or a foster family without a proper investigation or assessment of risk. When the agency strays beyond its policy, it risks having legal actions taken against it, which could be decided in favor of the other party. The risk is in being seen as doing something different for one client than for others.

Vignette: Wenatchee

In the 1990s a series of events highlighted the role of civil lawsuits in ending dramatic social events. Beginning in Wenatchee in 1992 and continuing through about 1995-1996, forty-three people were charged with 30,000 counts of child rape (Roberts, 1999; Lyon, 1998). The victims included about sixty children. A local detective became highly involved in catching perpetrators where crimes did not seem to have been committed. He began interviewing his own foster children and got them to admit being abused by others. Later they recanted those allegations. Before it was over, several social workers were fired for calling attention to the handling of the child abuse allegations. The result was a multitude of civil suits and financial settlements, including payments by the state for wrongful discharge to a social work supervisor and two social workers. The public reaction some six years later?

"Appeals court judges, as well as judges in the civil suits against the city of Wenatchee, have been astounded and outraged by the abusive procedures used to railroad people to prison" (Roberts, 1999, p. A15). However, while the prosecutor fought the release of the adults from prison, no other charges were filed against them. According to Roberts (1999), Prosecutor Gary Riesen "defends his cases and fights tooth and nail against every release of the wrongfully convicted. Even worse, the responsible CPS officials remain in office, one with a promotion" (p. A15).

At times agencies and/or geographical areas of the country go through a kind of awakening to "ritual abuse." Awakenings, often associated with revivalist activities (McLoughlin, 1980), represent cultural changes often taking the form of a disruption but actually involving a realignment of cultural values and social institutions. They typically begin with accumulated pressures and evolve to develop new social structures (McLoughlin, 1980). Given the religious ties of awakenings it is not surprising that they are often associated with allegations of satanic and/or ritual child abuse.

With these awakenings, persons, including professionals, find themselves not exactly sure about the natures of their own realities. At this point broad-ranging allegations of networks of cults sexually abusing children are apparently based upon faulty information. Theorists, practitioners, and researchers alike clearly indicate that no such cases of ritual sexual abuse have been found (Lanning, 1989a,b; Robbins, 1997). Even in the horrific cases of the 1980s involving day care, researchers have not substantiated abusive incidents despite the fact that many persons were convicted and served time for such offenses. They did find faulty interviewing protocols (Ceci and Bruck, 1993, 1995; Poole and Lamb, 1998).

Agencies may also stray from normal procedures as they move to increase administrative control over the child welfare system. For example, as agency management attempts to control children taken into custody, they may establish review panels. Such panels may work well in screening worker actions, but may not meet the test of law. For example, in a jurisdiction that requires a social worker or peace officer to determine that a child is in immediate danger before he or she is taken into temporary custody, the use of a screening committee for custody could be self-defeating and create a libelous situation for a child protective agency.

Implicit in this legal standard of "immediate danger" is the need to act in a timely manner. To establish an administrative review panel which seeks to determine that a child should be taken into custody based on immediate danger would likely result in a failure to respond in a timely manner. However, agency administrators attempting to control this action by social workers and then directing the social workers to take a child into custody could find themselves paying a legal settlement through a civil action.

ADMINISTRATIVE REVIEWS:
SCHOOLS, WELFARE, SOCIAL SERVICES, ETC.

A variety of reviews that are associated with the educational system, the eligibility system, and the social service delivery system are also important in various aspects of the social welfare system. These reviews are designed to support or supplement the parental role (Kadushin and Martin, 1988). As such they represent protocols which are aimed at ensuring that social institutions are responsive to parents. When the juvenile court as represented by a social worker becomes involved with a family, these other reviews for the most part become superfluous. Jacobs (1986) describes this confusion best in his study of special education services. He notes that the lack of clarity around the roles of these reviews confuses an already confusing situation. These reviews can serve as a check on the administrative element of the child welfare system; however, with the juvenile court involved this function is diminished.

CONCLUSION: COURTS AS A LABYRINTH

The cases that involve both protection and criminal action are some of the more difficult and complicated cases for social workers in public child welfare to handle. They involve the need to coordinate activities with a wide range of professionals, some of whom have significantly different value positions with respect to the prosecution, and sometimes the treatment, of perpetrators and victims. Professionals who work in the system on a day-to-day basis have difficulty sorting out the role and functions of the various courts, but it is virtually impossible for families to decipher them. During the transitional processes, it is extremely difficult for them to cope with the multiple systems. Since the social workers are often polarized as being on the prosecution's "side," they can at times offer very little help or support.

Chapter 9

The Concentric Systems View
of Child Welfare

INTRODUCTION

This chapter discusses the child protective system and begins by looking at the social production and reproduction of formal and informal social categories of abuse and neglect. It begins with the court work group, extends its argument into the child welfare community, and then discusses the reciprocal production and reproduction of the categories with its application to this model.

The model presents a view of the performance of the child protection system in terms of general categories of cases handled within the total system. This includes a look at child welfare system as a unit, i.e., as a whole. It represents a top-down view of the total system in terms of referrals and outcomes by general categories including those referrals that stay in the system and become cases.

The child protective system is defined simply as the child abuse and neglect report reception and action system. It includes referrals into a child protection system and action within about the first thirty days. Although the child protective agency system is comprised of multiple state and county jurisdictions, this work treats the child protective agency system as a national system. Although criminal justice literature streams use a progressive four-tier "wedding cake" model (Walker, 1989; Purpura, 1997) to describe cases and case handling, an adapted concentric systems model is used in this work. According to Walker (1989), this model emphasizes "differences *between* types of cases . . . [and shows] fairly consistent patterns of disposition *within* categories" (p. 30). The hierarchical layered wedding cake shows this nicely. This work modifies the four levels to explain the different use of resources within each category and to explain a potential way to triage cases in the child protection system. Concepts drawn from the commonly described 80/20 rule, Pareto's rule, or the ABC production model are thus incorporated in the wedding cake model. The basic concept in these three models is the idea that a small number of case situations use the majority of system resources. Stated explicitly, this model would suggest that some 20 percent of referrals into the system would use about 50 percent of the system's resources. Words such as systems, circles, levels, and layers are used interchangeably to refer to these concentric systems.

There are three of these systems. Each represents a general pattern that describes the handling of referrals into the child protective system. The first and third represent fairly clear-cut scenarios, while the middle system involves more complex and difficult situations for social workers. Scenarios in the first layer essentially enter the juvenile court system. Alternately, referrals described in the third layer typically do not enter the juvenile court system. Those in the second layer may either exit or enter the court system.

In general, the model is descriptive in that it simply tells what happens to particular types of cases. Certain types of cases can be placed in categories, or concentric systems, based on the perceived seriousness of the abuse or neglect and the perceived outcomes acceptable. In examining types of cases, it uses an "ideal model" that limits its use. It is meant to provide a measure of the total large system workload and action that constitutes the total child protective system.

It does not make allowances for the unique differences in monies spent, in laws between jurisdictions, or countless other factors that may argue for a reduced view of the total system and its performance. It relies on a political economy model that includes negotiated outcomes for some cases, based on assumptions of expected outcomes made by professionals.

BACKGROUND OR THEORETICAL UNDERPINNINGS

Historic View of the Model

The wedding cake model for viewing the criminal justice system was developed late in the nineteenth century by Lawrence Friedman and Robert V. Percival (Walker, 1989). It was the model used for "The Roots of Justice," a study of the history of criminal justice in Alameda County, California, from 1870 through 1910 (Walker, 1989). This model was also described in Michael and Don Gottfredson's *Decision Making in Criminal Justice* (Gottfredson and Gottfredson, 1988).

Child welfare experience and the limited research done on the juvenile court as a decision-making body is supportive of the use of this kind of model. For example, Hasenfeld (1985), using a political economy model, found multiple models involved in decision making within the juvenile delinquency court. These models suggest the kinds of interpersonal negotiations that occur between social workers, clients, supervisors, attorneys, and judges. These informal negotiations and negotiated case outcomes combined with formal court processes as trials constitute the major dimensions of the institutional response to allegations of child abuse and neglect. The model as originally developed is presented in a modified version in order to more adequately equate with the negotiated outcomes that occur in child welfare.

THE CONCENTRIC SYSTEMS MODEL

Social Category Production

This model describes actions and outcomes on case scenarios that depend on the fitting of case situations into social categories of abused or neglected children. It presumes these categories are determined by formal and informal social processes. It also presumes that these categories are in a general state of flux as professionals interact with one another and with clients of the child welfare system. This section describes how this construction process operates.

An inherent presumption within this model is the idea that social categories are produced and reproduced through collective thoughts, feelings, and actions, including dialogue expressed in language. Social workers respond to referrals by investigating and determining whether the allegations are substantiated, unsubstantiated, or indicated. These categories, set in federal reporting requirements, relate to findings of child maltreatment. Another category includes referrals/reports that are screened out, not investigated, etc. A U.S. Health and Human Services (2000, p. 3-1) report describes these as including those that "were out of the agency's jurisdiction; the perpetrator was not a caretaker; or, the parent or child in the referral could not be located."

In making such determinations, they are fitting the actions of the parent/caretaker into a social category of "abusive" or "neglectful" parent. Categorizing parents based on parental behavior establishes and reestablishes the social categories of abusive or neglectful parent within the administrative framework of the agency through a multiplicity of work actions (Swift, 1995). As social workers determine the kinds of behavior or action that fit each category, a critical consideration is that of the basic values held within the local child welfare system.

This idea of the production and reproduction of the social categories presumes the establishment of collective working level values within the local child welfare system. This is a question of the "integration" (from Parsons, 1965) of the social system, that is, the organizational group. Integration can be operationally defined as "activities directed to the adjustment of the relations of members to each other within the system" (Polsky et al., 1968, p. 8). It includes informal relationships of members to each other. It is not especially goal-oriented, related to fulfilling an adaptive task, or directly psychologically supportive. It includes "general conversations" and "bull sessions" that cement "internal relationships along specific values and themes" (Polsky, 1968, p. 10). This cementing of specific values and themes through collective dialogue forms the basis for determining the categories of abuse and neglect.

This system-level integration involves the establishment of value systems within communities that develop a general conception of the content of the social categories of abuse and neglect. Thus, the total members of the system, from a child protective social worker to an attorney representing a particular child, share some basic values regarding the acceptable and nonacceptable treatment of children. Along with this conception of these broad categories of acceptable and nonacceptable behavior is an informally agreed upon conception of what should happen to parents or caretakers when they fit the nonacceptable social category. The matching of the values attributed to the particular categories, that is, "acceptable" or nonacceptable" treatment of a child, and an acceptable outcome of "what should happen to the parent" provides the heart or centerpiece of this model in its historic usage.

The Grounding of the Child Welfare System

To understand more fully this production and reproduction of abuse and neglect categories, we must look at the court work group as the legitimating body that provides the foundation for collective stakeholder, that is, child welfare industry, dialogue. The work group provides the structure within which the community integrates its values and that, in turn, influence the work group's reproductions, both formal and informal, of these social categories.

The Court Work Group

The nature of the values within a social system or community is driven by the grounding of legitimate authority within the system with its values and beliefs. A dominant force in large systems that plays an important role is suggested by Parsons (1968), as he notes in a discussion of Pareto's work that force "may be said to determine the state of integration of a society" (p. 291). In short, the maintenance of a social system depends upon the integration of the system, and that depends upon a grounding or legitimating of authority and power related to the potential to get coercive compliance within the system.

In the child welfare system, the legitimate authority for intervening into family life is vested within the legal system and manifested with the juvenile court. This legitimated authority system essentially establishes the values and norms that operate to define and maintain the social categories associated with abuse and neglect. Although the exact legal categories are established in state legislation, the operational or interpreted definition of these categories is essentially left to the juvenile court, with its particular work group configuration.

An important aspect of understanding how this concentric systems model operates is to recognize that decisions within the court system are made based on implicit understandings and meanings associated with both the formal and informal descriptions of social categories. Although the court has a presiding judge that adjudicates cases, the court itself also operates as a social system. In the sense that it operates as an entity, it can be seen as a court work group. As an entity, this social system, over time, forms its own working level view of the presiding judge's style in the form of collective definitions of the social categories of abuse and neglect and their respective norms. Walker (1989, p. 33) describes the effect of this "courtroom work group" action as informally controlling "individual discretion" and providing "a high degree of consistency" within groups of cases/referrals.

The judge is the highest status person within the court work group. As such, he or she is the key member of the work group, and he or she sets the tone for the determinations of what constitutes the social categories overseen by the work group. The attorneys and social workers who work with a particular judge find, over time, his or her limits and expectations. They also learn of any particular views on particular case scenarios.

Although judges are the highest status persons in the court work group, they also have boundaries in terms of their ability to interpret and define the social categories into which parents and children may be fit. That is, judges must operate within the particular judicial system of which they are a part. First, they must function within the federal and state legal structure. Their findings and rulings are subject to appeal to higher courts. They must also adjudicate matters within the structures provided within the larger system of which they are a part. For example, they are located within a community. In such a setting, judges are typically evaluated informally by the community and sometimes formally by other attorneys.

However, the judge is only a part, albeit the critical part, of the total court context. In the juvenile court system, we typically see five different social roles that constitute the basic court system. These include the judge, the child's attorney, the agency or child protective agency attorney, the parent's attorney, and the social worker (the social worker's "membership" depends to a considerable extent upon the social service agency view of social work practice). With the exception of those jurisdictions that do not provide counsel for children and parents, the work group at minimum has these five formal roles. Although the roles are discernable within various jurisdictions, they are quite likely to have different titles attached. Also, particularly in rural areas, individuals may be playing multiple roles and it may be hard to differentiate these independent roles as played by particular individuals. For example, they may be labeled district attorney, public defender, etc.

Community Production and Reproduction
of Social Categories

Of utmost importance in understanding the operation of the court and the court processes from this concentric systems perspective is the idea of the court functioning as a community. It would be a community of meaning in Brueggemann's (2002) terms. These communities become the heart and soul of the larger community; they become centers of discourse and dialogue on ethics and justice and are embedded in the beliefs, values, and ideology of the wider culture (Brueggemann, 2002).

This would also apply to a wider view of the court community. Walker (1989, p. 51) suggests that the idea of a "courthouse community" can be a helpful way to view the court setting. From this perspective, all social workers in public child welfare are a part of court processes. Also, attorneys for parents, children, and agencies; judges; and others that attend court with any regularity constitute the court work group for dependency courts. Members of the child welfare community, that is, the "child abuse industry," or, as we might describe them, system stakeholders are also a part of this community.

Understanding this community is an important part of understanding action in the child protective agency system, since these members essentially construct and reconstruct, through collective dialogue and discourse, the informal meanings that become attached to the formal legal categories of abuse and neglect written in state law. These legal categories and the kinds of work processes involved in their establishment and maintenance, that is, their adjudication and disposition, constitute the ideological and dialogical gatekeeping structure for cases.

Interrelation of Community and Work Group Norms

Although the exact and formal definitions of social categories of abuse and neglect are written in law, the court work group effectively socially constructs the operational meanings that comprise each social category. From this perspective, the work group develops a shared value system as to the nature of cases within a category, that is, acceptable and nonacceptable treatment of a child, and the way those cases should be handled, that is, what should happen to the parent.

Walker (1989) describes this as "working together day in and day out, members of the courtroom work group reach a general consensus about how different cases should be handled. This involves a shared understanding" (p. 51). For child welfare, it includes a shared understanding of the kinds of cases that fit within each social and legal category within the jurisdiction. It also involves, as part of the adjudication process, the application of shared values related to the nature of abuse and the risk of the recurrence of abuse.

Through an interpersonal dialogue within the work group, collective meanings are constructed as to what constitutes abuse and neglect as it applies to the specific social categories. This dialogue involves the combining of formal definitions of the social categories of abuse and neglect with informal definitions, opinions, and values held by individual members of the work group. Swift (1995) notes that formal definitions of social categories serve as a primary route through which "instructions" for their understanding are conveyed in discourse. Definitional debates commonly emerge about the meanings of categories, and debates represent a struggle for competing meanings to prevail.

DYNAMICS OF THE MODEL

The concentric systems model is a descriptive model that is based on an analysis of what actually happens to referrals as they flow through the justice system. Two points are particularly important concerning the levels of involvement with referrals as they apply to the child welfare system. These include the idea that "there are significant differences between types of referrals, based on seriousness and other factors. . . [and there are] fairly consistent patterns of disposition . . . within each category" (Walker, 1989, p. 30). Generally, referrals fall into natural groupings based on this seriousness criteria, and with this comes some consistent patterns of dispositions of referrals. That is, there is a natural grouping of acceptable and nonacceptable treatment of children and a natural grouping of what should happen to parents, based on what happened to the child.

Purpura (1997) describes the model as stating that "officials handle different kinds of cases according to the informal rules of a particular" level (p. 5). The informal rules describe the outcomes of case situations based on a set of consensus or agreed upon rules and processes used by individuals within the child welfare system. The consensus may be established formally or informally. These rules and processes constitute both formal definitions and policies and informal rules and policies. These informal rules and policies are best understood as closely tied to the social production and reproductive processes described earlier. Thus, it is driven by collective dialogue and the action of defining and redefining social categories within the child welfare system work environment.

Vignette: Murder by Domestic Violence (A Level II Referral)

The stepfather of a six-year-old child is arrested by police after a ninety-mile-per-hour chase through the streets of Chicago. He is found to have murdered the child's mother. There is a large insurance policy on the mother, with the child as beneficiary, and no designated caretaker for the child. The child's father has had limited involvement with the child over the years and is afraid of the stepfather's family because of what he calls "mob" connections. The stepfather wants his own brother to become the child's caretaker. Should the juvenile court get involved in this situation? It depends. The juvenile court may become involved in an effort to protect the child. Its involvement can also include overseeing the legal issues involving the inheritance and ensuring that the child is adequately placed and cared for. Alternately, it could be argued that the stepfather will be in prison for many years and his brother could raise the child just fine.

Basic Dynamic of the Model

Walker's (1989) description of the model emphasizing degrees of seriousness and consistent patterns of dispositions can be described in concrete terms. These include the clustering of cases around the degree of seriousness of the abuse/neglect and the clustering of their outcomes. For example, cases involving very serious physical or sexual abuse would typically be considered a first level system or circle I in the concentric systems designation (see Figure 9.1), while minor situations would be handled according to the rules of system II or III.

Alternately, unsubstantiated cases would enter and exit system III as referrals only. One important distinction needs to be made. When

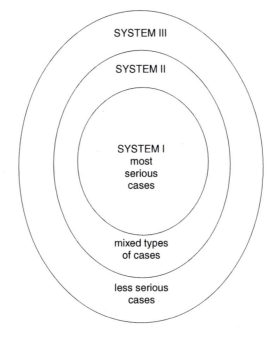

FIGURE 9.1. Concentric Systems Model

the criminal justice system is involved in potential prosecutions, the child protective agency system often acts as though the case is a high-risk or system I case. In this sense, the criminal justice system serves as the metaphoric dog that wags the child protection system. Taking the child into custody and filing a petition may help the prosecution's case, which thus improves the prosecuting attorney's political standing.

Although the two major variables discussed thus far are important in understanding the handling of referrals, three additional considerations are important. Cases are driven first and foremost by the perception within and without of the child protective agency system of the seriousness of the abuse. However, they are also driven by the perceptions and judgments regarding the likelihood of the abuse being repeated, the degree of publicity the case attracts or is expected to attract, the perceived collective norms of the court's work group, and the parents' resources.

Seriousness of Abuse

Issues as to the seriousness of the abuse affect how cases move through the system. Situations of egregious abuse are more likely than others to move through the total system, probably due to a confluence of factors, from the way the petition is framed to the parents' reluctance to settle the situation or the child's attorney or the social worker being unwilling to settle. An example of such a case might be one that results in the near death of a very young sibling as through battering or being shaken.

None of these systems factors can be viewed or understood in isolation. Rather, to understand their operation they need to be seen as linked with one another. They are certainly linked, as professionals within the confidential domain of the court, agency, and community become involved in dialogue regarding issues represented in any given situation.

Potential for Recurrence of Abuse

Generally, a major concern after the degree of seriousness of the abuse is the perception that the child maltreatment might be repeated. At the beginning point, that is, the intake section of the system, concerns for the safety of the child are invariably part of the social worker's consideration in taking action on referrals. Specifically, the concern is what happens to the child if intervention does not sufficiently change the family situation to make the child safe. This continues to be a concern as the situation moves through the child welfare system.

Whether a situation persists within the court system is, not surprisingly, related to the "fit" of the alleged abuse with what we could call the collective definitions of categories as produced and reproduced within the work group. Each case modifies or reaffirms these social categories. The actions of filing a petition and its movement within the court system constitute a ritual (a process to be discussed later) that affirms, reaffirms, or even disaffirms the legitimacy of collective values. Also, parental resources affect how cases move through the system. However, not many studies of this factor have been conducted, and the exact nature of their effects is unclear. With extensive resources, a family can bring in outside counsel, which essentially changes the work group and, consequently, the definitions of the social categories. However, an "outsider" who is not familiar with the laws, processes, and actions of the juvenile court domain may be at a disadvantage.

Degree of Media Involvement

The publicity a particular case attracts highlights the way the court, functioning in a confidential environment, operates. A point of clarification needs to be made regarding the confidentiality of the cases. Although the court's actions are confidential, because of crossovers to the criminal prosecution of adults for abuse, information to some extent in these cases becomes public. Although the child may have a confidential hearing in juvenile court, the father, mother, or caretaker may have a highly publicized hearing in criminal court.

For example, a case in which a caretaker is charged with the severe physical abuse of a child can be reasonably expected to make headlines in communities. Those stories typically mention details that have been gathered through the adult proceedings. Although reports on these proceedings usually preserve the confidentiality of the child's name and, to some extent, the details of the abuse, most people within the child's immediate environment recognize the situation. Information carried in the media is based to a considerable extent upon the parallel movement of a case in the criminal justice system. With more victims presenting their views to the criminal court, this crossover is probably increasing rather than decreasing.

Although media involvement may be limited, it is very powerful in its effects. For the most part, major stories about individual children and the system's performance or lack of performance, particularly in developed communities, tend to highlight critical problems or publicly perceived problems and may result in major organizational changes and staff reshuffling. For example, a story about a baby girl taken into custody and the system's inability to protect her from being beaten to death a few months later is big news and may very easily lead to changes in a child welfare organization's management. Although the national media may cover these cases, they actually occur less frequently on a local level.

APPLYING THE MODEL

The model as adapted here views types of cases as they enter the system at intake, as they are reported, and as they move to the point of staying in or exiting the system. The numbers used in Table 9.1 have been calculated from figures presented in the U.S. Health and Human Services report (2000) "Child Maltreatment 1998." The figures they presented were used as a base for calculating and presenting this information on a national level. The author is alone responsible for combining the information into the following categories. Every effort was made to relate outcomes to the total number of referrals. Although the report tells us that a number of referrals were screened out, many have been used in these calculations due to their inclusion in the model. The screening out noted by the study was because they "did not meet the statutory definition of maltreatment, did not contain sufficient information upon which to proceed, and/or did not pertain to the service population of the agency" (p. 3-1).

In the view presented here, the DHHS is accurate in what it reports. The referrals are not disputed; however, as we look at the whole system's operation, all data are important. This information is important

TABLE 9.1. Child Maltreatment Figures

Action Taken	Disposition of reports	Total Number of Referrals or Reports	Percent of Total Referrals
Total referrals or reports received		2,806,000	100.0
Not investigated	954,040		34.0
Closed, finding unclear			
Other, reasons unknown	381,616		13.6
Unsubstantiated	1,041,388		37.1
Subtotal: No investigation or unsubstantiated		2,377,044	84.7
Subtotal: Investigated and substantiated		532,063	19.0
Total referrals counted		2,909,107	

Note: Total number of referrals and the number of those not investigated or unsubstantiated is based on a report by the U.S. Department of Health and Human Services (2000). All other numbers are based on calculations from these figures. The numbers represent a variety of items being counted and therefore do not total 100 percent. This variety includes such matters as child counts, event counts, double counts, and family counts, as well as differences in definitions of the terms.

in that resources are required to act on nonfitting referrals. These resources might be expended elsewhere. For example, someone had to take the call, write some data down, and then send it in a report for it to be added to and then dropped from the calculations. In this analysis, these referrals have been calculated because they represent an important aspect of total system performance. The study's estimates used later in this book for the filing of petitions and placements in foster care have been used even though these are, at best, estimates based on extremely limited data.

This model provides us with a fairly simple view of the total operation of the child protection system. It shows that approximately 85 percent of the referrals were either not investigated, were unsubstantiated, or were closed for some unknown reason. Thus, for a variety of reasons, social workers were not involved in direct interventions in over 85 percent of all referrals. This model suggests a total system that is loosely focused in terms of the kinds of referrals it receives. It suggests that resource expenditures are not well focused and it hints at the frustrations social workers experience as they respond to many unsubstantiated and vague allegations. This analysis supports the view that the child abuse reporting system casts a very broad net. This also fails to deal with issues of what happens to people innocently caught up in the child welfare system. Often agencies do not have protocols in place for purging records. Alternatively and on the other extreme of these cases are the less than 10 percent of referrals that are either taken into custody or have had petitions filed in juvenile court. This represents the top layer of the metaphoric wedding cake. These referrals and situations necessitate a high expenditure of economic resources, involve the most emotional turmoil for professionals, and typically represent the greatest risk of continued or repeated child maltreatment. Although the U.S. Health and Human Services (2000) identified only 7 and 5 percent, respectively, of referrals that were in this category, their estimates had limited respondents.

The Model: Strengths

The concentric systems model is strongest in describing the general pattern of cases and the processes that are involved in their movement through the system. The fact that it deals with overall patterns makes it a good model to analyze systems performance from a management perspective. It is essentially a top-down model of how any particular system is performing at least in terms of quantitative considerations. It is valuable in that it gives a picture of the degree of utilization of all resources. For example, if a great deal of social worker attention is focused on allegations of minor abuse, the organization can be restructured through policies and procedures to improve its use of personnel.

This model also has implications for uniting formal and informal norms and perspectives of the child protective agency system as it operates in the implementation of abstracted norms (laws). Purpura (1997) describes the informal rules or processes used by officials as differing by the particular circle or layer. The rules at each circle are based on value judgments as to the types of cases that belong there "based on seriousness and other factors . . . [and there are] fairly consistent patterns of disposition . . . within each category" (Walker, 1989, p. 30).

A SYSTEM OVERVIEW
USING THE CONCENTRIC SYSTEMS MODEL

System I: High-Risk or Highly Involved Public, High-Profile, and Severe Abuse Cases

Walker (1989), in writing of the criminal justice system, refers to the highly publicized cases, the typical top layer, as "celebrated cases." To him, the O. J. Simpson case was "the all-time celebrated case" (p. 30). In child welfare, "the all-time celebrated case" status belongs to the Mary Ellen Wilson case. This case, heard in 1874, led to the formation of the first child protective agency (Costin, Karger, and Stoesz, 1996; Sagatun and Edwards, 1995).

This level also includes what Walker (1989) calls "heavy" cases. These are serious abuse or neglect cases. Although "heavy" cases differ by jurisdiction, a two-year-old with a spiral fracture would probably be a "heavy" case in most jurisdictions. The child welfare system works with the child and to some extent the parent/adult victims of the system I cases. These situations typically move through the child protective agency system and involve the filing of petitions with the juvenile court. In general, cases that fall in this layer are ones that involve a strong consensus as to the style of the litigation process and, at times, even the potential outcome of the case. To some extent, these cases tend to be fairly clear-cut. They tend to be situations that fit the particular value set of the agency, the law, and the social categories established within the court work group and the child welfare community in a way that the formal court processes are exactingly followed. In this sense, the rational view (discussed in Chapter 10) of the court process becomes the framework or structure in which action takes place. Certain cases are quickly recognized by line social workers as fitting this category and they act accordingly. For example, a shaken baby or an infant with spiral fractures and other unexplained broken bones at various stages of healing will typically be taken into custody and will proceed through the system as part of this layer of cases. Applying the model to these cases, we find that they represent less than 10 percent of cases that enter the system as reports or referrals, yet they require the most system resources. The U.S. Health and Human Services (2000) study identified approximately 5 percent of the children that were taken into custody. They also identified 7 percent of the children that had petitions filed in the juvenile court on their behalf. These represent this "heavy" level of case. Coming into custody is not only traumatic for children and their parents but also is expensive in that it involves alternate care facilities, specialized staff to handle care and legal requirements, etc. Those children that remain in custody and their parents typically would become involved in court proceedings, need legal representation, and incur expenses due to litigation such as time off work, case preparation, and investigation.

Cases in this group also include high-profile, media-covered situations, those that are unique to the statutes of a particular jurisdiction or that involve constitutional issues that may or simply could be appealed. Media situations speak for themselves in that the court work group has its own reference group observing its behavior. What is done within the confidential domain of the juvenile court is visible to some extent to people within the general community. The entire community gets a view of the particular case if only through the criminal prosecution of a perpetrator. Everyone in the work group has a stake in the case being handled properly, that is, according to the letter of the law as interpreted within the community including the court work group.

These cases typically appear in the media because of the inflammatory nature, that is, the egregious nature of the abusive situation. Included in these cases are the most atrocious situations such as babies being abandoned in garbage cans, birthed in public airplanes, left in public buildings, locked up in cages, thrown from windows, thrown against walls, etc. It also may include cases involving the wealthy and famous of our society. For example, the Woody Allen situation of the early 1990s would fit this category. In such cases, the court would need to be sensitive to the potential that a public personality may be viewed as being treated different from other clients.

Generally, these high-profile cases are handled in a manner that closely fits the rationalist model discussed in Chapter 10. These cases typically have legal representation for all parties. They typically include attorneys for all parties, experts as needed, and appeals. Although the media is limited in its capacity to report on the juvenile court processes involving these children, what they do learn fits the model of how the system is supposed to work. This learning is through a symbolic interpretation and experience of the criminal justice system. Gusfield (1981) depicts this action very nicely in his study of drunken driving arrests.

Cases that are clearly headed for potential appeals and/or involve constitutional issues also are included as a part of this layer. This includes situations such as when adoption appears to be a reasonably expected outcome or when religious practice looks like potential "abuse." Adoption cases typically involve multiple court jurisdictions and varying time lines for appeals. Thus, a "simple" adoption case going through the whole range of court scenarios necessary for finalization may take five or six years. Typically, at each step the court will ensure that every known situation has been treated with the utmost of diligence by the social service and legal system workers. That is, the judge will make sure that all of the metaphoric "i"s are dotted and the "t"s are crossed.

Similarly, unusual cases involving religious practices are seen in this layer. An example is those religious groups that oppose blood transfusion. Many jurisdictions provide for limited judicial jurisdiction for approval of the medical needs of the child while not making the child a dependent of the court. Thus, with the exception of the medical treatment, such as a blood transfusion, the parents maintain their parental role. A second example would be practitioners of a religion such as Santeria, which involves animal sacrifices. The involvement of a child in such a religious service would not typically be construed as detrimental to the child, depending upon how the parent(s) handled it with the child. Either of these scenarios could easily lead to an appeal to higher court levels. Thus, the court can reasonably be expected to handle these with the utmost attention to formal processes.

Vignette: A New Case

Arturo, a child protective agency social worker, reads the local paper in the morning before going to work. Today's paper included a story about an eighteen-month-old child that was taken into custody by a social worker and the police. The mother was arrested for child endangerment. According to the newspaper, the child's weight was only twelve pounds. One hour later Arturo found himself at work and with this case assigned to him. The child was taken into custody because of failure to thrive. The mother had had five other children removed from her care, primarily due to neglect. They had stayed in the foster care system and were receiving services from the permanency placement program. Three of the five were in residential treatment programs due to the severity of their emotional problems. Arturo knew that he had no choice but to file a petition on this referral. If his assessment suggested some mitigating circumstances, he could recommend that the court dismiss the petition or return the child home with court supervision. Otherwise, he would recommend removal from the parent.

System II: Mixed Risk

This level includes a mixture of cases typically sharing a complex array of factors that make it difficult for the system to sort out what is happening to a child and who or what is responsible. Said another way, these typically include cases which involve variables that confound the determination of the nature of the situation. The issues raised by this particular group of cases are harder to sort out than those system I cases. They present conflicting values issues that make them hard for everyone involved to "categorize."

Although the first group can easily be recognized as cases that must appear before the juvenile court for adjudication, this group contains some that must be presented to the court and others that might simply be offered or provided services or supervision. The exact investigative outcome is much less clear than the level I cases. They present, at times, highly ambiguous situations.

These are often "gray area" cases. These are situations in which it is difficult for social workers and/or the court work group to develop a consensus on a wide range of complex phenomena. In contrast with values-based issues in severe abuse cases, these situations are less clear-cut and may include "emotional maltreatment" cases. The former are clear in that the abuse is often provable by forensic evidence. Physical evidence often proves the abuse of a child. Forensic work on burns, for example, is highly developed in terms of the nature, extent, and effects. Social workers/police can measure the temperature of water heaters and the length of time involved in filling tubs, and doctors can tell the expected degree of the burns based on such variables.

In contrast, forensic work on emotional maltreatment is not available. Emotional maltreatment is not so clearly defined and its cause is less provably related to parental behavior. After all, a child's emotional problems, if present, may be related to genetic factors. Also, there are a wide range of theories of emotions—ideas about their construction, their manifestation in behavior, etc.—with no one consensus as to the veracity of any one theoretical perspective. These are difficult case scenarios for the larger child welfare community to deal with. For the most part, professional practice theories, what DeRoos (1990) refers to as "practice wisdom," may lead the workers to conclude that the child clearly has been emotionally abused. However, such theories are not definitive.

Sexual abuse cases, unless they are clear-cut, probably belong in this area. Clear-cut situations involve a witness, a confession by the perpetrator, a statement of the abuse by the victim, or undisputable physical evidence. In the absence of critical pieces of evidence, it is difficult to establish that the victim has been sexually abused. The evidence available depends on the nature of the sexual abuse, the time elapsed between the molestation event and the collection of the evidence, and the expertise of the examining doctor. These factors can be confounded by a victim's testimony about the abuse. For example, a child may or may not be considered a good witness. Similarly, other persons testifying, such as the alleged perpetrator, or the other parent or caretaker, can also confound the issue for the social worker and the court.

What happens to referrals in this system II level depends upon one or another unknown variable. Case situations in this layer typically do not have a clear consensus within the work group and limited actual or potential media attention, and the parents usually have limited resources. How these situations are handled depends on a variety of factors. In particular, it depends on how the assigned social worker sees the situation, how it is framed in petitions, the court work group's norm regarding the allegations as presented and framed, and even the time, attention, and persons present on a given day in the work group.* At times the outcome will also depend upon the work group's norms regarding the nature and causation of such things as "emotional maltreatment," the sophistication of the work group regarding international law including the rights of people from other countries, and the community's general stance toward "beyond control" children and family conflict involving family court processes.

Vignette: Private Problems versus Public Issues

The referent, apparently a relative of the mother of an eight-year-old, states that the mother gets "stoned" every weekend. She says that this has been going on for the past six months. The mother currently uses marijuana, and has since her marriage ended six months ago. When asked about the children's care while the mother is reportedly under the influence of marijuana, the reporting relative, who wants to remain anonymous, states, "Oh, they are okay. She always leaves the kids with her mother." The referent has no additional information to provide to the hotline worker. The child welfare worker gives the referent the names of some treatment programs "just in case she has contact with the mom."

This kind of case could be closed at intake if a referral is taken, especially if there is no prior history of reports. Why? There is no apparent detriment. In fact, the anonymous referent seems particularly sure the children are okay. Although it is unknown who the referent

---

*The model that at times has been noted as operating in a court environment is described by Mohr (1976) and suggested by Hasenfeld (1985) is the "organized anarchy" model of organizational decision making. In this model, decisions are likely to be made by "flight" or "oversight" and are driven by such factors as the persons present, the attention given by those persons, the problems and solutions they are carrying with them, and the time available for the task at hand.

is, what may be known is whether the ethos of the court work group accepts marijuana usage as prima facia evidence of a substance abuse problem. Rather, they may see it as similar to alcohol. The question then is the detriment to the child and as presented here it does not appear to be to the child's detriment. If the agency has abundant resources, a child welfare worker could approach the mother and offer voluntary treatment and services.

Referrals at this metaphoric layer of the system are typically handled one of two ways. The first is through an assessment at the "hotline." Referrals are taken from mandated referents, based on their view of the necessity for reporting. Then, the hotline worker assesses the situation using an agency protocol and determines that it does not need to be assigned to a child welfare worker for response. The protocol typically provides guidance in terms of referent, number of past referrals, review of past case histories, and current report. With supervisory approval, these referrals may be closed at intake.

The second group of referrals are assigned to social workers. A social worker may make one and sometimes many more visits and then decide not to involve legal protection for the child or children. Regarding contact with a parent or caretaker, referrals are often made and potential clients are connected with some of the vast array of service providers that constitute what Costin, Karger, and Stoesz (1996) refer to as the child abuse industry.

System III: Highly Value Laden

In system III are referrals that, for the most part, exit the child protective agency system or, at most, receive voluntary services. These constitute the vast majority of referrals. Actual figures as shown previously present 85 percent of referrals in this category. This includes a number of referrals for possible neglect and some that cannot be substantiated. It also may include some situations in which families need services due to a considerable risk of abuse or neglect. These figures also include approximately one-third of all referrals that are not investigated. Simply stated, one-third of national child welfare reports do not belong in the system.

These cases are highly dependent on local norms impacting action on them. Some of these situations may have petitions filed on them if they involve issues that are important to the interpretations of the court's role within the community. For example, if a child is living with a nonguardian grandparent and the mother is in jail and the father's whereabouts is unknown, some administrative policy positions would prohibit providing services, and some court work groups would believe they had a responsibility to protect the child legally. Of course, whether this happens depends upon the norms of the child welfare organization and the court work group. At times, these norms may essentially dictate a hands-off approach, while at other times they may essentially demand the court's involvement.

For the most part, these situations present a much smaller level of perceived danger to a child from abuse or neglect. These situations involve clear-cut decisions, like in the first layer. These situations typically do not belong in the child protective system. No evidence of abuse or neglect would support pursuit of action within the juvenile court. Alternately, at times no demographic information is available to allow anyone to find the potential client.

This group of referrals includes a mixed group of situations that have in common the lack of intent to abuse the child. It includes situations that involve parents with extremely high expectations for their children and at times are particularly strident in wanting children to achieve them. It also includes referrals for such things as "Mongolian spots," the "coining" of children, or the use of a variety of alternative health care measures. It also includes situations in which a parent may call requesting assistance in providing for his or her children. In such situations, the parent may simply feel overwhelmed and call for support.

Vignette: Health Care

Julie, a Hmong child protective agency social worker, received a referral from a school worker on a seven-year-old Vietnamese girl that had severe bruising on her back. The school nurse reported it. Also, it was noted that the girl had missed a couple of days of school reportedly due to illness. Upon seeing the girl and the bruises, Julie knew immediately what the situation was. The girl's mother "coined" the child's back. This is an alternative form of medical treatment common to some Asian peoples. She planned to visit the mother and explain to her that she needed to find another way to treat the child's medical condition. This was the third one of these calls Julie had had this month.

Vignette: Parental Expectations

Andrew, a child protective agency social worker, introduces himself to the father and mother and explains the reason for his visit. He is responding to a report from the school that a nine-year-old boy appears to be extremely afraid of his father. The call came after the school was closed so the visit was to the parents' home. During the course of the visit, the parents, of Asian heritage, well educated and affluent, were clearly upset yet controlled their feelings with the social worker. They carefully controlled their discussion not to reveal anything that could be used against them. Also, they made it very clear that if this matter went any further, they would have an attorney with them. They acknowledged having high expectations for their son's educational attainment. They acknowledged punishing him for poor performance but denied ever abusing him. After completing the interview with the parents and the child and reviewing agency records, the social worker indicated in his assessment that the child was fearful of failing his parents' expectations; however, this did not seem to be the result of any kind of overt physical punishment. Rather, it seemed related to their high expectations driven by their experiences in American culture.

SUMMARY

In this chapter we examined the total child welfare system. The model that was used was adapted from a criminal justice system model. It provides a way to describe action taken on referrals within the total system. Action in the model is dependent upon a combination of internal dialogic processes and actual or anticipated environmental actions, such as media attention to situations. The model was described and then illustrated through an application to the national child welfare system.

Chapter 10

The Rationalization
of Child Welfare Intervention

INTRODUCTION

The second model depicts the child welfare system as it is outlined in most state legal systems. It is probably best described as a highly rational model. It highlights one part of the total child welfare system, the legitimacy or sanction for intervening in family life. The view taken in this discussion of the legal system is from the social worker's and/or client's view of the system. The model assumes and depicts the process of legal intervention as a rational process.

This model shows the alternative steps or pathways a particular referral/case takes as it enters the system. It delineates the general flow of referrals and cases through the system from an administrative and legal perspective. For the uninitiated, that is, the non-child protective worker, the court process appears to be a maze. This model is often used to train newcomers to child welfare services. New social workers in the child protective agency can find that years are needed to understand all the pathways that are involved in the labyrinth. Although it seems so highly rational, it also at times presents alternate personas. Due at least in part to these alternate personas, even social workers seasoned in child welfare strive to avoid being involved with it. In this sense, it certainly epitomizes one force that drives social workers out of child welfare practice to what Specht and Courtney (1994) describe as a search for autonomy and what Costin, Karger, and Stoesz (1996) refer to as the social worker's retreat from authority.

THE RATIONAL MODEL

What the Model Shows

While the concentric systems model describes the way the system performs, the rational model describes how it works according to the stages or steps within the legal system. This is the model prescribed by law. It entitles any person involved in the child protective agency system to traverse its many detailed pathways. This is a legal right of those accused of abusing or neglecting a child and even of the children themselves. Thus, any one referral of a child based on allegations of abuse or neglect can go through the entire court system. The time for this to be completed can vary from a short appearance of a few weeks with a child staying at home in the interim, to a multiyear process that may lead to the adoption of a child.

In actual application, all referrals into a hotline have a chance of going through each step of the model; however, only some do. Calculations based on estimates from McDonald and associates (2000) suggest that only 7 percent of total referrals and about 35 percent of all substantiated referrals go to court. This chapter provides a brief, five-step overview of the rational model of court action. It tracks the legal flow of cases in and through a typical social service agency and through a typical juvenile court. It highlights key decision points and provides a view of the action that occurs at these points.

The Rational Model: The Legal System As Structure

The rational model is comprised of a set of what might be called judicial stages. The stages are demarked by legal steps that occur in a logical order, and can be conceptualized as key decision points, usually associated with particular types of hearings. For example, there are detention hearings, jurisdictional hearings, dispositional hearings, etc. The determination as to whether a situation passes through a particular step is determined either by a negotiated withdrawal of a situation from the court process or by the presiding court judge. If a negotiated exit is not completed, the judge applies a mandated set of decision rules, that is, standards of proof, as he or she looks at the evidence and determines whether the case fits the legal categories. If so, it continues within the court process; if not, it is dismissed and may be closed for services.

In addition, the concept of the "burden of proof" explains who must prove the case to the judge. The burden of proof varies with the particular type of hearing and the stage the case is in the system. The steps, standards of proof, and burden of proof are governed by law and are themselves a part of the legal system, an abstract system. They provide a way to understand the legal processes through which a child may be removed from a parent or caretaker, be detained, come under the jurisdiction of the court, be returned to the family or placed with strangers (foster care), and ultimately be returned to the family or permanently placed in an adoptive home.

The Steps: The Dominant Rules and the Kinds of Formal Action That Occur

Reports

The first step in the model involves the receipt of a report by the child protective agency. The receipt of a report begins a series of ticking time clocks. From this time onward the steps are required within definite time frames. Working within these time frames is crucial for maintaining legal sanction and for funding purposes. However, although the time frames involved in intervention are exact, the judge, as part of the adjudication process and based upon good cause, can waive time requirements. The result is a system that demands clear time frames and yet allows for exceptions that appear noncompliant with time frames.

The person making the report can be a mandated reporter, a member of a family, or an anonymous reporter. Mandated reporters are required by law to report suspected abuse and neglect. For example, in California mandated reporters are required to do this when they "reasonably suspect" a child has been abused or neglected. Generally, the concept of reasonable suspicion means that a professional person of like training and experience would believe similarly regarding the suspicion that the child may be abused. This requirement to report child abuse and neglect is a legal mandate that takes precedence over the "privileged" relationship between therapist and client.

Mandatory reporters are not typically authorized to investigate whether allegations are true; they are expected only to report if they "reasonably suspect" the allegations are true. They are not expected to make a final judgment as to the absolute truth of the allegations. This puts them in a position where they can better accept the client's side of the issue and continue to strengthen their relationships with their clients.

Vignette: Reasonable Person As a Level
of Reasonable Suspicion

A medical doctor, an expert in child abuse and neglect issues, recently moved to a major metropolitan area. She saw a client she believed had been sexually molested; however, she did not have the equipment to do a thorough exam as she had in her previous work location. She called the reporting section to inquire about her reporting requirements. She believed that her level of expertise raised the bar in terms of her needing to report the incident. That is, since she had additional education and training in recognizing sexual abuse in children, her "reasonable suspicion" would be typically higher than other physicians with less education and experience. She was told that she was correct.

Investigation: Risk Assessment

The second step within this model involves a social worker contacting the child and his or her family. This contact involves investigating the allegations in the report to determine if they are valid. If determined to be valid, the social worker is expected to do risk and safety assessments. The first is designed to assist the social worker to determine the degree of risk that the child will be abused. Some agencies use a risk assessment device to determine whether a social worker should be assigned, while others use it at the point of contact with the child/family. These devices are simply tools and cannot, in and of themselves, determine the proper action on a case.

Three general "ideal types" risk assessment devices are used across the country. These include actuarial models, clinical models, and theory-based models. The former work well, within limits, in developing correlations of macrolevel risk factors and abuse or neglect for the general population of referrals. Using this model, agencies can, in broad and general terms, and, with an adequate foundation of data, determine the probability of various kinds of outcomes at intake based on significant variables. They are best used to look at the total referrals coming into the system. When combined with a time-series calculation, they can be effective in predicting overall levels of intake into large agencies. These are a good management level tool.

The clinical model is a consensus model. It is typically built through the use of group processes that involve expert level social workers in child welfare determining the factors important in deciding the risk of abuse or neglect. For line level workers, although not as an administrative tool, this model may be the most usable. It provides a good baseline for working with subjective data—that is, socially constructed definitions of abuse and neglect tied to local value systems.

The theory-based model is based on theories of behavior and action. It is designed around various theoretical perspectives and may involve extensive paper requirements that can provide management with a tool to directly impact line level workers' actions. This usage can be extremely burdensome in terms of paperwork requirements. It makes sense to scholars but has less practical value for line social workers.

Safety Assessment: Custody/No Custody

If founded or substantiated, the social worker must determine if the child is safe in the family home. In some jurisdictions social workers can take children into custody, while in other jurisdictions only peace officers are authorized to do so. Alternately, in some jurisdictions a court order is necessary to place a child in custody. Generally, the social worker or police must consider whether the child is in immediate danger of being abused or neglected to affect custody.

A safety assessment is focused on determining whether a child is safe in the current living environment. If not assessed as being safe, the social worker is expected to take action to ensure the safety of the child. This may mean custody for the child or, dependent upon agency policy and the situation, an alternate living environment for the child or even a parent or caretaker. Sexual abuse situations are typically assessed as too unstable to settle with voluntary or temporary relocations of the child or perpetrator. They create situations that simply disintegrate after a few days or weeks.

The next step involves the social worker either terminating from the contact or referring the family for services. If the report is not substantiated, but the child is assessed as at risk of being abused or neglected, services can be provided to the family on a voluntary basis. The social worker and agency do not have the authority to require the family to do anything about their personal problems without some macrolevel sanction for intervention. Ultimately, if the outcome of the investigation is that the allegations are true, the social worker would make note in agency records that the referral was "founded" or "substantiated," terms that are used interchangeably in this work.

Child in Custody

A child being taken into custody begins the ticking of the judicial clock. This begins a series of legal points at which particular court actions are required. The "judicial clock," as used here, refers to the time frames written in law and accounted for by the local court clerk. Thus, if a particular day is a holiday for the court clerk, it would typically not count as a "judicial day." These are a continuation of the time streams that began with the initial report to the child protective agency.

The time when a child is taken into custody represents a key point at which the parent's right to due process begins. Although custody triggers this in most jurisdictions, some jurisdictions are sensitive to the effects of the sharing of information between the child protective agency and the police. In these jurisdictions, social workers are required to notify parents, before their first interview with the parents, that anything said or learned about their child's situation may be used against them in criminal court. However, once the child is in custody, for the most part, case law following the *Gault* case makes due process available to children and their parents.

A number of jurisdictions have developed a wide range of procedures and protocols to ensure that the child protective agency workers are sensitive to parents. These include requiring the taping of interviews, the notifying of a parent by letter after the child has been in custody for six or more hours, and even having parents sign notification of possible rights issues.

Filing a Petition

The filing of a petition constitutes the next step and begins the court process. After a child is taken into custody, the parents' rights include a legal notice of the reasons for custody and of their legal rights and hearing dates and times. The petition typically alleges that the child has been abused or neglected as defined in state law. It also must have the social worker attest, through a sworn statement, to its accuracy in presenting the facts involved in the matter. Some agencies use attorneys to write petitions.

Detention Hearing As the Second Step in the Court Process

A detention hearing represents the second step in the court process. The focus of this hearing is the court's consideration of the temporary custody of the child pending the jurisdictional/dispositional hearing. The timing of the detention hearing varies by jurisdiction. California, for example, requires a petition to be filed within forty-eight court hours of custody and the detention hearing to be the next day.

At a detention hearing, the standard of proof is often probable cause. Probable cause means that the judge has enough evidence to believe that the child would be in significant danger if he or she remains home until the case is tried. If the judge thinks there is a high probability that the child would be hurt if returned home, the child would be kept in custody.

If the judge decides the child shall continue in temporary custody, at times and in some jurisdictions, the social services agency is authorized to place the child in a foster home. In other jurisdictions there may be considerable litigation before the agency can take such a step. In the latter cases, the court may hold the view that placement in a foster home constitutes a determination within the court's direct control and cannot be done until jurisdiction is established and the need for out-of-home placement has been ascertained.

Vignette: Opening of a Detention Hearing

The bailiff stands and says to the courtroom, "Will everyone please stand." The judge enters the courtroom and sits down. The bailiff

(continued)

(continued)

states, "Will everyone please be seated." The judge notes, "We have before us today case number nine nine nine nine involving the minor Jessica Unknown. Has everyone had a chance to read the petition?"

The judge ends the hearing, stating, "The court finds prima facia evidence to support the petition and the minor would be at risk of further abuse or neglect if returned to the parents' custody. Therefore, the minor will continue in custody with the department of social services to supervise, pending the jurisdictional hearing."

At any time within the court process settlement of a situation can be negotiated. Such a settlement would involve agreement by all parties and the judge. The resolution would also typically include a particular action or even changes and then action on the petition.

Jurisdictional Hearing

At the jurisdictional hearing, the next step in the legal process, the judge must determine, according to the standard of proof, whether the child comes under the jurisdiction of the juvenile court. It does so by establishing that the child comes under the jurisdiction, as spelled out in state statutes and case law of the state.

In most states, at the jurisdictional hearing, the preponderance of the evidence standard dominates. The preponderance standard requires that evidence supporting the idea that the child has been abused or neglected outweighs evidence arguing against abuse or neglect. A commonly used illustration of this concept is "tipping the scales." If the metaphoric scales of justice tip slightly to one side when loaded with all of the evidence, the preponderance of evidence is on that side. If 51 percent of the evidence presented in court favors one side of the case, then that side of the case has been established by a preponderance of the evidence.

Jurisdictional hearings involve the social worker writing an evidentiary report and sometimes a social study. Evidentiary reports simply present the evidence that supports the petition, in a written report form. Social studies are a court adaptation of what social workers know as a biopsychosocial report. However, the laws of various jurisdictions and case law limit what goes into these assessments. In fact, to some extent, legal proceedings limit the actions social workers take with clients. Work by social workers must be within the boundaries established by the law as interpreted by the court.

If the dispositional hearing is combined with the jurisdictional hearing then the social study would be included in this report. This would include a recommended dispositional order. In some places, such as California, the social study may be used to prove the petition (Sagatun and Edwards, 1995).

For the petition alleging the abuse or neglect of a child to go to the next stage, the court must find that the petition as filed or amended is true. At times, the matter may "go to trial." Trials are typically before a judge and involve a full range of witnesses being called, with attorneys examining and cross-examining witnesses. Witnesses can also include "expert witnesses," those professionals who can be qualified under court rules as experts in addition to evidentiary witnesses. Expert witnesses can present their professional opinion while nonexperts are limited to expressing facts of which they have firsthand knowledge. Some social workers can be qualified as expert witnesses.

Dispositional Hearing

If at the jurisdictional hearing the court finds that the allegations are true and that the child comes under the court's authority, the matter moves to disposition. The next step for the judge is to decide what should be done to preserve the child's welfare. This is done at the dispositional hearing. The judge may conduct the dispositional hearing at the same time as the jurisdictional hearing. Technically, the jurisdictional hearing must precede the dispositional phase. Logically, in order to make a decision, aka order, for a particular child, the judge must have the power to make such an order. Jurisdiction gives the judge the right to make an order under the dispositional phase. When these two are handled together, it ranges from difficult to impossible for new social workers or parents to differentiate between them as they may move very quickly.

Vignette: Severing the Legal Tie

The mother of fourteen-year-old Todd is explaining to the child's grandparents after a trial, "My attorney told me that what the judge did today was to 'cut the invisible legal tie' that I have to my son. Maybe, since it is done, I should say 'the son that I had.' I guess that means he is no longer my son. At least, that's what the attorney said. For both of you, Mom and Dad, that means that Todd is no longer your grandson. The attorney said that if anything should happen in the future and if Todd was ever to live with us again, we would need to be licensed as foster parents. How weird! A son that's no longer a son. Or, a mother without a child."

At the dispositional hearing, the court determines, among other things, the living situation that is best for the child, reunification plans, and mandated services.

Vignette: A Child in Custody, but No Grounds for Termination of Rights

A parent says to her attorney, "It doesn't make sense to me. They use a weaker standard of proof to take my Jeannie away from me. Then at each step, the standards get harder to meet. However, in the end, with the same minimal evidence, the judge seems to be deciding that there was more evidence there the first time. It seems to me they didn't have enough evidence to terminate my rights in the first place and so they go through this ruse to make it seem like more in the end."

Review Hearings

Reviews of the child's situation and progress toward reunification are conducted every six months (court and calendar time combined). This is done by administrative review teams in some jurisdictions. Typically, teams are appointed by the agency head and would include persons from outside the social worker's administrative line. Alternately, periodic reviews are conducted by the juvenile court.

Permanency Planning Hearing

Federal law requires a permanency planning hearing within twelve months of the date of custody. These time requirements are subject to exceptional circumstances determined by the judge at the various hearings. At this hearing, the judge may order the child returned to the parent, a limited continuation of reunification services, or a permanent placement plan. At this hearing, if the child cannot be returned to the parent, the judge is required to consider alternate permanent plans for the child. These include a preference hierarchy of adoption, guardianship, or long-term foster care (this also may include relative or kinship care as foster care). The judge is expected to ensure the greatest degree of legal permanency. Thus, a relative home is seen as "less permanent" than an adoptive home.

Vignette: A Seventeen-Year-Old to Be Adopted

A parent was telling her sister about the court's action at a permanency planning hearing. "Gloria is seventeen years old and living with her grandmother. I don't know why the judge would order her to be adopted. That means she needs to move. She tells me that when she is eighteen years old, she is coming back to live with me. I can't stop her, so I guess she will be back here. After all, she constantly runs away from Mom's house, goes to those wild parties, and what she does with those boys! It is a wonder that she's not pregnant. The whole thing just doesn't make a lot of sense to me."

Criminal Court Hearings/Trials, Etc.

Some dependency matters also move, by way of parents being charged with the violation of criminal laws, into criminal courts. Although not a subject of this work, it is important to understand the standards of proof that dominate this arena. In contrast to juvenile courts, criminal courts typically have a higher standard of proof to find a person guilty of filed charges. The standard is typically that of "beyond a reasonable doubt." Because it is so difficult to eliminate all reasonable doubts in the mind of a judge or jury, this standard of proof makes criminal cases the hardest type to prove.

For child welfare, this difference between the courts is significant. A parent can be charged and found "not guilty" in criminal court because the evidence does not rise to the level required, yet at the same time the child can become a dependent of the juvenile court where the standard of proof is at a lesser level.

Parents may understandably have a hard time with this discrepancy. For example, they will often say something such as, "I was not convicted of abusing my child. I want her back." The facts may be that the child was taken away from the parent based on the juvenile court's lower standard of proof, while the charges against the parent were not sustainable at the higher level of proof. Parents have difficulty understanding this complex and abstract concept.

Family Courts and Guardianships

Family courts use the standard of proof of the "best interests" of the child in making determinations as to guardianships. "Best interests" is a term that is highly valued by child savers; however, it is a lower standard than those typically required in juvenile court. The net result is that the family court can establish guardianship of a child with a lower level of evidence than the juvenile court would require for involvement with a child. For example, a mother with a long history of substance abuse is in jail and decides that she wants a relative to become the child's caretaker. She is afraid that if she does not take this action, the juvenile court may get involved. The probate court, using the best interests standard, can establish a guardianship. In the same situation, the juvenile court may not be able to take action because of its higher standard of proof. From the probate court's perspective, the mother is adequately providing for her child by having the relative provide care and supervision.

Vignette: Grandmother Gets Guardianship

Mrs. G. files for guardianship of her ten-year-old grandson, Arthur. Arthur's mother is in jail for what seems like the tenth time or so. Each time, Arthur has lived with his grandmother. This time, school workers are hassling the grandmother because she is not his guardian and they say they need him to have a parent, a guardian, or a court order to

(continued)

(continued)

be enrolled in their school. The guardianship, with the mother's agreement, would clearly be in his best interests and in all likelihood would be ordered by the court. This keeps this family case out of juvenile court, which could be expected to make Arthur's placement with his caretaker permanent despite his, the grandmother's, or the mother's desires. However, such a guardianship would be fairly easy to terminate in order to allow the parent to resume her parental obligations when she is out of jail.

Conflict Within the System: Internal Actions

At times there is considerable conflict within the court system. Although the formal structure provides the context for action in the juvenile court, the informal processes, including dialogue and action, are more variable. They are important in defining the norms and values that explain the working level interpretations of the social categories of abuse and neglect. At times, attorneys, social workers, and even parents, will invest considerable energy on attempts to change the outcome of a particular case by changing the work group, that is, the players. This can take the form of hiring alternate attorneys or even clients asking for a new social worker and alleging unfairness or bias. Impossible to substantiate, but politically potentially damaging, such efforts work at times. Not only will clients ask for different social workers, but attorneys may take action to get a new judge. This can take the form of manipulations to control the court assignment if such an action is possible.

To protect against influences on the court processes, courts generally establish tight procedural controls. These are aimed at controlling manipulations to obtain a perceived advantage within the legal system. Judges or commissioners may find they have a conflict of interest and will recuse themselves from particular cases. Recusal is the action of disqualifying oneself from participation in a decision due to an actual or perceived conflict of interest.

Social Worker Role

The social worker role is simply a part of the intervention approach under this model. The social worker's role is to act as an extension of the court, that is, as the eyes and ears of the court. In addition, the social worker is to add his or her expertise within boundaries established by the court. These boundaries are similar to those police follow, including a focused investigation expanding through the exposure of details in the original investigation, social histories within the context of state law and court expectations, and service plans driven by deficits uncovered through investigations.

THE COURT PERSONNEL

Judge

Judges are either elected or appointed; some are appointed and subsequently elected. The judges are the highest status persons within the court work group. This is the result of their key roles as "trier of the facts" and their function of "adjudicating" the petition (i.e., the matter).

Depending on the unique nuances that are part of a particular jurisdiction, appointments to juvenile courts are limited. For the most part, judges get the juvenile court setting as part of the court assignment process. Judges within various jurisdictions rotate assignments on a periodic basis. Judges may stay for a considerable amount of time in juvenile court. The juvenile court, while cloaked in confidentiality, can be a highly visible position within the community.

Sometimes cases are heard before commissioners or referees. These differ from judges in that rather than being appointed or elected, they are typically hired through civil service systems. Typically, the appeal process of commissioners' actions begins with an appeal to the presiding judge of the court.

Social Worker

The social worker is typically responsible for investigating reports of abuse and neglect, developing case material, writing petitions, preparing and presenting evidence, following through on the orders of the court, and providing services as required not only by the court but by his or her department. Simply stated, the social worker has an important role in keeping the court process operating.

As we look at the social worker as a part of the court's metaphoric work group, it is important to note the limits of the social worker's role. In particular, administrators and advocacy groups at times question the latitude or discretion the social worker has in making decisions. Although social workers seem to have significant power to take a child into custody, or at least influence that action, they actually serve in a complex web of relationships that effectively constrain their actions.

For example, in some situations, if the social worker does not remove a child, the supervisor passes judgment on the actions. The worker could be sent to review the situation or requested to write additional material to support his or her action, etc. With that supervisory scrutiny, all parties are aware that they are dealing with potential life and death decisions. Similarly, if the decision is to remove a child, petition the court, gather evidence, write social studies, etc., the situation is poured over meticulously by everyone in the work group. Simply stated, social workers, like police, have little discretion. Walker (1989) describes the limits of police officers:

> The decisions of individual officials are heavily influenced by the bureaucratic setting in which they work. Even though a police officer has enormous discretion to make an arrest, he or she will usually have to have a supervisor sign off on it. A prosecutor will examine the arrest report, and a defense attorney may challenge the arrest or the accompanying search. A judge will rule on a number of issues. The actions of these other officials act as a major constraint on the police officer's actions. (p. 51)

Social workers have the same limitations as police in addition to other constraints. The supervisor must sign off on the action. A receiving center social worker and supervisor must also agree, in addition to the various attorneys and the judges within the child welfare system. Also, other social workers or attorneys are part of writing petitions for court action and thereby exercise a screening function. Social worker discretion is controlled through formal check and balance processes, but like that of police, it is "controlled informally" (Walker, 1989, p. 33).

THE SOCIAL SERVICE

Department's Attorney

The agency employing the social worker typically has an attorney represent it in court actions. In some areas the attorney is not likely to be present in all matters. However, in some settings, this attorney or a representative is likely to be in court for most hearings. The attorney typically represents the agency interests as represented by its agent, the social worker. This attorney's role is to represent the social worker's position. At times conflict of interest issues are involved in determining who represents who in what court. For the department's attorneys, the daily role is to represent the department on case situations; however, they sometimes also represent the department on administrative matters.

Thus, the department's interest may appear different at different organizational levels. At those times, another attorney would need to represent either the social worker or the administration. Thus, the social worker could be represented by one attorney and an administrator in the department may be represented by another.

Vignette: Attorneys

Beginning an expected two-week trial, the judge was exploring the adequacy of counsel. A central issue was the child services division's legal counsel. On occasion, the attorney, Trudy Counselor, had represented the division on administrative matters. An expected point of contention in the trial was anticipated to be a department administrator's involvement in a line worker's decision to make a placement. The administrator had allegedly ordered the worker to remove a child from the Sanchez family home and place her in the Mendoza family home. The Sanchez family had appealed that decision. Now the question for the court was whether the attorney, Ms. Counselor, could fairly represent the social worker, who reportedly claimed to have made an independent decision to place the child with the Mendozas.

The Children's Attorney

The children's attorney is charged with representing the child in the juvenile court. Depending on the jurisdiction, this varies from a departmental employee to an attorney with a contract agency. Different jurisdictions have different administrative arrangements to provide for this function. At times, this is provided by the prosecuting attorney's office or the counsel of the department. At other times, this function may be provided under contract to a private nonprofit or profit-making agency. Although the exact administrative function may vary, the role is generally constant—to represent the child's interests. This typically involves the perceived best interests of the child and, if the child is competent and of sufficient age, are defined by the client, the child. Thus, the attorney may be advocating what the social worker may or may not see as in the child's best interest. This conflict is clear in the cases of adolescents who are presenting behaviors that effectively leave them outside of the capacity of their parents to control them. At times, these children want a degree of freedom and independence not possible with their parents, in foster homes, group homes, or virtually in any setting within the dependency system. However, the attorney is then faced with the issue of advocating for a nonexistent alternative that the teenager wants.

The conflict in the roles also comes center stage within the court setting as the child, through his or her attorney, may join in advocacy with the parents against the social worker. At other times, the sides may shift. This shifting of roles and alliances is commonplace in litigated court processes.

Public Defender: Parent's Attorney

The parent's attorney is usually an appointed public defender. Typically, this is a full-time employee of the public sector. It can also be a contract position and may be an appointed private attorney from a panel of attorneys volunteering for this work and on a per case basis. In a much smaller number of cases, the attorney is a private attorney whose services are paid for by the family. The attorney is expected to represent the parents' interest in the matter. Therefore, depending upon the circumstances of the case and the nature of the parents' relationship, each parent may need an attorney. For example, if the parents are divorced, the noncustodial parent could get custody of the child. There would also be a chance that each parent may lose his or her rights to the child, so each parent needs legal representation.

> **Vignette: Emotional Maltreatment**
>
> Dorothy and Gene are the parents of four-year-old Alesia, appearing before the court on a petition alleging emotional maltreatment. The parents are currently separated, although they are married and have been for five years. At the detention hearing, this information is presented to the court. The judge said to the parents, "I see that you are both represented by Ms. Garcia of the public defender's office. However, I also see that you are living separately. Because of that, I see a potential conflict of interest and order the public defender's office to obtain additional counsel for one of you."

Hidden in the "Emotional Maltreatment" scenario is the possibility of the court changing the legal custody of Alesia as a long-term plan. In such a case, dealing with legal representation issues at the beginning facilitates a timely achievement of this goal for the child.

Others in the Court System

The group just described constitutes the main working group within the court system. In addition, a number of other persons are critical to the ongoing action of the court. Following are some of those that are typically very important in the operation of the court.

Court Appointed Special Advocates (CASAs)

Since about 1989 courts have used court appointed special advocates (CASAs). The Victims of Child Abuse Act of 1990 introduced changes in the child welfare system including the use of these advocates. This act provided for improving the investigation and prosecution of cases, the use of court appointed special advocates, child abuse training programs for judicial personnel and practitioners, provision for an adult attendant in court for children in cases where the child is testifying, and provisions for live child's testimony via television, etc. (Sagatun and Edwards, 1995).

CASAs are meant to provide the judge with an unbiased view of the court proceedings from the child's perspective—essentially, to represent the child's position from the perspective of what is truly best for the child from a community layperson's perspective. These are community volunteers that are provided special training and who then meet with children and their families on a regular basis. Some jurisdictions use these and guardian ad litems to represent children in court.

Guardian ad Litem

Initially authorized under the Child Abuse Prevention and Treatment Act of 1974, guardians ad litem (GALs), are meant to represent the legal interests of children before the court. The Victims of Child Abuse Act of 1990 expanded the use of GALs by providing federal funds to state protective agencies to meet the requirement that every child involved in a child welfare proceeding have a court appointed guardian ad litem (Sagatun and Edwards, 1995). Also, special education programs require GALs as part of the educational process including the development of individualized educational plans (IEPs).

Court Clerks

The court clerk role is probably the most important role in the handling of the ebb and flow of cases. Most important to social workers, they are the official "gatekeepers" of the system. Social workers file initial petitions with the court clerk. They also take supplemental petitions and schedule all hearings before the court.

In addition, the court clerk typically maintains court records, prepares daily calendars, and generally manages the movement of paper, including legal documents, into the case records. Their particular importance comes from their critical role as gatekeepers for the court system, including the judges. That is, to get something scheduled on the daily calendar, aka "calendared," it must go through the clerk. In this sense, they are critical to keeping the plethora of legal detail accurate. They are also a key social role in handling the massive amounts of paperwork that move between the juvenile court and the departments' case records. In short, they are critical in understanding the technical operation of the juvenile court.

Bailiffs

The bailiff has one of the most visible roles in the court environment. He or she is often a retired police officer and serves to maintain order and decorum within the courtroom. Often senior deputies, they may be armed and vigilant in maintaining order. They also perform a variety of additional activities at the request of the judge.

Court Reporters

The court reporters record official dialogue within the courtroom. Some courts use tape recorders for this function, and others rely on people. These persons typically use machine writers that imprint coded letters on tape. When a person is called upon to testify, the court reporters document the testimony. They maintain the official record of the proceedings and if anyone has questions about the proceedings, they are the source of the original and official records.

CONCLUSION

The rational action model presents steps in the legal system through which a small percent of all referrals to the child protective agency system enter. This model is based on a conception of the American child welfare system as driven by the court system. This approach conceives of social work practice in a host setting, aka the legal system. Although the court system sees only a small percent of child welfare clients, its power within the system lies in its potential for involvement in any one particular referral. The central concept that connects macrolevel systems with individuals is the concept from Weber (1978b, pp. 978-979) of law as an "abstracted norm." The court system, more than any other part of the child welfare system, treats alleged transgressions of child care norms by parents or caretakers as violations of law. Within this context, the court adjudicates these allegations with a model that involves an emotionally detached and highly rational process. This model represents this part of the child welfare system with its highly ordered and exacting steps, tight legal and paper controls, and closely bounded actions on cases.

Chapter 11

Life in Narrative and Drama: Meaning, Self, and Identity

INTRODUCTION

The third model for viewing action in the child welfare system is the ritualized process model. This model highlights psychological and sociological perspectives of client behavior. This chapter provides some understanding of the psychological and sociological views of behavior important in understanding the model.

This chapter introduces some ideas related to "private" and "public" presentations, narrative constructions of reality, and their role in developing and maintaining individual identities. It emphasizes the role of narrative in individual and family life and its action as it demarks behavior by locations in which it is performed. It also discusses the concept of social dramas as eruptions of tension occurring as part of the violation of social or family norms. These eruptions contribute to the interventions by social institutions into family life. This chapter provides the foundation for understanding the ritual process model described in Chapter 12.

BEHAVIOR AS DRAMA AND NARRATIVE

Vignette: Don, Scene I

Don wasn't sure what happened. He simply had an argument with his fifteen-year-old son. Somehow, the argument got out of control and they ended up physically fighting. His son was actually stronger than

(continued)

(continued)

he was these days, but Don got in a "lucky" hit and hit him in the face. CPS was called and responded with the police. Don was arrested for felony child abuse. Since he was a teacher, a conviction could terminate his career. At forty-four years of age and with a history of about twenty years of teaching, he wasn't sure what he could do. He knew he shouldn't have been fighting with his son, but how was he supposed to keep him in line? Didn't he have a responsibility as the boy's father? These questions were important, but nothing seemed more important than the crisis with which he was now involved.

Abstracted and Virtual Space Involving Privacy

The ritual process model highlights the action of individuals within families as social institutions enter their social narratives and interrupt ongoing "private" and "public" events. Private events relate to events that are essentially secret (Imber-Black, 1998) or at least not publicly shared by the family with the larger public, those persons within the family's environment. For example, a wife complaining about a neighbor's behavior would not ordinarily be shared by her spouse with the neighbor.

In contrast, public events, to a family, relate to those events that are shared with or done with persons outside the family. For example, a wife visits with a neighbor for coffee and talks about community affairs. Such a contact is typically "open" to the community in that either participant can reasonably expect that such expressed views might be shared with other persons.

Both private and public events can be viewed as occurring in actual or abstracted spatial domains or regions (Goffman, 1959, 1961). The events, both private and public, constitute stories or narratives that individuals and families enact and reenact in thoughts, feelings, and actions on a daily basis. Some examples of physical regions are noted in the following list:

Backstage	Front stage
Bedroom/home office	Living rooms
Judge's chambers	Juvenile courtroom
House	Neighborhood

Home	Church
Private thoughts	Public statements
Actual role in extended family	Presented role in extended family
Past criminal record	Current problems with legal system
Family	Nonfamily
Private room	Common room

Abstracted or virtual regions can occur anywhere. The formation of these virtual regions is dependent upon control of who receives the communication. Regions are not limited to physical space but can also include simple domains of communications. An example is people communicating by telephone. Here two people can have a discussion in which they are the only communicators. By conversing with individuals over the telephone, they are the only persons privy to the conversation. Similarly, even on street corners, individuals can control for other persons' proximity and communicate privately in their own virtual or abstracted space. As long as they are the only communicators, it is a private dialogue. Of course, if it is shared with others it becomes public. Sharing, of course, can be by plan, by poor controlling for privacy, or by someone eavesdropping.

Private and public discourse combine with other discourse to modify narratives that constitute our personal and private realities. This conception of narrative has, for some theorists, replaced conceptions of status and role as explaining our social world (Calhoun, 1996). Essentially, narrative as used here involves a storied description of reality. It is built on an epistemological foundation and includes current behavior within a complex array of historic behaviors and events that include views of causal action. In this sense, we strive to make sense of the world, and we do this by constructing, and ultimately living within, our narratives. In this sense social life is viewed as comprised of a web of narratives and metanarratives, which represent an underlayment to abstract systems. They contribute to feelings of security safety. They represent, as metanarrative, the context for intellectual inquiry (Somers and Gibson, 1996).

This collective conception of social reality as narrative evolves as these dialogues take place selectively in private and public domains. Through these narratives we construct not only our theoretical knowledge, but also our individual social identities (Saari, 1991). Private and public narratives together constitute an individual narrative view of social reality—a view in which each individual experiences a reality just a little bit different than another, that is, his or her own reality (Calhoun, 1996). These narratives at times evolve into social dramas. Dramas are temporary eruptions in the narratives of social life that evolve within a particular system and interrupt the normal process form of the social narrative (Turner, 1982).

CHILD WELFARE AS INTERVENTION IN SOCIAL DRAMAS

A child welfare worker's intervention into family life involves intervening in these family narratives on behalf of the larger society. The child welfare worker acts as an agent for social institutions, objectified, within the child welfare system sanctioned through the legal system. Interventions in this context change family narratives that are erupting in dramas, including the relationship of family members to one another. As intervention occurs over time and includes court action or the threat of court action, the child welfare worker increasingly comes to know the family's most hidden or private activities or secrets. This model explains how these private or secret narratives and dramas occur, how they become public, and ultimately how they affect what Terkelsen (1989) calls second order transformations in families, and end with the ultimate stigmatization of perpetrators and victims alike (Goffman, 1963).

Vignette: Don, Scene II

Don thought he had a good relationship with his children and his wife. He also thought he had good relationships with community members including those from his church and even his school. Somehow, as Don sat in jail and the social worker made contact with all of these folks, things looked different. From what Don was hearing, his wife and sixteen-year-old daughter were afraid of his temper, his church friends remembered his yelling at a church member, and even his principal wasn't sure Don had everything under control. In Don's view, these

(continued)

(continued)

things had been fine; now it seems people were sharing a lot of "hidden" issues or concerns with the social worker. As the trial progressed he even heard about an early event in his twenty-year marriage when, during an argument, he flushed his wife's prized down pillow down the toilet when she threatened to pour paint on his car. It was juvenile, but he thought it was simply part of going through the early stages of marriage. He didn't understand why it came out now.

Private and Public Behavior As Dependent on People Present and Locations

Inherent in this view of private and public behavior is the concept of barriers to perception which can be viewed as external to the individual and working to limit a particular person's or persons' access to a particular communication. For example, at a large public dinner, if two guests whisper to each other, their conversation is, for the most part, confined to them. As long as they speak so only they can hear what is said, others may know a conversation is going on but will not know the content of that dialogue.

This concept suggests that private and public behavior is dependent upon the mix of people and locations in which the behavior occurs. It addresses the question of who is present and who is a participant to the behavior. That is, public and private behaviors or events are relative to the people present and/or those able to perceive them. Participation of persons involved in the communication can be controlled by the setting up of spatial locations, both physical and abstracted. For example, people outside of the family, the public, would not be able to see private family behavior. Family behavior at its most private is done within a "back region" or "stage" relative to outsiders. However, this is dependent upon family members maintaining the boundaries that limit access to viewing the behavior.

Back region behavior within the family would involve private behavior by individuals and subgroups such as parents or siblings. To these subgroups, the behavior would be private and occurring in their front region, although it would be back region behavior to other family members who were not a party to it. Again, this requires controlling access to the behavior. For example, a supervisor has a private conference with a social worker. This is private to them and back region to other social workers in the work unit. However, if the supervisor does not control access to the communication, the social worker can come out of the meeting and share this private dialogue and it will become public to the work group, although it will remain private to people outside the work group. What is shared is simply an "extracted" view of the actual behavior. The worker described with language his or her interpretation of the meeting. This is not the same as other persons being able to view the meeting themselves. Thus, what is shared as public is only a partial or limited view of what transpired.

Joint behavior within the public space of the family would be public to family and private to the larger community. The front region refers to where the performance of behavior is given, while the back region refers to where it is rehearsed or prepared and even where hidden, suppressed, or where secret items reside. The areas that do not include these two regions are referred to as "the outside" (Goffman, 1959, p. 135) (see Figure 11.1). This, of course, would include all of those persons who reside outside of the family and their friends and acquaintances.

Vignette: Don, Scene III

As Don is reflecting on the events that landed him in jail, he remembers the first minutes when the CPS social worker and the police arrived. He was sure that he had told them the story the way it had happened. He was sure that he had only told them about things of which he was certain. He also recalled that he hadn't told them about a couple of additional blowups that he had had with his son. His lawyer was coming to see him soon. He needed to think this through so that he could get his story straight.

Neither Private nor Public Behavior Is Protected from Intrusion

At any point in time, any event can be viewed as actually observable or at least potentially viewable in a public arena. Whether the content of something is observable is dependent, to some extent, on another person's ability to perceive it. That is, everyone's actual or

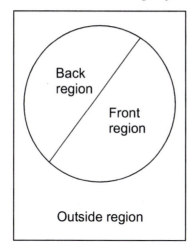

FIGURE 11.1. Behavior Regions

potential capacity to see beneath Lefebvre's (1968) "veil of appearances" (p. 47) is the same. Some people can see through it more clearly than others. Social workers, if they receive good training, can see beyond the presented behavior.

As private behavior becomes visible publicly, the boundaries separating or maintaining private and public space dissolve for individuals. This is what happens with institutional responses to allegations of child abuse and neglect. The behavior, even though it was either intended to be private or believed to be private, becomes public as it is ferreted out by social workers or police. As narrative erupts into social drama, the social worker is able to see the underlying tensions clearly. This is what is happening to Don. As his personal narratives erupted into drama within the family, the boundaries of private and public have become blurred. He is confused about which is which. Other people are sharing information publicly that he thought was private.

For example, a mother disciplining her son by spanking him in a supermarket would be enacting public or front region behavior to everyone who could perceive or witness it. This is in contrast to the spanking of the child at home, the back region to the public and normally private or concealed from public view.

The social worker's task, if the spanking was reported as abuse and assessed as needing a response, would be to investigate what happened in an attempt to find out what, when, and why the activity actually occurred. In investigating the public behavior of the mom spanking the child in the supermarket, the social worker would typically investigate other private behavior that may have been abusive to the child. This investigation increases the tensions within the family and may result in an eruption of narrative into social drama. By this action, private behavior can become public.

Vignette: The Hat, Scene I

Mary Jane, as she got ready for the evening with the Jones family, turned to her husband and said, "Now Al, if Estelle wears her funny pink hat, what are you supposed to say?"

Al looks at her as she buttons her skirt and answers, "That is a very nice hat that you have."

"Very good," says Mary Jane.

Here we have preparations for front region or "on stage" behavior that takes place in the back region. Mary Jane and Al share a secret about Estelle's hat, and they are prepared to cover this up with their on stage performance at the evening's social event. They are practicing this cover-up in the back region of their home, the location of the upcoming performance.

At any particular point in time, an event happening within a particular system is theoretically viewable as the back region, where the performance of a routine is prepared, or in the front region, where the performance is presented. However, access to these regions is controlled by the participants. It is controlled backstage to prevent the audience from seeing its preparation. For example, presumably no one else is present as Mary Jane and Al have this conversation. If someone else is present, the conversation would probably be different. Secrets, or private behavior, can be maintained as access to the front region is controlled to prevent outsiders from coming into a performance that is not designed for them.

Vignette: The Hat, Scene II

The doorbell rings and Mary Jane answers the door. Her friend Beth, who is visiting, comments on Estelle's "ugly" pink hat. Mary Jane brushes it off and says, "Estelle can wear whatever she wants." After a brief period of time, Beth leaves. Mary Jane returns to the bedroom where Al is getting dressed. She tells him, "Beth thinks the hat is ugly too. But we still need to tell Estelle we like it."

Here Mary Jane is unwilling to let Beth in on her and Al's secret. However, Beth might see or perceive some noncognitive clues as to Mary Jane's private practicing and thoughts about the hat. However, while Beth is present there is no further backstage rehearsal of the night's activities. As soon as Beth is gone, the rehearsal backstage continues and is not visible to Beth or anyone else on the front stage.

Vignette: The Hat, Scene III

That evening Al greets Estelle. "Well, hello, Estelle. It is very nice to see you. I see you have your very nice pink hat on." Estelle replies quickly, "Hi, Al. It is nice to see you too. But I'll bet Mary Jane told you to say something nice about my hat." Al is surprised but catches himself and says, "Well, she tells me a lot of things to do, but she doesn't usually give me direction in commenting on ladies' hats."

In Scene III, we see that Estelle may have seen through Al's initial public performance. However, Al was able, through extemporaneous action, to divert her from learning about the backstage practicing they had done. Depending on Estelle's sensitivity to Al's comments, she may have glimpsed the back region practice that Mary Jane and Al had done. Again, social workers are expected to be trained to recognize these subtle actions and reactions.

This concept, as noted earlier, adapted from Goffman, conceptualizes action as involving varying degrees of publicness. For example, denying the spanking of a child to a social worker while admitting it to one's spouse could be seen as affirming the private nature of the spanking within the family and disaffirming a public narrative for the investigating child welfare worker. However, if or when the social worker learns about the spanking and the hiding of it as a family secret, other motivations might be attributed to the parent.

How Private Narratives and Secrets Become Public

Secrets become public as people tell about them. With institutional intervention, tensions hidden or expressed in narratives tend to erupt. The eruptions of these tensions result in a reformulating or reconstructing of the multiple narratives associated with individuals' social identities. This eruption of narratives into dramas results in the temporary permeability of boundaries between private and public narratives. These boundaries will remain unclear until new narratives are constructed that include and explain the eruption of narrative into social drama. Individuals, when interviewed by institutional agents such as social workers that represent larger social narratives, metanarratives (Somers and Gibson, 1996), share narratives from both private and public regions. After all, that is what the metanarratives call for. Sharing information with authorities is a part of this larger narrative. For example, "protecting children is everyone's duty, isn't it?"

Probably the greatest strength of this model is that it stresses the ebb and flow of feelings, action, information, and power within the child welfare system, the family, and even within the agency. In particular, it highlights seemingly ephemeral aspects of human behavior and their ultimate change through the action of macrolevel forces. Even in enmeshed families, long-held secrets may become public within the social institutional intervention into the family system as perpetrators and victims interact within the legal structure of those institutions.

Vignette: Shaken Baby, Scene I

The social worker left the mother's home. The six-month old child was in the hospital, the victim of "shaken baby" syndrome. The interview with the mom was generally nonproductive. The social worker thought to herself, "She is not telling me all that she knows. It's as if she is covering for someone. But who is she covering for? Her boyfriend?"

Vignette: Shaken Baby, Scene II

As time progresses and the case moves through the legal system, the social worker has contact with the extended family, in addition to the mom and even the mom's boyfriend. Finally, one day the mom tells her grandmother that the boyfriend was in the house when the baby was "hurt."

Vignette: Shaken Baby, Scene III

The grandmother tells her niece, who tells the social worker, who confronts the mom with the information. The mom then tells the social worker that she left the child with her boyfriend for a few hours the morning when she was shaken. She just hadn't thought to mention it to the social worker or the police.

The Child Welfare Worker Is Required to Enter the Family System and Learn About Back Region Events and Activities

Child welfare workers are required to enter the family system and to determine the nature of events that allegedly involve abuse or neglect. The family's denying the existence of the events does not discharge the social worker's responsibility. Based on what the child welfare worker is able to learn, he or she may close the case as unsubstantiated or he or she may need to pursue other "institutional" actions to learn about the event(s). This is what we saw with the "Shaken Baby" vignette. These institutional actions could include talking with neighbors, friends, or extended family members. They also could involve the police and the filing of a petition with the juvenile court. As each of these actions take place, increased tensions are experienced within the family about the event(s).

With this institutional response, tension in the family builds. Individuals, experiencing increased anxiety for themselves and other family members, find themselves reflecting and evaluating assumptions they have made about previously perceived scenes and activities. As they reflect on past scenes, they find themselves rethinking the meaning they have accorded to those events. As this process goes on, they draw logical inferences and often share this information publicly. In this way, there is a collective reflection and reconstruction of events that have occurred. This represents an aspect of what Brueggemann (2002) calls "social thinking," a collective thinking about events. Depending on what the social worker learns from this intervention, this dialogic activity may increase intervention into the family system. Such an increase in intervention heightens tensions within the family system and makes it harder for past and current narratives to explain what is happening. This would typically lead to increased reflection and reconstruction of events from the past and their interpretation within the boundaries of the family narratives and the metanarratives of the larger society.

From Narratives to Social Dramas

Social interaction as described here takes place within these social narratives. It includes events, scenes, and acts. A narrative would typically represent the enactment of sets of scenes that occur over several acts. As tensions build in narratives, the system becomes ready for an eruption and a shifting of the narrative to social drama. For example, the molestation of a child could progress as narrative. The acts leading up to and including the molestation could easily be conceptualized as act 1, act 2, act 3, etc. Within each act could be one or more scenes that involve molesting behavior. Each of these could involve social interaction and take place within a complex web of individual and family narratives.

Using the concept of narrative opens up the social worker's way of conceptualizing behavior. The social worker, to be effective, must have the capacity to recognize events within a process stream. Looking at one isolated event can obscure other elements that are important in understanding a particular situation. For example, the next vignette shows the beginning of a molestation of a child.

Vignette: The Molestation of Sherry, Scene I

Bart, Sherry's stepgrandfather, stands up, waves his hand at eight-year-old Sherry and walks out to the garage from the living room. In the garage, he signals for her to sit down on a comfortable chair he

(continued)

(continued)

has there. He sits next to her and says, "I want to show you something very nice. But you need to agree that this will be our little secret." She is a little puzzled, but trusts and loves her grandpa and says, "Okay." He then pulls out a picture of a recent *Family Square* magazine and points to a picture of a female model. He tells Sherry that this model is very pretty, is a girl just like her, and that the model likes showing off her body to men. He also tells Sherry, "As you grow older you will like this too. I will help you to learn about this." He then tells Sherry what a nice girl she is, gives her a platonic hug, and they return to the living room.

This is the beginning of a pedophile's approach to a young girl. It constitutes an initial activity directed at a future scene that will include the perpetrator's behavior in which the child is sexually molested. The act is the first in a molestation narrative involving this perpetrator and this victim. The first scene occurs in the living room where Bart encourages the child to follow him. The second scene is in the garage and involves Bart's encouraging the child to sit next to him and his sharing the picture(s) with her and the words he used. The scenes may stay the same; however, the events can be expected to change as Bart grooms Sherry for a new social role as victim. All scenes and events taken together constitute a narrative. They take place within the context of several other narratives. Specifically, Bart, Sherry, and each family member has his or her own narrative of daily life that was incorporated in the beginning of the molestation narrative. For example, a sister, sitting in the room when Bart called Sherry, may have incorporated the action into a narrative of "Sherry is Grandpa's favorite; what he is doing with her now is just another example of this." Alternately, the grandmother may have concluded "There goes Bart again, singling out one of the grandchildren for special attention. I wish he wouldn't do that," etc. Social workers need to understand that each member lives within and enacts his or her own narrative.

Vignette: The Molestation of Sherry, Scene II

Bart has progressed with his "socializing" of Sherry. In the evening, while watching television, he now gives her a secret hand signal and she comes and sits on his lap. He fondles her over her clothes even as other family members watch television in the same room. No one seems to notice this "special touching" of Sherry.

Through the socialization process (potentially months or years later), Bart has developed his relationship with Sherry to the point that he can maintain a private relationship with her in what is ordinarily public space. He has conditioned her to the point that she believes that everyone knows what he is doing and that they believe it is okay. However, other family members simply do not know what he is doing to her. He has essentially developed a barrier to their perceptions through the careful structuring of their narrative scenes. For example, a simple belief, narrative subtheme, that he would not do anything wrong can lead family members not to see what is happening.

Vignette: The Breach of Norms Is Made Public

Betty, Sherry's older sister, now sixteen years old, has just been placed in the grandparents' home by a social worker. Betty had also been socialized and molested by Bart. Now, her first night back, she avoids Bart, but sees the social interaction between Bart and Sherry and the shared secret hand movements. Her perceptions are not obscured by narratives about the presumed innocence of Bart's behavior. She corners Sherry and asks her what is happening. Sherry shares her "little secret" with Betty. Betty runs away from the family home and calls the social worker to report Bart's past molestation of her and current molestation of Sherry. The social worker responds with the police. The stepgrandfather, Bart, is arrested and the children are taken into protective custody.

Betty is able to recognize exactly what was happening. Her personal narrative included the molestation she experienced by Bart. She was quickly able to incorporate the important elements in the molestation narrative into her personal narrative. She was able to pick up on the hidden cues because she knew the shorthand that was used by

Bart with Sherry. She did not have the same barriers to perception that the family members had. Although she could not deal with it in the family home, she was able to call it to the attention of the authorities, a part of the larger metanarrative, knowing that they would take action. This essentially made the private drama public. The question then is what happens next.

Individual Identity and Narrative

As we have seen, narratives as used in this work are far more than simply stories. Although narratives have historically been viewed as a storied representation of the world, more recently they have been recognized by social workers, among others, as being far more substantive. Theorists are determining that social life is itself "storied" and that stories guide action, construct identities, constitute experience, and in general help individuals make sense of the world (Somers and Gibson, 1996). Narratives as conceptualized here include a discursive action that combines conceptions of time, space, and relationality (Somers and Gibson, 1996). In this sense, narrative and narrativity are "concepts of social epistemology and social ontology" (Somers and Gibson, 1996, p. 58). Through this dialogic process we come to "know, understand, and make sense of the social world" (Somers and Gibson, 1996, p. 59) and form our social identities. Moreover, these narratives are an aspect of how individual identities are formed and are, for the most part, not effectively studied as objective entities since they are based on individual meanings (Saari, 1991).

Narratives vary in the levels of action of which they treat. They can be viewed as metanarratives that constitute the underpinnings of worldviews (Somers and Gibson, 1996) or simply as stories that include individual worldviews within them (Saari, 1991). Generally, the latter view is emphasized in this model. Narratives simply provide a way to understand individual behavior as it occurs in a processing form over time. It is a way to understand social interaction that has occurred and is germane to child welfare. Narratives also suggest the underlying importance of individual meaning to those who are incumbents of the particular social roles.

The Model Described in Narrative

The central idea of the ritual process model discussed in Chapter 12 is that some social role changes are driven by social institutional interventions in the lives of individuals. When they involve interventions into family life, they may change the structure of families, including changes in the major family narratives. The central force driving these institutional interventions is a collective value set manifested in public policy and the child welfare system. The authority for legal intervention lies in state statutes and is overseen by the juvenile court. In this view, the court represents what Shils (1982) might call a symbolic center of our culture. As such, it is a center of authority presiding over the application of the governing laws of its respective domain. It also is a body to which we attribute sacred powers to determine the efficacy of matters brought before it. The governance metaphor that leads to this conception of the legal system is part of metanarratives that we live within and that are grounded in conceptions of the nation.

When institutional interventions involve children and parents, the effect is to open the family system to the agents of social institutions, the legal system, and the court. The ultimate outcome is potentially a change in social roles and narratives. These changes in social roles and narratives may involve a concomitant change in individual identity that leaves the individual with a changed sense of who he or she is. Along with this internal state, an "identity" comes with a new narrative that explains the situation.

When narratives erupt into social drama, the social worker may be able to develop a view of the underlying tensions and thus understand the kinds of narratives that are present within the family system. It also creates confusion for family members as their ongoing narratives clash with metanarratives. This results in confusion as to the nature of reality and uncertainty of the proper idea of private and public narratives. This confusion in relation to the institutional intervention results in not only an increase in the tension within the family system, but also the sharing of information with legitimate authorities.

The result is a continuing dialogue among family members and persons close to the family. These dialogues involve a deconstructing of the events of the narrative that brought the child welfare system into the family. As individuals deconstruct these narratives, they see connections that were not initially seen. The net effect of this deconstruction and reconstruction of the collective narratives is a sharing of additional information with the investigating social worker. As this information is shared, intervention continues. The social worker is provided with additional pieces of the total narrative, thus helping disembed the social interaction involving the molestation. This allows for a more accurate reconstruction of the events and their re-embedding within the social service agency and the legal system, that is, the juvenile court.

This leads to a collective reconstruction and reenactment of allegations and, ultimately, a challenging or affirming of collective values. As these values or norms have been violated, the court takes action to ensure that the transgression does not recur. As this process continues through the phases of ritualization, there is a shift of power within the family and at times within the community. The ultimate completion of the process is one that may lead to a second order transformation (Terkelsen, 1989) within the family. That is, it may lead to a change in the family's fundamental structure. This changes the power relationships within the family and attaches new social labels to family members. In particular, the new social labels of "perpetrator" and "victim" stand out within the family and the general community.

This shifting of roles and power, as part of this second order change, is relative to family members with one another. Ultimately, the participants take on new roles with varying degrees of stigma. For example, a molesting stepgrandfather prior to exposure of his molesting behavior may be seen as a moral, just, compassionate, parental figure to his family and even to his church congregation. He may be everyone's ideal of a grandparent. After his arrest and conviction for felony child molestation, he is considered a sexual offender and can expect to serve time in prison.

Simultaneously, the alleged victim, who is initially empowered by the intervention process, ultimately experiences her own stigmatizing as she is accorded the official social role of victim. For example, Sherry moves from being a "nice young lady" to being that "poor thing" or "the victim of that horrid man." Within the role set of the victim, she gains many things that were not previously available to her and that may not be available to others. For example, she moves to the top of the list for some agency counseling programs, she gets first consideration for some school placements, and she receives pity from those who know or suspect they know about the events. The positive part is that she gets these special programs. However, the negative part is that in order to get these "benefits" she must be officially classified in the social role of victim, a role that has a negative evaluation (Goffman, 1963) attached.

Through the court process(es) each participant gradually attains a level of comfort with his or her new role. Even the perpetrator gains some level of comfort with the passage of time and his public displays at hearings, trials, etc. Similarly, Sherry and other family members gain a degree of comfort in their new roles through these same hearings, attending normal functions in the community, etc. This adjustment is through a shifting of individual identities driven by the addition of new narratives. These displays provide a social context for the individuals to become familiar with new thoughts, feelings, and actions. For example, "what happened could have been a lot worse," "we must go on," etc. In short, the new narratives incorporate the molesting event within the families' major narratives, and these new narratives now are congruent with the metanarratives of the larger social group.

The idea is that a series of institutional or macrolevel actions occur. These are discussed in Chapter 12. These can be described as phases; however, they are not determinant or mutually exclusive. They are interconnected and continuous. Each phase does not need to happen in each situation in the same way. They seem to happen often enough that the model has applicability to child protection. The original report and issue involving abuse or neglect can often mask or hide other phases or steps.

CONCLUSION

This chapter lays the foundation for understanding the effects of intervention into family systems as illustrated by the ritualized process model. Behavior in this model is driven by social action, as described in part by Erving Goffman's view of social interaction, Victor Turner's anthropological views of symbolic interaction, drama, and ritual action and views of social narrative (Calhoun, 1996). Inherent in this approach is the idea that individuals' actions are seen as driven by thoughts, feelings, and actions expressed in language and symbols and enacted within and through narrative.

Chapter 12

Social Intervention
As Ritualized Action

INTRODUCTION

In the last chapter the ritual process model was alluded to and some of its philosophical and theoretical ideas were presented. In particular, the theoretical perspectives regarding individual behavior were presented. This included concepts such as "private" and "public" spaces and ideas such as "social narratives" and "social dramas" that contribute to the formation of social identities.

This chapter turns to the institutional processes of intervention into families. It builds on conceptualizations of the child welfare system as an expert system that is constructed by experts in policy and law. It now provides an abstracted legal structure that, for the most part, we consider as sacred and yet take for granted. The ritual process model views behavior alternately from an individual perspective and from a social institutional perspective. Expert systems, as discussed in the preceding chapter, are conceptualized as constructions within meta-narratives.

THE RITUAL PROCESS MODEL

There are five ritual phases. These include a breach, a precipitating event that makes the breach public, an institutional response, a ritualized examination of the event and an analysis of its place within the larger community, and, ultimately, reintegration within that community.

Overview

The ritual process model involves the previous phases, steps, or processes as described by Turner (1969) and these processes result in generally understandable patterns of behavior. There is a different kind of social interaction at each stage or phase of the ritual intervention process, that is, intervention of the social and legal systems. Although these are presented in a sequential pattern, some of these stages or phases can occur simultaneously.

The steps or phases of the ritualized process model are as follows:

1. Breach
2. Precipitating event
3. Institutional response
4. Ritualized analysis
5. Reintegration

Simply stated, the model presents a view of child abuse as involving a violation of a social norm, which becomes public as an allegation of abuse or neglect and is investigated by a social worker. The social worker examines in minute detail the social interaction that occurred. The social worker ferrets out the "facts" of the matter, that is, he or she extracts or dissembeds the interaction from its original time and place, and reconstructs it with symbols including language.

As the social worker completes this disembedding process, he or she sets it to language in the form of his or her own thought structures and, ultimately, in case recording. The case recording essentially reconstitutes or reembeds the social interaction for storage. The social worker determines if the allegations are true and, if so, probably petitions the juvenile court in an effort to protect the child. The petition must present a verbal "picture" of the abuse/neglect, the extracted social narrative or "social interaction" that suggests the need for protection.

The petition (an abstract depiction of the social interaction, the abuse or neglect) becomes the focus of a dialogic processes within the structure of the court (the court work group). This structure and these processes take place in an environment that provides safety and security for participants.

This action can be briefly described as including a process that involves a social worker identifying and investigating an alleged event of abuse or neglect; raising the event(s) from its original moorage in time and space; and transporting it in the form of a language or word picture to the juvenile court where it enters a "distanciated" (Giddens, 1990, p. 14) time and space. The parents and child follow this action because of a basic level of trust in the higher principles described within metanarratives derived within the Constitution and held within the legal system as represented by the court.

Breach or Violation of Social Norm

The first phase refers to the act of breaking or violating a norm. This may or may not be visible within a family. The spanking of a child in a supermarket would be public, while the beginning phases of pedophilia socialization would not be public. That is, the latter happens privately within the family and often "backstage" to both the family and the community. "Backstage," as in the Sherry vignette, means a kind of "virtual domain," that is, an artificially created separate communication system between Sherry and the stepgrandfather. Thus, the stepgrandfather's grooming of his victim would be done overtly to some extent, although it could be unknown to others living in the home. Not clear from the vignette is whether he broke family norms with his behavior.

When "grooming" moved to "sexual touching" by the stepgrandfather, his actions breached community norms, even if not family norms. However, until it was "exposed" to the public, it would not result in an institutional response. Given this context, the secret with the granddaughter would be what Imber-Black (1998) calls a "poison secret," one that is withheld from other family members and has a deleterious effect on the family. An underlying tension within the multiple narratives of family life was created.

The setting up of secrets, at times tied to threatening verbal statements to the victim, makes the victim feel helpless. For example, the child may be told, "You better not tell anybody because if you do, you will be sent to a foster home and I will be sent to jail. You don't want that, do you?" The victim is simultaneously given to feel he or she has "full control" of the situation, but is also told that he or she is responsible for all the bad that could come from it. The result is often that the victim is incapable of action. Typically, this becomes symbolized by the perpetrator as part of the molestation narrative as "Well, let's just keep this as our little secret!" The social worker must ferret out the particular metaphor the perpetrator uses with his or her victim in order to understand and track how the narrative has evolved. This refers to the "secret" language the perpetrator uses to symbolize the total molestation narrative. This can be any metaphor; however, through the socialization process it comes to have special, secret meaning to the perpetrator and the victim. That is, it constitutes their own particular narrative. Whether the perpetrator uses metaphors such as "secret," "having fun," or "playing," etc., the important element is the collective meaning that it contains for the victim and perpetrator.

At times, the developing of signals between the perpetrator and the victim can become very complex and highly ritualized. As shown in the vignette, the initiating scene is one involving a complex symbol system whereby the perpetrator signals the victim as to future actions she is to take. For example, certain hand movements done in public, that is, in open view of all family members, can signal a victim that "I will visit you in bed tonight," or, as in the vignette, can mean "follow me." Implicit in each signal is the message that the perpetrator will do certain sexual things with the victim.

Thus, the perpetrator communicates with his victim publicly while each is performing other roles on stage with other family members. The public actions in these cases set up private acts that are to occur in the "back region." At times, other family members may catch the signals. If they do but do not know the secret meanings, they may become unknowing accomplices to the victimization of the child. For example, if the child sees that the family member caught the signal, but the child is not able to separate public and private meanings, he or she may believe they know what the grandfather is doing with him or her. This solidifies the victim role even more deeply within the total narrative. Alternatively, family members may come to recognize the meaning behind the "public" signal as something that violates family norms and may take action that makes the event public (a precipitating event). In the previous vignette, the older sister, Betty, intercepted these signals and called public attention to what was happening.

The effect of breaching, or breaking family norms, is at minimum the creation of an open tension, open rift, or the eruption of social drama within the family. It can also lead to protective actions within the family such as keeping the perpetrator away from the child, etc. Sometimes these are effective and at other times they are not.

Other family members may become part of the molestation narrative for the child through actions or inactions without their knowledge of the abuse narrative. For example, a girl may wonder whether she should tell the mother even though the stepfather may have pleaded with her or even threatened her with the breakup of the family if she were ever to tell the mother. The victim may even rehearse or "try out" telling her mother the story. For example, she may say something to her mother, often when the mother is very busy, such as "Mom, what if I told you something very bad?" Unfortunately, her "test" to determine if she should tell her mother would be based on her mixed feelings of fear, guilt, and alliance with the stepfather. At times, it is virtually impossible for the best of mothers to pass this test. At the least, this family tension would operate noncognitively at the level of the family system and would affect all family members.

Precipitating Event

The term "precipitating event" refers to an event that occurs to make a breach within a system move from a private to a public domain. The understanding of the nature of precipitating events and their underlying meanings are classical aspects of assessments within the social work domain. The context and process that results in the precipitating event tells social workers much about what is happening within the particular family system. In this context, at some point the "secret" is let out of the perpetrator-victim subsystem and into the larger institutional system. For example, Betty's catching the hand signals from Bart brought her into the virtual domain that was private to Bart and Sherry. Betty had a range of choices and, ultimately, the action she took brought children's protective services, the social institutional response system, into the family system.

At some point, the victim of sexual abuse is likely to report the behavior to someone else. The child may methodically plan a scenario in which he or she tells someone about the molestation or the child may let out a "spontaneous utterance." It may be to another family member or to school authorities, a therapist, etc. The events that make this private behavior public could include, for example, another touching event, an expansion of the degree of severity of the molestation, a second perpetrator attempting to touch the child, a presentation by a child abuse prevention team at school, a friend reporting his or her friend as a victim, the result of a fight between the victim and the perpetrator, or a variety of other factors that somehow raise in the victim's mind the need to take action. The victim could experience feelings of fear, of getting even, of safety, or even trust in the recipient of information. The important point is that a precipitating event typically brings the private issue into a public arena, which may result in an institutional response.

Institutional Response

The metaphor of social institutional response refers to the third stage or phase of the ritual process and involves a response to the report by official forces including child protective workers, police, investigators, etc. As the institutional forces intervene, the tension may erupt into social drama or even to open conflict. The exact nature of the response varies according to what is reported, who reports it, and who it is reported to. If the report suggests the child was abused and is in danger of being abused again, has bruises (providing evidence of a law violation), or if the perpetrator is expected to have access to the child in the near future, an immediate response is usually done.

The Disembedding, Moving, and Reformulating of Events of Social Interaction

As already noted, the responding social worker, on behalf of the agency and the legal system, is expected to investigate the allegations, complete a risk and safety assessment, and document the results in a social narrative. Depending on the situation, the worker also could be involved in petitioning the court for intervention on the child's behalf.

Further Interventions

A typical report may be from local school personnel after a child abuse prevention (CAP) team has made a prevention presentation. The report would usually be made to children's protective services. Upon receipt, the social worker would typically respond to the school. Since sexual molestation is a crime, police would also be involved so they can begin a criminal investigation.

In most jurisdictions of the country, for sexual molestation cases, an initial interview is followed by an in-depth interview by a larger collaborative team. A first interview might be done by a social worker and a police officer. This would in all likelihood be a forensic field interview. The child protective worker and police officer, at this point in the process, would focus on validating factual information received in the report and learning additional information that is immediately available on the individual and family background. If this information is validated, the interview process moves to the second phase.

The second interview is a more intensive forensic interview with a larger multidisciplinary team, typically consisting of child welfare social workers, police, and attorneys. In order to provide a comfortable environment and to minimize the trauma of the interview for the child, a neutral child-centered setting is typically used for this in-depth and, at times, video-recorded interview. Representatives of all systems that have a need to interview the child would be present and typically would include a prosecuting attorney, a police officer, a child advocate, and a social worker. One team member would be designated the interviewer, while others would observe behind a one-way mirror. The physical structure of the setting would need to accommodate these participants and would typically include a one-way mirror, recording equipment, etc. The purpose of this second interview is to obtain all available information as to what, when, and where from the child as to the events of the molestation. The recording ensures that the interview techniques support an objective forensic style interview. Forensic interviews are typically theory free. They are focused on obtaining information from the child. They are not in any way therapeutic and thus a clinical style methodology or approach is not appropriate (Ceci and Bruck, 1993; Ceci and Bruck, 1995; Poole and Lamb, 1998).

At this step or immediately following this interview, the safety assessment would need to be conducted. Presuming the report is substantiated, the assessors would look at risk factors and anticipated plans for legal action and arrive at a determination as to the least restrictive environment in which the child would be safe.

An important question here is whether the level of evidence available could lead to the arrest of the alleged perpetrator. That is, does evidence warrant such an arrest? If not, a determination must be made as to whether the victim would be safe in his or her home from the perpetrator. Should the child be taken into custody? A significant part of this would be an assessment of the home situation. This would include answers to such questions as will the mother keep the father away from the child? Can she keep him out of the home?

The focal point of institutional action at this phase of this model is to stop or seal off or repel the advancing breach in community norms. Action taken now must quickly highlight the community's willingness to respond to such transgressions of law. Making sure the child is safe and possibly arresting the suspect would accomplish this. However, the perpetrator will probably be released within a few days, so the child must be considered safe even if the suspect is not in jail.

This step involves the child being examined by medical personnel. Although this could be done earlier, it would typically follow the more in-depth interview. This colposcopic examination should be performed by experienced medical examiners with a sensitivity to the child's needs. This process might provide information that a trained physician could use to determine a probability that a child has been molested. Since the determination as to whether a child has been molested is tied to statistical research, the medical examiner can only determine a molestation by correlation, that is, the probability of the certainty that the child has been molested.

Steps in the Investigative Process

This extracting of the event(s), that is, the disembedding and subsequent reconstruction and presentation of this material, from the social worker's perspective can be described in steps as follows:

1. The social worker investigates the allegations by talking to all parties, witnesses, etc. This includes examining other such events within the family setting. This provides a "picture" to the social worker, becomes an abstracted symbolic representation or "symbolic token" of the actual event that happened.
2. In a sexual abuse case, a joint interview is done with a sexual abuse response team and further information about the event is learned.
3. The child is taken into custody and is seen by a medical doctor. For example, if a child has been hit in the face by a parent, pictures are taken of the handprint (to serve as evidence of abuse). The social worker interviews doctors and nurses that may have gathered evidence. This adds to the symbolic depiction of the

event(s). This helps to complete and validate, or invalidate, parts of the narrative the social worker has already gathered.

4. The social worker uses proper forms to create a written record of the narrative of the social interaction and documents all contacts in keeping with agency policies and procedures. This stores the abstracted version of the event within the language of the agency culture.

5. The social worker writes a petition that essentially serves as a "word picture" of the event(s). This symbolic representation of the event is presented to the court for adjudication. This moves the abstracted material to the special time and spatial locations of the court, a respected and revered part of our culture.

6. This adjudication works to re-create and examine the social interaction, and to determine if it is true. That is, the judge must determine whether there is a factual basis to the allegations of abuse or neglect experienced by the child. If the judge makes this determination, it then becomes a "social fact."

Changes in the Family

With the institutional response, the family system begins to change. A social worker and police begin to ask questions about private, intimate details of individuals' lives. The focus is on finding out what has been happening to the alleged victim, that is, who did what to who and who knew or should have known about it? The result is a blurring of the boundaries of the private and public narratives and the beginning of the creation of new symbols as a projection and transference of meaning.

For the victim, the feelings of helplessness shift to feelings of being able to cause changes and also feelings of guilt and responsibility for the effects. Also, the private and poisonous secret of the molestation shifts to the public stage on which the way the perpetrator used the relationship with the victim is highlighted. The same kinds of shifts occur for other family members. At times, the institutional response takes on mythic proportions for the family members as they rewrite and reorganize temporal narratives around the happenings of the response. For example, in describing important events within the family, a child or sibling or even a parent may refer to it as "That was before Sherry reported what her stepgrandfather did to her."

Ritualization Analysis

The fourth phase of the process involves the ritualization narrative and refers to what happens from this point to when the court case is dismissed. The structure for this part of the action is essentially that as outlined in the rational model. This typically includes detention, jurisdictional, dispositional, and even review hearings. This ritualization process also applies to actions in other courts such as in criminal and family courts, but this chapter deals only with juvenile court.

With the filing of the petition, the total process enters a new stage. When the social worker files the petition, the court work group becomes part of the total process. In this sense, the social worker loses what control he or she may have had over the investigation, the processes, or the outcome. For this reason, the social worker, in terms of relationship building, must be sensitive to his or her limits and not give anyone a false sense of security with any particular outcome. The social worker cannot even make a good guess at the outcome.

Four major processes are involved in this phase and they are continuous and interrelated processes. They include reconstruction, replication, reenactment, and evaluation. Each of these involve working with previously private information in the court setting (in the public of the child welfare system). The juvenile court, from this perspective, while maintaining the confidentiality of the information, is conceptually a public arena, for its participants. That is, those persons within the court environment are entitled to hear the personal information involved in the case and are expected to keep it confidential.

Reconstructed or Reassembled Events

This phase involves the presentation of evidence gained in the investigation that supports the word story of the event that was petitioned. The pieces of evidence should fit together in a cohesive, logical web. The evidence must match the event as reconstructed by the social worker. The reconstruction is typically reported within documents that are part of the agency records and those that are submitted to the court.

The Reembedding of Extracted Material Within Court Domain

The petitioned facts with supporting evidence then become part of the judicial process, as the court adjudicates their accuracy. Notice is provided to the parents and to the child as to the allegations. This process makes the narrative presentation, which is by now social drama, public within the court setting. This constitutes public dialogue that involves a symbolic repeating and replication of the alleged events that occurred within the family's back region. The reenactment occurs within the front region of the court setting. Here, the judge is the finder and determiner of the facts of the matter. What were at one time private actions by the alleged perpetrator toward the child are now disclosed and discussed in the confidential, safe, and protected environment of the court. All of those who were a party to the initial allegations are themselves drawn into the process, if not verbally at least in terms of thoughts and feelings.

Reenactment of Norm Violations

Although the material is confidential to the outer world, it is not to the court personnel. During the course of court proceedings the facts are brought forth within the rules of court. The events surrounding the abusive incidents are reconstructed and reenacted symbolically through dialogue with the use of language. The court and all participants are involved with the critiquing of the efficacy of the material presented by the social worker. Ultimately the judge, through the process of adjudicating the truth or falsity of the petition, determines the facts that are presented in the case.

Shifting of Power Relationships Within the Family: Changing Family Structure

During this phase there is power relationships shift within the family. When the alleged norm violations, the sexual molestation events, were occurring, the perpetrator clearly was "in control." The child was dependent upon him or her for care, support, and adequate supervision.

In the typical family structure, the mother and father are the authority figures. Within this court process, they continue to be authority figures, but they have limited power. The judge presides and, in this sense, is "in control" and makes decisions based on the rules of court and rules of evidence (these rules being grounded within the community standards and laws). Speaking on the alleged victim's behalf is his or her attorney. With this representation, the victim becomes empowered to take part in the legal aspects of the hearings. The attorney represents the victim's interests, which may or may not be in harmony with those of his or her parents. As the victim's interests are being represented on a coequal basis before a neutral and powerful authority figure, the victim is coequal with her parents. This shifting of power relations through the court process is shown in Figure 12.1 (adapted from Turner, 1977).

Evaluation/Examination

Ultimately, the judge must make a finding. The finding is in relationship to the private behavior as petitioned, and its applicability to the code of the state. Is the petition true (substantiated) or untrue (not substantiated)? If true, then how well does it fit with respect to the code's definition of a child who has been abused or neglected? Also, if true, what kinds of services, etc., are needed to ensure the safety of the child? Ancillary issues include reunification plans, visiting arrangements, and service plans if the child is deemed unsafe in the family home.

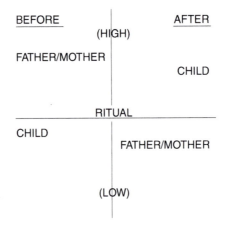

FIGURE 12.1. Court Process Power Axis

Reintegration

The last phase of the ritual involves the reintegration of individuals within roles, status, and relationships with new or rewritten narratives and new social structures. Following the action in juvenile court and in criminal court, the victim and perpetrator have new social roles, that is, new social identities ascribed to them. Specifically through the finding of the court that the child has been the victim of sexual abuse, the child would be labeled officially a "victim." With this changed status, as noted earlier, the child would be eligible for a variety of programs. Similarly, the perpetrator would have been labeled a child molester and, if is convicted in criminal court, he or she could become socially classified as a child molester. Molesters' relationships and roles within their families and the community would change considerably. Jail or prison time is possible and later they must notify authorities of their current residences and possibly lose civil rights regarding, among other things, voting.

For the family system, there has been what Terkelson (1989) calls a second order structural change. Assuming the court has affirmed the molestation and the stepgrandfather is convicted in criminal court, the family's main economic provider, the breadwinner, goes to prison. They need another source of income. If the mother becomes an employed parent, the household income can be expected to drop as the mother typically has limited skills and will have to pay for child care. Other family members will need to take on new roles and relationships with one another to keep the family system operating. The family will also need to work through whatever issues or concerns that the prior events brought up for them. They can be expected to develop a new set of symbols in the form of narratives including changes in language they use to describe their changed relationships with one another. Also, they may incorporate the past events through rituals and myths associated with temporal dimensions of experience, such as "Well, that happened before we found out about Sherry!"

For the social institutions, there has been a reaffirmation of their viability in confronting this attack on community order as represented in public laws. They have been successful in beating back this threat to the mores of the community. As the responding system, the hearings and processes that took place simply affirm the system's values of the desirability of protecting children from sex abuse. They were successful in protecting the social order from what Mary Douglas (1966) would call polluting elements, such as sexual molestation, that is, metaphoric "dirt."

CONCLUSION

The ritualized process model highlights the interaction of macro-level social institutions and their effects on individuals and families within the juvenile court system. In the sense that it involves social interaction and its effects, it highlights various narratives including aspects of social roles, social role performance, and individual behavior and action. It also shows how individuals through institutional adjudication process transition from one social role to another, often significantly different, social role.

It draws on theories from a variety of dramaturgical and post-modernist streams. In particular it draws from such authors as Victor Turner (1969), Terence Turner (1977), Edward Shils (1982), Edgar Schein (1985), and Erving Goffman (1959). The theory explains the processes of change within the dependency system in terms of the effects of intervention, including the investigation phase through court adjudication. It emphasizes the effects on spatial and temporal dimensions in families. Of primary concern from this perspective is the way the individuals present themselves and their activities with others, the ways in which they guide and control the impression they form, and the kinds of things they may or may not do in sustaining their performances (Goffman, 1959).

Thus, the dramaturgical perspective provides a way to view individuals, families, and even communities from a collectivist or macro-level perspective in addition to helping to understand the dynamics by which individual actors shift and change social roles and narratives. Such changes are seen as resulting from shifts in the perceptions of others and the individual's sense of his or her own identity. It also provides an understanding of boundaries that maintain private and public spaces and helps to understand how these are maintained by performances that take place over time.

SECTION III:
ETHICS, VALUES, AND CONCLUSIONS

Chapter 13

Ethics, Values, and Integrity

INTRODUCTION

The entire field of child welfare is rampant with ethical and values issues. Three central and related ethical and value-based concerns can be conceptualized, including the concept of client self-determination, the value of informed consent, and the idea of the social worker's fiduciary responsibilities. These rise to the level of being central grounding values or principles. Here the idea of client self-determination with its intricately related concept of informed consent, the power of due process and normative law, and the need for limited paternalistic behaviors contributes to the development and maintenance of sound fiduciary relationships. This chapter examines these three concepts and related issues.

Self-determination is particularly important simply because child welfare is for the most part a nonvoluntary service delivery system. A reciprocal of self-determination is the concept of paternalism. Paternalism in this sense is negatively related to self-determination. Viewed from the perspective of clients, one might say that the child welfare system is by its nature paternalistic. It works through a societal mandate to ensure the attainment of socially constructed values. In this sense, the social collective determines what is best for those who come under its jurisdiction.

The value of informed consent compliments the emphasis on client self-determination. It ensures that when clients are adequately informed of the processes involved in child welfare they are enabled to effectively participate in significant decisions affecting themselves and their families. This value, if afforded to clients, does much to level the field of operation as the individual interacts with those who work for social institutions.

When we discuss values or ethics in nonvoluntary service systems, we inadvertently must talk about the social worker's fiduciary responsibility. Unlike some areas of social work, the fiduciary responsibility in child welfare involves multiple dimensions, all of which are important to the practitioner and the client.

SELF-DETERMINATION AND PATERNALISM

Client self-determination and paternalism are alternate sides of the same metaphoric coin. Separated by concepts such as "informed decision making" and "due process," they constitute the legal and ethical boundary of the fiduciary relationship in child welfare practice. This is not to say that they carry more weight than other values, such as confidentiality, service provision, competence, etc. However, they provide a behavioral framework that, when applied to practice, helps to ensure that those other values and ethics are a part of practice.

Self-Determination

Self-determination is one of the truly dominant values in professional social work. It can be understood as "The practical recognition of the right and need of clients to freedom in making their own choices and decisions" (Biestek, 1957, p. 103). In practical terms it means that clients should, as far as they are able and within the limits of collective values expressed in policy, be able to control their own lives, that is, their destinies.*

However, within the nonvoluntary child welfare system, this right is bounded. For example, the NASW (1996) *Code of Ethics* notes that obligations to society, or other legal situations, may limit the expression of this right. That is, these macrolevel obligations may supersede the client's right to self-determine his or her fate. Biestek also notes that this right is limited. In his words, "The client's right to self-deter-

---

*The child welfare worker must respect the individual's right to self-determine his or her own present and future. Such self-determination must be based on the client's own perceptions and understandings of the world and upon information on the child welfare system provided by the social worker. Parents, like others of us, have opinions as to what they want or do not want including their hopes and aspirations for their futures. To ignore this is to treat parents as children.

mination . . . is limited by the client's capacity for positive and constructive decision making [and] by the framework of civil and moral law" (1957, p. 103).

In child welfare, the client has this right to self-determination regarding the receipt of services within the limits provided by the legal system. The client is able to make selective choices as to a variety of items. Once court jurisdiction is established, this right is circumscribed by the legal orders of the court. That is, the court, within its legal role, may limit a client in the sense of mandating certain behaviors as a "condition" of having something else happen, such as a child be returned to him or her. In such a situation, the court determines some elements of, for example, a treatment plan. These, within the context of court intervention, become fixed or nonnegotiable. At the same time, the client can make some choices. In particular, clients have a right to participate in determining negotiable parts of their treatment plans.

The social worker must be respectful of clients and be professionally able to engage clients in making these self-determining parts of service plans (Rooney, 1988, 1992). Although clients, particularly parents, have the right to participate in such things as formulating service plans, they also have the de facto right to only partially participate or even not to participate in the plans designed for their improved functioning. In this situation, they are invariably risking the consequences of adverse court action.

Even when choices seem nonnegotiable, they often have negotiable features. For example, if the court orders a parenting class, the parent can choose which program, assuming it meets the court's expectations. This is limited or "bounded" self-determination.

Paternalism

One of the more powerful ways the child welfare system and child welfare workers can keep parents from exercising self-determination is through what Reamer (1983) calls paternalism. Paternalism is essentially a limitation placed on a person's exercise of the right of self-determination. Paternalism involves someone, such as a social worker, interfering with a person's right of self-determination typically for that person's "own good" as perceived by the other, that is, by the social worker.

Paternalism operates when the social worker, an authority figure, limits "client self-determination for a person's own good rather than the good of a third party" (Rooney, 1992, p. 55). For example, the social worker tells the client "You don't have to know what is happening in court. All you have to do is go to counseling." In the operation of paternalism, the social worker imposes his or her own standard of what is good for the client.

Vignette: Self-Determination As Making Choices

Martha was meeting with Jennifer, the mother of two-year-old Cindi. Cindi was made a dependent of the court based on the mother's not providing adequate medical care for her. Jennifer did not seem able to recognize the illnesses that seemed to be plaguing her daughter. The court had ordered her, among other things, to attend a parenting class that focused on educating parents about adequate medical care for children. Martha had been able to find such a program. She explained this to Jennifer. Jennifer responded, "But I wanted to go to my church's parenting class." Martha said, "Well, the court has ordered that you attend a particular type of program, but [recognizing client self-determination, she added] if you really prefer that program, I can look into it for you."

Just because paternalism suggests a limit or boundary to self-determination, it is not always inappropriate. Reamer (1983) notes that an appropriate use of paternalism would be in circumstances that involve the good of another person. For example, if a person is perceived as taking action to harm another person, paternalism, that is, limiting self-determination, would be justified. This, of course, is the heart and soul of child welfare intervention. Intervention is based on the belief that the child's right to protection takes precedence over the parent's right to parent the child. The important question is that of just who makes this determination? The answer in our child welfare system is the court.

Alternately, paternalism in the sense of its being an inappropriate action takes at least three forms. These include deliberately opposing clients' wishes, withholding pertinent information from clients, and manipulating clients through providing misinformation to them (Rooney, 1992). These forms have in common the central idea that the social worker, as an authority figure, knows what is truly best for the client. However, in a world in which more is unknown than known, it is hard to say that anyone can say what is truly best for another person.

In child welfare, the first form of inappropriate paternalism, deliberately opposing a client's wishes, can operate as simply as saying to a client, "You have no choice," when in fact the client does have a choice. This operates through the social worker dismissing particular choices of treatment or training programs that the client wishes to be involved in, and also can take the form of ignoring the fact that a client always has a choice. All choices have outcomes and either the social worker or the parent may be uncomfortable with a particular outcome. However, the choices are still real despite their potential consequences being undesirable. For example, despite a court order, a parent has a choice to complete or not complete a drug treatment program. However, in some cases if the parent does not complete the program, he or she may serve jail time or may not have children returned. Social workers must remember that clients always have choices.

Vignette: He's Too Fragile to Hear the Truth

Jane, the social worker for a twelve-year-old boy, Toby, and his fifteen-year-old brother, Eric, finished talking with Eric's foster mother. She turned to her desk mate and said, "Eric has run away again. I am going to see Toby, and he will probably ask about his brother. When I tell him about Eric, I am just sure that he is going to run away too."

When she met with Toby, he asked about his brother. Jane told him that Eric was doing really fine in his foster home. She went on to say that he hasn't had any running away incidents in about six months. Jane didn't know that Toby had the phone number for Eric's best friend and later called to check on his brother. He learned that he was a runaway. He said to the friend, "Those social workers are always lying to you. I think they are afraid that if I know about Eric being on the run, I will run away. That's nuts! I wish I would get a social worker that would just tell the truth." When asked about it later, the social worker told her supervisor that she told Toby that Eric was fine, because she didn't want to upset him.

This vignette illustrates the second kind of paternalism, a deliberate withholding of information combined with lying to the client. The social worker stated that she was afraid of what Toby would do. However, the worker's actions may have had more to do with her own fears and anxieties around dealing with Toby's feelings than fears about what Toby might do. By "protecting" the child, the social worker may be setting into operation another set of forces that may make the situation significantly worse. By telling Toby what she knew, she could have helped him deal with any feelings he had that might affect his behavior. This could, by itself, result in his running away. Also, and at least as important, he is not likely to trust social workers more after this experience.

The third form of paternalism involves providing misinformation. A good example is one in which social workers attempt to "frame" situations to get parental compliance with requests. For example, for a social worker to say something like, "If you follow through and do drug testing like the judge has ordered, then the judge will return your son to you," is misleading to a parent. The problem is that the social worker has no foreknowledge about what the judge will do. Other factors may lead the judge to make a different determination and order. Social workers who mislead their clients end up with clients who are very upset, not trusting of them or subsequent social workers, and who are disempowered by their experience with social workers.

Vignette: If You Help Me, Everything Will Be All Right

The mother was distraught. The social worker wanted to take her children into custody. The mother had moved with her children without telling the social worker. Technically, this was "child stealing." Now the social worker had found her and the children. He believed the children should be in custody. He knew that the judge was very unlikely to quickly return children to parents who had disappeared with their children while under court supervision. Now, the social worker told the mother, "If you help me take your children to the children's shelter, the judge will return them to you the day after tomorrow at the detention hearing." The social worker said it with a voice of authority and essentially led the mother to believe he could control what the judge would order at the detention hearing.

This third form of paternalism is most apt to happen in child welfare when children are taken into custody. Social workers, in order to get the parent's support for the removal, sometimes provide misinformation such as "Well, if you cooperate with our taking the children into custody, I am sure the judge will return the children to you tomorrow." This has two problems. First, there is no way to know if the judge will return the children to the parent. Social workers make only recommendations to the court, not decisions for the court. Second, the social worker providing this information may reasonably suspect that the child will be held in custody no matter the degree of parental cooperation.

Vignette: If You Help Me, Everything Will Be All Right, Part II

Alternately, the social worker could have openly and honestly solicited the mom's participation by providing her with informed consent. The social worker could have told the parent exactly what the social worker could do and discuss concerns about possible outcomes. For example, "Based on your working with me today, I would expect to make a recommendation for the return of the children tomorrow. I don't know if the judge will follow it. In fact, I do know that the judge sometimes feels strongly about these kinds of situations, but I really can't tell you what he will do. What is truly important, and I believe we both agree on this, is that the children need to be safe and secure and to know that you are concerned about them."

INFORMED CONSENT

If we accept the basic social work values of self-determination and paternalism as two sides of the same coin, we can see that informed consent serves as a kind of metaphoric bridge between the two. Informed consent described as a fiduciary principle (Kutchins, 1998), as coupled with due process (Rooney, 1992), or as an ethical standard (NASW, 1996), essentially describes an underlying philosophy of working with clients in a respectful way. Child welfare practice, in this view, must be conceptualized as helping clients work within a choice-making framework. Social workers have an obligation to share what they know about the case, what they see as problems or issues, what they see as choices facing the client, and what the potential outcome of each choice might be. An extremely important aspect of this is the idea of "potential outcome." At times, social workers believe they can predict the outcome. However, there is no way to predict the outcome of virtually any particular choice with 100 percent certainty.

This process of helping clients make informed decisions includes soliciting a client's participation in listing alternative action choices and potential outcomes. This also helps clients to learn how to sort out choices for themselves. As it applies to counseling or treatment, it would also include explaining items such as risks, benefits, costs, and alternatives so that the client may select the most effective treatment, thereby making an informed choice (Kutchins, 1998).

Ideas about informed consent are well developed in medical practice. In particular, Morreim (1995) argues that individuals should be involved in their own decisions. While she talks about economic issues dealing with insurance, she notes that patients should be provided with the information needed to make decisions, including medical treatment. This view holds that "patients can be respected as free and responsible agents" (Khushf, 1998, p. 111).

Probably the most important aspect of informed consent in child welfare is informing clients of their due process rights, with possible outcomes. At times this can be threatening to social workers. In some situations the social worker may be helping the client to fight or oppose recommendations that the worker is making to the court for the parent's child(ren).

In past chapters, we have discussed due process issues. Due process rights are essentially legal rights that are protected by the Constitution. In addition, the proceedings in the juvenile court are predicated on the legal concept of due process. Rooney (1992) notes that "as each citizen is Constitutionally entitled to due process before rights can be endangered, all clients are entitled to be informed about rights and programs for which they are eligible, as well as limitations to those rights and programs" (p. 58). In the child welfare system, the right to be informed about one's due process rights is probably the most basic ethical standard that practitioners must follow. This is the foundation of trust in the working relationship between the social worker and the client. It is also perhaps the most empowering aspect of working with clients in this setting.

Vignette: Costs of Care

Glenn, the father of David, an eight-year-old boy with severe emotional problems, is talking with Eileen, a children's protective service intake social worker who has responded to a report from the school about David's severe emotional problems. Eileen, having completed her assessment, is saying to the father, "We can make David a dependent of the court, based on his emotional problems, if you wish and agree. If we do, the court can order that he is placed in a residential treatment center. This kind of center would help both David and your family. They will provide not only education for David but also therapy for him and your family. You will need to participate in the treatment program and in court proceedings. With the juvenile court order, payment is made through the department. The usual cost of care is about seven thousand dollars per month. Do I have your agreement?" The father, believing he has been fully informed, agrees.

[Six months later, on a Friday evening about 9:00 p.m.] David has been in a residential treatment center for the past five months and the family is participating in the program. The family is watching television and there is a knock on the door. The father answers the door and is greeted by a sheriff's deputy, who serves the father with a summons. The father finds that he is being sued for the total cost of care for David. He calls his social worker the following Monday and learns that the department considers this a child support case and that he should get an attorney to negotiate a court-ordered payment. Otherwise, he will have to pay the total cost of care.

FIDUCIARY RELATIONSHIPS

The concept of a fiduciary relationship is most often thought of in everyday discourse as related to a financial professional's ethical and legal responsibility to clients. In this parlance, an investment advisor, a certified public accountant, or similar person has a special responsibility to clients, which is related to the idea of being trustworthy. That is, the client is expected to be able to trust the professional to maintain the client's interest as first and foremost in dealings on his or her behalf.

However, the fiduciary concept extends beyond financial transactions and includes other professionals and other service contexts as considerations. Fiduciary relationships, as used here, are described as the legal foundation of the social worker's relationship with clients. What constitutes a fiduciary relationship? *Black's Law Dictionary*

(1979) defines a fiduciary relationship as one that includes formal and informal arrangements "which exist wherever one man trusts in or relies upon another. One founded on trust or confidence reposed by one person in the integrity and fidelity of another" (p. 564).

This certainly applies to child welfare in that the client is dependent upon the social worker to present accurate and vital information to the court along with well-thought-out recommendations. The social worker, acting as an extension of the juvenile court, is expected to be trustworthy in all transactions.

Relationship Issues: Truth Telling

If informed consent works as a bridge between self-determination and paternalism, then it also serves as an introduction to fiduciary issues in social work. Informed consent provides a central piece upon which the social work relationship with a nonvoluntary client can be built. The key element in this working relationship is the concept of trust. Trust, in this sense, is driven by clarity of boundaries. The social worker must be clear about his or her boundaries while working with clients. This includes respecting the boundaries of clients.

The concept of trust is widely recognized in social work as being important in relationships. This idea of informed consent, grounded through court decisions and in ethical and fiduciary issues of social work practice, establishes the need for truth telling by social workers.

> This duty to tell the truth is the basis of the informed consent doctrine that obligates professionals to explain the risks, benefits, costs, and alternatives, which at least gives clients the right to know what the most effective intervention is and to make an informed choice to accept or reject a proposed alternative. (Kutchins, 1998, p. 620)

Relationship-Based Practice As Based on Trust, aka Fiduciary Relationships

This conceptualization of child welfare practice fits well with a relationship-based perspective to serving clients. The helping relationship is the primary vehicle in providing effective "helping" services to people (Kutchins, 1998; Zastrow, 2000). This is noted not only in social work, but also in psychology by Baron (1998), as being one of four central concepts important in making systems of therapy effective. Baron notes that this seems to be universal in various forms of therapy.

> All forms of therapy involve clients in what has been termed the therapeutic alliance—a partnership in which powerful emotional bonds are forged between persons seeking help and their therapist. This relationship is marked by mutual respect and trust, and it can be a big plus for people who previously felt helpless, hopeless, and alone. (Baron, 1998, p. 518)

However, the concept goes beyond therapy to be part of the total relationship between client and social workers. For example, Galambos (1999) notes that fiduciary relationships involve trust and confidence in actions. She cites Darr (1991) when describing the fiduciary relationship as one "in which confidence and trust on one side results in superiority and influence on the other" (p. 2). The responsibility for maintaining this fiduciary relationship, from this perspective, is with the social worker, the person helping the other person. Darr (1991) goes on to note that with the "presence of superiority and influence [go] . . . the duties of loyalty and responsibility" (p. 2). In short, there is a kind of reciprocal and mutual alliance, a fiduciary relationship, between clients and child welfare social workers.

Fiduciary Relationship As Tied to the Conceptions of the Client

What, if any, are the limits of this relationship? Just as there is a limit to self-determination, there is also an exception to this fiduciary relationship noted in the National Association of Social Workers' (NASW) *Code of Ethics* (1996). The exception is that the social worker's fiduciary responsibility to the larger society is considered primary and superseding the loyalty owed to clients under some circumstances. However, it does require that clients be informed of this limitation. Informed in this sense implicitly means "informed consent."

Although this position within NASW appears clear, an important additional question is regarding the limits of society in directing action within child welfare. For example, most social work practice typically involves situations in which the nature of the client is clear-cut. However, in child welfare this is not the case.

Here the question is that of just who is the social worker's client and who is "society" from a child welfare practice perspective? The child welfare system itself aims to protect children from abuse and neglect; however, the child is dependent upon his or her parents and, of course, lives within a family and a community. We also find the social worker is employed by an agency, located within a cultural, social, and political community, to work with the child, the parent(s), the family, the community, and the legal system. Thus, it is unclear who the client is and who society is. This is particularly true when we look at legislative mandates to preserve families and to protect children all within the context of the stakeholders of the child welfare system.

THE SOCIAL WORKER'S "DOUBLE AGENTRY"

One of the ways to look at this is to examine the concept of "double agentry" as it applies to child welfare. To understand some aspects of fiduciary responsibilities within the child welfare environment, we can learn from the context of private practitioners working with managed care systems. These practitioners serve at least two competing "client" systems. They are expected by their "employer," the managed care organization, to hold costs down. Simultaneously they are trusted by the client to provide the best help and care available.

These competing forces within managed care call on the practitioner to function within a context in which they serve as a kind of double agent. Galambos (1999) identifies these dual roles for social workers in managed care systems and notes that Durham (1994) refers to these as "double agentry" situations. In these relationships, providers, such as social workers, would be seen as acting in dual roles as caregivers and agents of managed care companies. Each role has a "different set of loyalties and responsibilities" (Galambos, 1999, p. 2). Whether this is doable or even reasonable, it is an accurate conceptualization of this kind of relationship.

Vignette: The Call from the Senator

Bill, working on finding a suitable placement within the placement preferences of the Indian Child Welfare Act for two Native American children, was frustrated. He had tried virtually all of the agency's resources. Not only was he under pressure from his administration, but also from the children's shelter, his own attorney, the current non-Indian foster parents, who wanted the children to stay with them, another agency that was providing courtesy supervision, and the Indian community representative and their legal counsel. Well, he would continue to try his best. The telephone rang, and he answered, "Bill Adams speaking." It was a woman from U.S. Senator Brown's office who was calling to find out what was happening on this case. She had already talked to Bill's supervisor. She was asking for an update on efforts to find an appropriate family for the children!

COMPETING INSTITUTIONAL LOYALTIES WITHIN CHILD WELFARE

Of course, the managed care situation is different from child welfare; however, there are some similar connections. The connection between managed care, the client, and the social worker is one that is tied together by money. In child welfare, by and large, social workers are separated from economic costs associated with choices.

However, the costs and funding for programs throughout a typical community create a multiplicity of social and financial linkages among programs. For example, public funds pay for education, recreation, children's protective services, utilities, etc. Similarly, group homes and residential treatment centers are dependent on the child welfare system for referrals, etc. Financial ties exist among multiple social networks in children's protective services; however, the influence of money as tying these networks together is indirect at best.

More important in understanding this concept of a fiduciary responsibility tied to the concept of society are the collaborative working relationships between people and systems. The child abuse industry is a multiplicity of forces, which are tied together around broad goals such as providing services to children and families. In this context, the practice of child welfare is essentially representative of a multiplicity of social institutional forces. In this sense, we must understand that individuals and social/political groups have a stake

(Mitroff, 1983) in the child welfare system. These are the members of Costin, Karger, and Stoesz's (1991) "child abuse industry." These individuals and social groups, in their own way, provide the context in which the social worker is called upon to work with each individual client.

These relationships exist for the practitioner, as they work with the organizations that are a part of the working process, and as they work with their client systems. For example, a referent may have a preconceived notion of the best plan for the child and become extremely upset if the social worker works in an alternate direction with a parent. Thus, a school principal who believes a child should be removed from a parent can be expected to be upset when the child is back with the parent the day following the report. The problem in providing services is when the principal is unwilling to help work with the parent and the child. The principal needs to be considered as part of the "action system" in helping the parent, child, and the family to improve their functioning. Note that the principal is simply to be "considered," not that the social worker "must acquiesce to his or her demands."

Being sensitive to these stakeholders is often extremely important in providing services and in empowering clients. They, just as much as the client, must be engaged as much as possible as a part of the helping process in order to create the best working relationships for the social worker, the child, and the parents. Without the support of these "partners," the process of helping parents becomes much more difficult.

Although there is a lack of research into the "legal aspects of the relationships between workers and clients" (Kutchins, 1991, p. 106), these are critical to practitioners in public child welfare. They are important in that they can help us understand the boundary issues that may actually or potentially need to be defended by the social worker, the agency's administrators, or the court as action moves within the child welfare system. A critical piece of practice in public child welfare is establishing and maintaining these fiduciary boundaries.

Centers of "Conflicting Loyalties" or "Multiple Agentry"

These competing forces in child welfare constitute centers of power within the general community and, as part of forming a helping alliance with the social worker and the family, place their own direct or indirect demands on social workers in child welfare. These centers or networks manifest in a variety of ways, including direct contact with social workers and indirect contact through organizational administrators or individuals serving on a variety of teams, committees, or other groups within the child welfare environment. For example, death review teams and multidisciplinary case review teams typically include a wide range of community members.

These centers are best conceptualized as centers of conflicting loyalties for the social worker. These forces competing for the loyalty of the social worker include his or her agency, the juvenile court, the criminal justice system, community groups, the general community, fellow professionals, advocacy groups, and clients, including children, parents, and/or families. These compete around the values they hold with respect to suitable care and treatment of children. In this sense they become an "outside work group" that establishes, with the social worker, through dialogue, the norms that ultimately permeate the court work group. They are part of the dialogic production and reproduction of the social categories of child abuse and neglect and of the categorization of particular clients.

THE NETWORK OF FORCES PROVIDING THE CONTEXT OF CHILD WELFARE PRACTICE

These forces constitute the decision-making context in which a child welfare worker practices. In this view, as soon as a case is assigned, a set of forces metaphorically coalesces to provide the context in which the social worker is expected to practice. *Force* is used here to mean a propensity for a specific type of action. These forces essentially provide direct or indirect pressure on the social workers to act in certain ways, to document their actions for funding and litigation purposes, and to comply with agency and community standards, both explicit and implicit.

These forces provide the context in which the social worker is viewed as the main operator. As the main operator, the social worker's assumed role is to work with the client, that is, the child, the child's parents, and the family network. This involves an implicit, if not explicit, understanding of values and expectations. Of course, these are mitigated by the role of the agency and the court within the community. While these forces are not technically clients within the child welfare system, they are advocates that hold strong value positions and require the social worker to negotiate with them respectfully and ethically.

Five sets of external structures must be incorporated in developing family-centered interventions in the child welfare system. These include the client system, the parents and child, the agency employing the social worker, the juvenile court that makes case by case decisions regarding families and children, and the general community of child welfare advocates and professionals. These are described along with their connection to the social worker in the following list:

Social Group	Center of Loyalty
Client system	Primary fiduciary reciprocity
Agency/administration	As employee, employer "pays the bills"
Juvenile court	As legitimate authority for recommending action
Criminal justice system	As legitimate authority within the community
Community	Interest groups, parent, child, family, etc.; advocates; social worker as public servant

The Client System

The relationship between the social worker and the client, both parents and children, has been discussed extensively in this work. The concern in terms of fiduciary relationships is the need to stay clearly focused on protecting the child and working with the child's family. In doing so, it is also crucial to work respectfully and honestly with the parents. Both are the clients of the social worker.

The Agency: The Administrative Organization

The social worker's employing organization is important because of its charge to administer the child welfare programs. The organization itself has dual and conflicting responsibilities for providing income maintenance and child protection programs. Income maintenance programs involve complex, standardized, and efficient screening and paying systems. These are very task oriented and involve virtually no worker discretion. Alternately, the child welfare system, by nature of its complex, highly value laden, and diverse clientele requires worker discretion in making value-based decisions.

For child welfare social workers within their organizations, the primary effect of this tension is that they become mediators of the administrative pressures for standardization, while being called upon to work with unique and diverse clientele. To do this, workers must realize that the collective tension is ongoing and that the client is caught as much in this process as the social worker is. To survive this tension and be effective in working with clients requires an acceptance of the limits of human knowledge of governance and its concomitant effect on individuals.

Vignette: Priorities

Flora Tightly, the supervisor, interrupted Molly Compassionate as she was talking with an eight-year-old boy, a client for whom Ms. Compassionate was developing a placement. The boy had just been "kicked out" of his foster home where he had lived for two years. The action was done without advance notice being given as required by the foster parent agreement, and Ms. Compassionate had no way of anticipating that it would happen. The boy does not have a place to sleep tonight and is carrying all of his possessions in a black trash bag.

Ms. Tightly handed a copy of a court report to Ms. Compassionate and said, "I have read this report. It needs some changes, which I have written down. The report should have been in yesterday, but if you get it in today I won't write you up."

Criminal Justice System

A second major system of forces that sets up abstracted systems and makes demands on child welfare workers is the criminal justice system. The child welfare worker interfaces with various members of the criminal justice system. In fact, the social worker often functions in a team relationship with police and prosecuting attorneys on some cases they share. This adds a personal element to professional relationships and contributes to a joint dialogic process that helps in informally defining and constructing social deviance within the formal legal definitions in the legal system.

The criminal justice system focuses on the enforcement of criminal laws within the purview of the criminal court, while the child welfare worker seeks to protect children within the context of the juvenile court. Cases that are shared involve a potential violation of criminal statutes through an action or inaction by a parent or caretaker who injures a child. Generally, these involve provable allegations of abuse or neglect.

Although seemingly straightforward, the actions involving the criminal justice system are varied and at times very difficult to work with. Purpura (1997), for example, notes that although the criminal justice system is often portrayed as very organized and acting harmoniously, it is laden with conflict. He notes that

> this reality has led to a conflict model which emphasizes varying degrees of mutual distrust and even hostility among criminal justice agencies. Police often view the courts as being too lenient and corrections as being ineffective. Courts view with suspicion the evidence gathering techniques of police. Corrections agencies blame judges for sentencing practices that cause overcrowding in prisons. Criminal justice agencies are engaged in a never-ending effort to preserve their budgets as they work on their own agendas, compete for scarce resources, and strive to preserve their power. (pp. 4-5)

Although Purpura was describing criminal justice systems conflicts, his analysis differs for the child welfare system only in terms of intensity and is particularly germane as the criminal court impinges on child welfare clients. For example, a social worker may believe that a parent should be home to provide for a child, while the police or prosecuting attorney believe the parent should be in jail. Who wins? No one! The social workers must be able to recognize and be involved to the extent that it furthers their clients' goals within the context of the criminal justice system.

Vignette: When Case Collaboration Breaks Down

Two hours ago, Raphael, a children's protective worker, released a nine-month-old girl to her mother. He completed his investigation and an assessment of the individual and family issues. With the agreement of his supervisor, he determined to release the child and provide family maintenance services to the mother and child. Officer Upset of the Lost City Police Department was distraught with the social worker's release of the child. He was convinced that the mother was a drug user and that he just had not been able to find the evidence. As the mother drove from the shelter, the officer stopped her, searched the car, and placed the child in custody for the second time in two days. The social worker filed a petition with the juvenile court, and the next day the judge determined that the child was safe with the mother and scheduled further hearings.

Juvenile Court

The court work group, with its established formal and informal norms, also provides a force that the social worker must consider while working with clients. The social worker is essentially an agent of the court. However, the social worker is also a gatekeeper for the court. As a gatekeeper, he or she must be able to accurately recognize case situations that demand court attention. The social worker is expected to participate in and enforce the orders of the court. In this sense, the social worker must respond within what Shils (1982) might call the central value system of the court.

Vignette: The Child Protection Culture

Tina, a social worker in children's protective service, is visiting a mother whose daughter is a dependent child of the court. The mother missed her last drug test. In much of the child welfare culture, a missed test is considered a positive test. However, just this morning she heard from a court liaison that the court did not want social workers to automatically take children into custody based on only one missed test. To take a child into custody, more evidence would be required.

Community

The community also provides a point of support and a point of co-operation and pressure for certain kinds of action. The child welfare community must be engaged in an appropriate manner in each plan for family intervention for it to be truly effective. Although each case is different, these community members, sometimes stakeholders, may include the following:

1. A principal who is making her sixth referral in the past month and is very upset that none of these children has been removed from their "terrible families."
2. A multidisciplinary team that reviews cases and has been following this case for five years. They have, on numerous occasions, recommended the children be removed. So far, ten previous social workers have not thought this was in the best interests of the children.
3. A pediatrician, new to the area and highly skilled in sex abuse investigations, believes this child has been abused, while the local expert can find no evidence of sexual abuse.
4. An angry neighbor who states that she has seen the father beating the children every day for the past month.
5. Upset relatives of the mayor of this major city, who list the mayor and all of the council members as character witnesses as to their wonderful capabilities as parents. This is in response to a child abuse report alleging abuse of their five-year-old son.
6. An upset parent involved in a custody dispute with an ex-spouse and who believes the social worker is siding with that spouse.
7. A member of a minority ethnic group who vehemently believes the system is out to get him just because of his ethnic group membership.

Vignette: Putting Together All of the Pieces

The social worker in children's protective services, Debra, has just been assigned an out-of-custody neglect case involving three children. The referral came as the result of a multidisciplinary team staff-

(continued)

(continued)

ing. The case is one that professionals have legitimate concerns about in terms of its slipping through the metaphoric cracks between the service domains of community agencies. Her first efforts on the case are to call for the case records, talk with previous social workers, telephone to other agencies in and out of state, and meet with local community members. This is in preparation for developing an intervention plan.

CONCLUSION

Practitioners in child welfare must be grounded in values and ethical considerations germane to this practice setting, including the need to maintain fiduciary relationships. In particular, they must be sensitive to concepts of self-determination, paternalism, and informed consent. At times adhering to these ethical and values issues can make their jobs, at least in the short term, more difficult because they may find themselves in the position of telling the clients how to oppose their recommendations in court.

Also important is maintaining a fiduciary relationship with clients amidst a vast and complex array of forces. These include the child and family, and also macrolevel forces including members of the community and social institutions. In short they could, on any given case, include the total of Coston, Karger, and Stoesz's (1991) child abuse industry. Each of these, in one way or another, may lay claim to a social worker's attention when working in child welfare on a particular case. Loyalties take the form of an adherence to the values and basic beliefs held by the group of which the child welfare worker is a part. Social workers need to be clear and respectful of the multiplicity of individuals, agencies, and other forces involved with them and with the client system.

Chapter 14

Conclusion

The analysis within this work highlights five perspectives that are important to the child welfare system in the United States. These include the idea that little substantive change has taken place in the overall functioning of the child welfare system since its early beginnings. Also, as much as we might like it to be otherwise, the concept of child abuse and neglect in today's world is a fluid concept, subject to multiple interpretations. The organizations that administer the child welfare programs are largely organized as an assembly line production process. Social work practice in these settings involves an "invisible army" of agency-trained social workers that the social work profession seeks to disavow. Despite the administrative context, child welfare practice as conducted today is essentially practice in a host setting, the legal setting.

CHILD WELFARE AS "CHILD SAVING TWENTY-FIRST-CENTURY STYLE"

From Saving the Cities to Saving the Moral Life of the Community

The American child welfare system in many ways looks like a twenty-first-century version of the child saving movement. Experience in child welfare suggests that we continue to take the children of the poor and minority populations into the child welfare system. It is different today in that the minorities are Black and Hispanic instead of Irish and Italian. It also differs from the early child savers in that their efforts were aimed toward the problem of poverty and social control in urban areas, while today's primary issue is focused on the war on drugs.

Like the early child savers, today's system is effective in removing children, but not in restoring families or returning children. The early child savers were unabashed in their goals of "draining the cities" of the threat to social order. In contrast to the nineteenth-century child savers, today's child welfare system seems to be more involved in what Giddens (1991) might call the "sequestration" of these marginalized children and families. Such a sequestration involves "connected processes of concealment which set apart the routines of ordinary life" (p. 156) for peoples that are different from mainstream populations. This is a kind of collective internalizing of a social problem, which works to minimize the ethical and moral issues involved with the problem as we presumably seek objective solutions to the problem. The child welfare system appears to protect children from parents and caretakers, but it is organized in a way that involves multidimensional forces and values that determine and focus its efforts.

We can understand this better if we look at what happens to the parents of the children taken into the child welfare system. The vast majority of referrals into the child welfare system today relate to the war on drugs. In particular, this war on drugs' reach is particularly deep into minority and poor populations. For the parents of children in the child welfare system, a clear "sequestration" is in process. Small (2001) describes this as "the 'war on drugs' has become the newest tool used to disrupt communities and generate today's slaves, aka prisoners" (p. 896). Not only does this war disrupt communities and generate prisoners, but it does so through what we can see as a clear sequestration process. Here the sequestration involves "connected processes of concealment" (Giddens, 1991, p. 156) that include what has been described by political economist John Flateau as

> metaphorically, the criminal justice pipeline is like a slave ship, transporting human cargo along interstate triangular trade routes from Black and Brown communities; through the middle passage of police precincts, holding pens, detention centers and courtrooms; to downstate jails or upstate prisons; back to communities as unrehabilitated escapees; and back to prison or jail in a vicious recidivist cycle. (Flateau, 1996)

What he does not say, but could say, is that this metaphoric pipeline is visible largely to its travelers, not to the larger society. We collectively talk about problems of social control, and simultaneously we maintain this metaphoric processing system.

Vignette: The Hero: Getting Backpacks for Foster Kids

The news channel managers pick their hero for the month. A teenaged girl led a drive at her high school to raise money so foster kids could have inexpensive backpacks to carry their possessions in. Foster kids, when they leave placements, are well known to pack their belongings in black plastic garbage bags. They don't have the resources to buy a suitcase and these placements are supposed to be only until a permanent placement is found. However, children move from home to home with great regularity. With the fund-raising effort, some of these children will get these backpacks.

Government, through the foster care program, has become, in effect, the institutional parent for these children that rotate through foster, group, and treatment homes. In the past, with the Children's Aid Society child savers, children would be placed in a foster home in the "West." When the children emancipated, they either stayed with the surrogate family, set off on their own course, or returned to their urban roots and their natural family. The modern child that is removed from his or her family travels between multiple placements carrying possessions in black plastic bags and, ultimately, is processed through an independent living program to emancipate at a far younger age than their more affluent counterparts not removed from their families.

Vignette: The Relationship with the Foster Family Is Too Close

Carrie, a children's protective agency social worker, calls Beverly, a foster care agency social worker, about Emma, a two-year-old foster child. She tells her, "Emma has to be moved from the Bowen foster home." Beverly asks, "Why? I just saw her yesterday and everything seemed fine with her and the family." Carrie replies, "She needs to be closer to her father." Emma is in reunification mode and could some day live with her father. Beverly responds, "But he is living in a home-

(continued)

(continued)

less shelter, is not drug testing as he has been mandated, and has a fifteen-year history of substance abuse. Also, Emma is bonding just fine with the Bowens." Carrie replies, "Well, that's the problem. She is getting too attached to that foster family; that's not good for her. Her case is in reunification mode and that means that she shouldn't develop good relationships with anyone besides her family. If you can't find another home, I can find another foster care agency. What do you want to do?"

THE PRODUCTION AND REPRODUCTION OF CHILD ABUSE AND NEGLECT

A second important consideration highlighted in this book is the idea that child abuse and neglect are socially constructed categories. Stated simply, they are not fixed categories in which certain people fit. Although their broadest contours are delimited, the categories are indeterminate and adaptive according to the parties defining them and determining the situations that fit into each. Unfortunately, abuse and neglect are not so easy to define as an illness or other malady caused by some kind of virus. Nonetheless, our researchers work tirelessly to find the cause of this socially defined phenomena. It is socially defined in law and in everyday transactions and dialogue among laypeople and professionals. However, it continues to be different for individuals within the same and or similar jurisdictions. The categories are subjectively determined by what Fleck (1970) might call thought collectives. These categories become part of our abstract social system, our megastructures.

THE INDUSTRIALIZATION OF CPS: TURNING STONES

The organizations that serve as agencies for practitioners in child welfare have become increasingly industrialized. This includes an assembly line operation in which the client moves between social workers providing specialized services. In such an environment, the social worker does not see the result of his or her professional work. All a social worker is organizationally able to see is the completion of his or her assignment. There is no feedback loop for the social worker and no substantive connection with the total service process for the client. The organization, with its time honored view of the need for efficient and standardized operations, demands uniformity and consistency even as it may speak about unique and "diverse" clients. The service delivery systems, that is, the agencies, pursue standardization of the means of serving clients over the effectiveness of their operations.

Similarly, these agencies are organized around a deficits view of human nature, even as they describe their strength- or resiliency-based approach. They must be so organized because the categorized programs that fund them stress the deficits approach to serving clients. The role of the agency is to recognize barriers clients have and provide specific task-focused specialized services to eliminate those barriers. Of course, the assumption is that a simple "task" can work to replace such fundamentals as money for the family (Epstein, 1995). It should not be surprising, in this context, that the means become more important than the ends. Marc Parent (1996) points out that child welfare workers simply and endlessly work to save children from hopeless situations. It is a hamster-like exercise wheel phenomena. The social worker continually moves the wheel in an endless and mindless pursuit of accomplishing "tasks." Over time, this becomes a kind of mind numbing turnstile of action and experience.

The result is clients who are not involved in assessments and service plans. Social workers do assessments and draw up service plans of things that parents are to do. These will often be written at the educational level of a college graduate, even though the clients may not have graduated from high school. The client then must keep track of twenty to thirty tasks he or she is supposed to do, take time away from his or her minimum wage job to attend multiple counseling and training sessions, and meet the social worker as he or she completes his or her own list of required tasks. The effect is alienation of clients and workers.

THE PRACTICE OF SOCIAL WORK: WHO STAFFS CHILD WELFARE?

Traditionally, child welfare has been conceptualized as a subgroup or specialty within the range of settings in which social workers practice. It has been viewed as a setting in which social workers are the dominant profession. In this traditional conception, social workers are viewed as individuals who have a professional degree from an accredited school of social work, a college or university.

The assumption that all social workers in child welfare must have a bachelor or masters degree in social work is not valid in today's world. At least three considerations support expanding our view of just who social workers are in child welfare. First, there are not enough social workers; second, agencies must provide supplemental training to all social work staff; and third, there is great need for interdisciplinary service delivery teams.

Only about 27 percent of the "social workers" and supervisors in child welfare have social work degrees. This figure has remained relatively unchanged for at least the past twenty years. Also, many agencies are turning to other educational programs to meet their needs for social workers. For example, many graduate programs are training human service professionals and family therapists for child welfare work.

The reality of child welfare work is that it is far too complex to be taught exclusively within a university setting. Given the complex requirements of the multiple layers of governance that direct the programs, agency directors must provide training on items specific to practice within the agency and the local community. Thus, no matter the extent to which a college or university focuses on training social workers for child welfare, agency-specific training is still needed. Partnerships between universities and agencies can help to bridge this gap; however, it is simply too broad to be transcended completely. In addition, to distinguish between individuals based on university training is unrealistic given the complexity of the child welfare system. Rather, another category such as "agency trained social workers," is needed. This brings us back to our early roots with agency-based training for some of the first social workers.

Also, given the level of complexity in child welfare coupled with the high staff turnover, it is important to reconceptualize practice as involving multidisciplinary teams. These collaborative entities are generally evolving even now. The next progression would call for a community-based and multidisciplinary approach to child protection services, which is discussed later in this chapter.

CHILD WELFARE AS PRACTICE
IN A "HOST SETTING"

Although child welfare practice is a subgroup within the larger field of social work practice, it is practice in a host setting and, for the most part, is actually practice within a social institutional network. First, the agency that typically employs the social worker is the welfare system. The primary business of this organization is income maintenance. In this sense, the income maintenance system is a "host setting" for social workers.

The income maintenance administrators, as we enter the twenty-first century, often do not hold social work degrees, and the emphasis of their programs is significantly different from that required for the child welfare program. The income maintenance component of the typical child protection agency demands a disproportionately high amount of time and attention from administrators. This side of the organization involves the largest dollar amounts of revenues and expenditures and serves the largest number of clients. In this sense, it continually gains the attention of administrators over the child welfare program. The child welfare program is effectively neglected in these mixed administrative organizations.

Historically, social workers saw themselves deriving sanction for practice from agencies; today's social worker in child welfare derives sanction for practice from the legal system. The brunt of the social worker's authority to intervene in family life is derived from his or her role with the juvenile court. Even when cases are not before the court, social workers must always be cognizant that their authority is derived from the legal system. Any one case scenario can be brought before the court and this impacts his or her performance in the field. In this context, the juvenile court judge makes the major decisions on individual cases. This makes the legal system the primary host setting, albeit a kind of "virtual" setting, for child welfare practice.

Social workers without education or training in basic legal processes may find themselves unable to understand the logical thought processes of attorneys and even judges. This, of course, is a confusion and a lack of understanding that they would have in common with many child welfare clients. This host setting has its own primary mental maps or philosophical assumptions that drive action within the court.

Social workers do not have the power or control over the helping of their clients that either they think they have or community members think they have. Social workers, despite their belief in the efficacy of psychotherapy, are limited in the juvenile court to making recommendations. Beliefs that social workers may hold today that they can fix problems of child abuse are as empty as the 1962 Kennedy-era welfare claims, that "psychoanalytic intervention could 'cure' the problem of motivation and strengthen the family" (Day, 2003, p. 330). In child welfare the judge makes the decisions. Within this setting, the emphasis is on concrete and provable facts, as opposed to ideas embedded in what DeRoos (1990) calls practice wisdom.

Social Workers As Gatekeepers for Juvenile Court

However, and importantly, social workers act as the "eyes and ears" of the court even as they function in a dual role with the agency as employer and the juvenile court as the director of cases. Social workers find themselves cast in the role of gatekeeper as a number of other agencies make referrals for action. These include concerned family members, alternate court systems, the police, and other professionals. Other courts dealing with children and families operate on basic underlying beliefs and philosophy that can be compared and contrasted with the juvenile court.

Problems Within the System's Operation

Although only illustrative, the three models suggest concerns with the numbers of referrals, the handling of the referrals, and the effects of the processes on clients. Of total referrals, most do not enter the court system; only a small percentage do. This suggests that the child welfare system indeed casts a wide net to catch referrals of children. The net result is that the system gets more referrals than it can handle.

The rationalist model provides a model that if adhered to can protect the rights of individuals. However, although the court may hold such promise, the costs are very high and reality is far different. For example, in an adequately staffed jurisdiction, a five-day trial will require preparation and court time for a judge, at minimum four attorneys, one social worker, a stenographer, a bailiff, and other court personnel. Although the trial lasts for five days, the time invested in preparation and evidence gathering drives the cost of the trial much higher. The problem is that court resources are variable within juris-dictions. Some provide extensive protections for children and par-ents, and others provide virtually no representation. In particular, ru-ral areas of the nation have difficulty providing a high level of representation. Courts are highly variable not only in terms of provid-ing due process rights, but also in their interpretations of state codes.

The ritualized process model powerfully shows the process where-by intervention into families is effective. It also highlights the power the adjudication process has and therefore suggests the ill effects of situations in which families are brought through the process based on poor assessments. This is implicit in the analysis. Moreover, it also calls attention to the fact that no one wins in court proceedings. The perpetrator goes to jail, the victim and his or her family are stigma-tized, the family goes through major structural changes, and the state pays the cost for confining the perpetrator and providing services to the victim. No one wins.

The Labyrinth

The child welfare system is a labyrinth that defies easy description by neophyte social workers, clients, and even experienced social work-ers, managers, and attorneys. When child welfare, including the legal system, is examined from a systems perspective, it is an extremely complex environment. It is not a user-friendly system for poor peo-ple, or virtually any peoples. In addition, the child welfare system as a whole is composed of a wide variety of self-interested advocates and providers of services. These constitute a wide range of competitive forces with differing levels of interest in any particular situation. For social workers and clients, the result is a variety of nebulous forces acting in unknown but often stressful ways.

Changes in the System

The child welfare system, viewed on a national level, is a confused, inefficient, and ineffective operation that does not adequately serve children who need protection or families who need help and support. On a national level it could benefit from a decentralizing of its opera-tion. It currently takes in more referrals than it can handle and most of them are closed without any action. This is a needless and senseless intervention into the lives of citizens and residents alike. To address this, the system needs to take in referrals that clearly involve abuse and neglect and, alternately, develop a way to serve children and families that need services.

The court system could be improved by integrating the functions within one body. This is currently being done experimentally in a number of jurisdictions. Costin, Karger, and Stoesz (1996) suggest a regional child protection authority. This makes sense, particularly for some of the more rural areas across the nation. The problem in these jurisdictions is that the numbers of referrals are small, the costs of expertise are high, and individual referrals are handled with little consistency of expertise from the court or even the child protection agency. By combining some of the smaller jurisdictions in creative ways, this detriment could be offset as a regional court and administrative structure are formed.

The agency-based organization of the child welfare system sets up structural phenomena that results in the incapacitating of its personnel. Social workers working within the bureaucratic and confusing structures develop a "trained incapacity" that effectively limits their effectiveness. Some are seemingly forever trapped in the metaphoric "box" of normal or conventional ways of thinking. The system emphasizes a production model that was developed for the manufacturing of products, an assembly line manufacturing system. This is self-defeating in an area in which effectiveness is tied to the "helping relationship" with the client. Transferring cases from station to station may work well in processing cases, but it falls short in building an individual's trust in the system.

Social Constructions

If we truly want to help people, we need to ask what is the best way to address these problems. We typically think of programs to address problems. Thus we identify problems as requiring programs to solve them. I suggest we need to look at the issues from a broader perspective: we need to identify "social problems" and think of ways the "people" can solve them. In an arena such as child welfare, in which the larger community constructs stigmatizing conditions and then labels and impresses these upon individuals, it would behoove us to be sensitive to the ways in which this is done. This is not an individual level phenomena, but rather an "institutional" level issue.

A broader approach to identifying service needs and responding to these needs would be beneficial to people. For example, stating that some people have "problems in living" is much less stigmatizing than saying that they have "abused" or "neglected" their children. Such a broad-based social category combined with federal block grants for local child welfare organizations could lead to more innovations than our current abuse and neglect categories. In particular, if these block grants were to combine categorical programs such as mental health, Temporary Assistance for Needy Families (TANF), substance abuse, child welfare, day care, health care, etc., services could be provided around this very general concept. That small percentage of cases involving the abuse and neglect of children could be referred directly to the court system.

The block grant concept is extremely important in child welfare. Child welfare as a categorical program is too big to administer on the federal level. For example, approaches that set a caseload standard nationally look very different between the job of a "dependency investigator" in a large city in New Mexico and the job of a "continuing social worker" in rural California. The one size fits all strategy does not fit many. Such grants or other alternate funding should be tied to broad outcomes to ensure continuity across the nation.

CHILDREN'S PROTECTION AS TAKING PLACE IN AN INSTITUTIONAL ENVIRONMENT

Whether we like it or not, and whether we agree or not, social work practice in public child welfare is deeply embedded in our multiple social institutions. It is not agency based as it is often perceived. Recognizing this on a practical and behavioral level could result in several shifts, including a shift to a conceptualization of practice as taking place in an institutional environment. This could include a shift from paternalistic practices with a new and stronger emphasis on informed consent as empowering clients. It also could include an increased involvement of families into the intervention process, the use of more community volunteers, elimination of mandatory reporting laws with continued immunity for professionals who report suspected situations of detriment to children, and the decriminalizing of the child abuse system.

Probably the most significant change that would be helpful, and one that Gelles has made and acknowledged that it borders on heresy (Gelles, 1996), is the dropping of the mandatory reporting requirement. In its place should be a voluntary reporting system through which professionals could report family or parent issues, that is, problems in living, directly to a community-based intervention unit. Such a unit could intervene, dependent upon the reported circumstances, by referring cases to a small court services agency or unit of the police. However, simultaneously and independently, they could intervene through the use of volunteers such as a team with child protection professionals, trained to multiple levels of competence, and private nonprofit agency service providers. The reporting center becomes a clearinghouse for not only child abuse or neglect, but also for situations in which individuals and families are experiencing problems in living.

As a unified and community-based system of services, such an organization should be grounded in the community and view the individual and the family as a unit within the larger social system. This could be a community, multilevel wraparound system of care, support, and services. Specht and Courtney (1994) are on the right track when they suggest a renewal of the settlement house concept. In this sense, it should be integrated with similar service intake systems as TANF, probation, health services, mental health, etc. Everyone in some manner or at some time has problems in living.

To counter the negative effects of the industrialization of the service delivery system, an organizational arrangement for these services would probably do better if separated from current categorical programs. New environments would present new problems of conceptualizing practice and these can lead to new client-centered services for which Brueggemann (2002) has so eloquently argued.

The family conferencing system that originated in New Zealand with the Maoris should be expanded in the United States. In this approach, the court, at a strategic part of the proceedings, turns the situation over to the native tribe—the family and other interested persons. This group is then expected to develop a plan to resolve the issues in the child's situation. They meet and develop a plan for the child and the family. Professionals are not typically involved in this process. In the American version of this program, the family conferencing programs, professionals meet with the parties to help in developing plans. These are different from the Indian Child Welfare Act requirements whereby a tribe can take jurisdiction from a court. All family members should be included in a variety of ways as case situations move into and through the child welfare system. We should consider the problems of children and their parents as serious issues. As serious issues, they should involve all other family members in addition to other individuals important to the child/family and even to the community. Family members, not just parents, should be involved in the legal processes that impact their total families.

Social Work Practice Conceptualized As Social Institutional Practice

The most marked consideration that should stand out from this presentation is that the child welfare system is conceptually a social institutional practice environment. Social workers as practitioners work less as "practitioners" within an agency and more as "practitioners" in a highly complex institutional set of arrangements. Costin, Karger, and Stoesz (1991) describe some of these institutional arrangements as the "child abuse industry." By an institutional frame for intervention, sanction for intervening in social problems is derived and expressed at the level of social institutions. The agency as the driving point for intervention does not fit with the complexity of work in child welfare.

This idea of the social institutional context of practice refers to the idea that there is a multiplicity of forces that act upon the practitioner as he or she responds to allegations of abuse and neglect. What is important then is the conceptual incorporation of these forces of pressure within the helping process, and this involves several shifts. This is a shift from a paternalistic practice system in which the social worker as the expert has the answers to the problems within the family, to a model in which the social worker is more of a partner and a leader of the helping process. Such practice could emphasize informed consent as self-determination and thus empower clients.

This process orientation to social work practice as conceptualized in this work represents one major stream of thought that serves as a cornerstone of social work practice. This stream is tied to the early settlement house movement and is similar to the argument presented by Specht and Courtney (1994) and described by Smalley (1967) as being a process-centered approach versus a practice based on a diagnostic or clinical model in which the practitioner conceptualizes practice as the application of a "repertoire of interventive acts" (p. 25).

CRIMINALIZATION

What It Is

The criminalization of abuse and neglect creates another set of forces and issues. These are addressed as part of each chapter as they have been considerations. The issues involved in the criminalization process relate to legal due process rights, the social worker's role in helping clients, and in the effects of the criminalized process.

Due process rights become problematic as potential clients, suspected perpetrator parents, are interviewed in situations in which the ramifications are not made clear to them. They are not typically informed as to the outcome of their involvement with authorities as they talk with the social worker and/or the police. With the sharing of information between child welfare agency workers and the police, discussions between parents and children with social workers become transparent to the criminal justice system.

Since information shared by parents with child protective workers is shared with police and prosecutors, parents are at times admitting legal guilt, while social workers view them as taking psychological "responsibility" for their actions. Social workers see a motivated and willing client; prosecutors see a "suspect" easy to convict. Stated simply, it is a "slam dunk." The parent ultimately serves time on probation or in jail. Depending on the outcome, the family experiences a major economic problem that simply complicates their already difficult problems in living. Pelton (1989) is right about the conflicting dual role of the social worker; however, he does not take it far enough.

What Should We Do?

Along with treating child abuse and neglect seriously, we ought to look at it as an important function of a modern society to provide help and support for children and families experiencing problems in living. We need to decide if we want to help families or send their members to jail. That is, we need to either separate the child welfare system and the criminal justice system or find a way to blend them that treats families more humanely. If we deem certain behaviors as criminal, then the police should handle the criminal justice investigations. If we deem them child welfare related, our broadened and community-based child welfare system should respond to them. It is not reasonable both to tell people we want to help them and then to bring them into the criminal justice system as part of our helping. This point is made more subtly by Pelton (1989) about the interfacing of the social worker's dual role as law enforcer and helper of families. For parents to admit legal "guilt" and have this used against them in criminal court breeds not only distaste and disgust at the child protection system but also plants seeds of distrust. Why should parents trust a social worker when they have experienced this or have known of others that have experienced this trickery?

SUMMARY

Child welfare American style is different than child welfare in other nations. This work locates the American child welfare system within the administrative context of the nation. It began by locating child welfare within a larger paradigm concerned with the well-being of children in general. Child well-being was identified as being an institutional level protection or safeguard for children. As such, it was comprised of rules that were meant to protect children from a variety of factors associated with the market economy. In the United States, probably the best example of such an institutional level safeguard is the child labor laws. These are meant to protect children from the harm they might experience in a market economy that used them as labor.

In the United States and several other developed countries, child welfare has come to be seen in common parlance as children's protective services. This child protection system is focused almost exclusively on protecting children from the actions of their parents/caretakers. This view of child welfare as being child protective services is built on an internationally recognized perception that some children fall in the social categories of child abuse and neglect. These categories are socially constructed categories. The primary point at defining them is the legal system. The legal system establishes a basic elaboration of the contents of each category.

Each referral into the child welfare system goes through a sorting action. The first level sorting involves determining the particular kinds of elements that are involved in the situation. This involves a determination of the kinds of court systems that might be best for the particular child/family. These could include a family, probate, criminal, civil, or juvenile court. The juvenile court, for children, is the most powerful in terms of being able to intervene on behalf of the child's needs for protection.

The legal categories are defined and delineated through social processes that include organizational actions as the manufacturing of the members of each category. This action is illustrated by Swift (1995) in her work on manufacturing bad mothers. In addition to child welfare agencies' involvement in manufacturing the contents of these categories, the court work groups of various domains also are a part of further determining the contents of each category. The action of the court system in manufacturing these categories is one that relies on extracting social events, storing them in case records, and then adjudicating them through petitions.

Through this adjudication process the court, as the environmental context, transforms individual identities into those associated with new social categories. For example, a child may, through this process, move from a social category of "normal child" to the social category of "victim of abuse or neglect." As an incumbent of the social role of "victim" he or she is often entitled to special consideration such as being given priority for counseling or for school placements, etc. The same is true for the perpetrator. After this transformation he or she may be the incumbent of a social role such as "convicted felon," "child molester," etc. These roles become part of each person and include an assorted set of thoughts, feelings, and actions that work to preserve their adherence to these role sets.

Implicit in the idea of the need for university-trained professionals is an assumption that all social workers are autonomous practitioners. That is, only university-trained practitioners can function as private practitioners much as doctors practice medicine. However, what we have seen here is that child welfare practice now is much more complex than at any time in its history. Also, given the relationship basis of effective social work practice, it is only reasonable that new configurations of social workers are used to provide services. In this sense, social workers must be separated from their one-on-one relationship with individual cases and provide services as parts of multidisciplinary teams. Consistency of relationships is critical in working with clients effectively.

References

Alexander, J. C. (1990). *Durkheimian Sociology: Cultural Studies.* New York: Cambridge University Press.

Arendt, H. (1986). *On Revolution.* New York: Pelican Books.

Barker, R. L. and Branson, D. M. (1993). *Forensic Social Work: Legal Aspects of Professional Practice.* Binghamton, NY: The Haworth Press.

Baron, R. (1998). *Essentials of Psychology.* Boston, MA: Allyn and Bacon.

Bauman, Z. (1994). *Intimations of Postmodernity.* New York: Routledge.

Becker, H. S. (1966). *Outsiders: Studies in the Sociology of Deviance.* New York: The Free Press.

Bell, C. (1992). *Ritual Theory, Ritual Practice.* New York: Oxford University Press.

Bellah, R. N. (1985). *Habits of the Heart: Individualism and Commitment in American Life.* Berkeley: University of California Press.

Bender, T. (1978). *Community and Social Change in America.* New Brunswick, NJ: Rutgers University Press.

Berger, P. L. and Luckmann, T. (1967). *The Social Construction of Reality: A Treatise in the Sociology of Knowledge.* New York: Doubleday and Company, Inc.

Berrick, J. D. and Gilbert, N. (1991). *With the Best of Intentions: The Child Sexual Abuse Prevention Movement.* New York: Guilford Press.

Biestek, F. P. (1957). *The Casework Relationship.* Chicago, IL: Loyola University Press.

Black, H. C. (1979). *Black's Law Dictionary.* St. Paul, MN: West Publishing Co.

Boli-Bennett, J. and Meyer, J. (1978). The Ideology of Childhood and the State: Rules Distinguishing Children in National Constitutions, 1870-1970. *American Sociological Review, 43*(December), 797-812.

Brace, C. L. (1973). *The Dangerous Classes of New York.* New York: Wynkoop and Hallenbeck.

Braverman, H. (1974). *Labor and Monopoly Capital: The Degradation of Work in the Twentieth Century.* New York: Monthly Review Press.

Bremmer, R. H. (Ed.) (1970). *Children and Youth in America: A Documentary History.* Cambridge, MA: Harvard University Press.

Brendan, T. P., Gedrich, A. E., Jacoby, S. E., Tardy, M. J., and Tyson, K. B. (1986). Forensic Social Work: Practice and Vision. *Social Casework: The Journal of Contemporary Social Work, 67*(6), 340-350.

Brueggemann, W. G. (1996). *The Practice of Macro Social Work.* Chicago: Nelson-Hall Publishers.

Brueggemann, W. G. (2002). *The Practice of Macro Social Work,* Second Edition. Belmont, CA: Brooks/Cole.

Burke, K. (1984). *Permanence and Change: An Anatomy of Purpose,* Third Edition. Berkeley: University of California Press.

Calhoun, C. (1996). *Social Theory and the Politics of Identity.* Cambridge, MA: Blackwell.

Ceci, S. and Bruck, M. (1993). Suggestibility of the Child Witness: A Historical Review and Synthesis. *Psychological Bulletin, 113*(3), 403-439.

Ceci, S. J. and Bruck, M. (1995). *Jeopardy in the Courtroom: A Scientific Analysis of Children's Testimony.* Washington, DC: American Psychological Association.

Cook, J. D. and Cook, L. (1963). The Lawyer and the Social Worker: Compatible Conflict. *Buffalo Law Review, 12,* 410.

Cornell University Legal Information Institute. (1993). Bill of rights. Available at <www.law.cornell.edu/constitution/constitution.billofrights.html>.

Corrigan, P. (1987). *In/Forming Schooling.* New York: Bergin and Garvey.

Costin, L. B., Karger, H. J., and Stoesz, D. (1996). *The Politics of Child Abuse in America.* New York: Columbia University Press.

Darr, K. (1991). *Ethics in Health Services Management.* Baltimore, MD: Health Professions Press.

Day, P. (2003). *A New History of Social Welfare.* San Francisco: Allyn and Bacon.

Dean, R. G. and Fenby, B. L. (1989). Exploring Epistemologies: Social Work Action As a Reflection of Philosophical Assumptions. *Journal of Social Work Education, winter* (1), 46-54.

Decherd, C. (2001). U.S. Denies Visas to Adopted Children Bought from Parents. *Las Vegas Review-Journal,* November 21, p. 21A.

DeRoos, Y. (1990). The Development of Practice Wisdom Through Human Problem-Solving Processes. *Social Service Review,* (June) 276-287.

Dewey, J. (1954). *The Public and Its Problems.* Chicago: Swallow Press.

Dobelstein, A. W. (2003). *Social Welfare: Policy and Analysis.* Pacific Grove, CA: Thompson/Brooks Cole.

Dolgoff, R., Feldstein, D. and Skolnik, L. (1997). *Understanding Social Welfare,* Fourth Edition. New York: Addison Wesley Longman, Inc.

Douglas, M. (1966). *Purity and Danger: An Analysis of the Concepts of Pollution and Taboo.* New York: Routledge.

Douglas, M. (1986). *How Institutions Think.* New York: Syracuse University Press.

Douglas, M. (1994). Institutions Are the Product. Sixth International Conference on Socio-Economics, Jouy-en-Josas, France.

Downs, S. W., Costin, L. B., and McFadden, E. J. (1996). *Child Welfare and Family Services: Policies and Practice,* Fifth Edition. White Plains, NY: Longman Publishers USA.

Durham, M. L. (1994). Healthcare's greatest challenge: Providing services for people with severe mental illness in managed care. *Behavioral Sciences and the Law, 12,* 331-341.

Early, T. and GlenMaye, L. (2000). Valuing Families: Social Work Practice with Families from a Strengths Perspective. *Social Work, 45*(2), 118-130.

Edelman, M. J. (1967). *The Symbolic Uses of Politics.* Urbana: University of Illinois Press.

Edelman, M. J. (1977). *Political Language: Words That Succeed and Policies That Fail.* New York: Academic Press.

Edelman, M. J. (1988). *Constructing the Political Spectacle.* Chicago: University of Chicago Press.

Edwards, L. P. (1987). The Relationship of Family and Juvenile Courts in Child Abuse Cases. *Santa Clara Law Review, 27*(2), 201-278.

Eliade, M. (1975). *Myth and Reality* (Revised Edition) (Trans. W. R. Trask). San Francisco: Harper and Row.

Emerson, R. M. (1983). Holistic Effects in Social Control Decision Making. *Law and Society Review, 17*, 425-455.

Ephross, P. H. and Vassil, T. V. (1988). *Groups That Work: Structure and Process.* New York: Columbia University Press.

Epstein, W. M. (1995). *The Illusion of Psychotherapy.* New Brunswick: Transaction Publishers.

Farazmand, A. (1999). Globalization and Public Administration. *Public Administration Review, 59*(6), 509-522.

Farrell, R. and Holmes, M. D. (1991). The Social and Cognitive Structure of Legal Decision-Making. *The Sociological Quarterly, 32*(4), 529-542.

Finkelhor, D. (1983). Removing the Child–Prosecuting the Offender in Cases of Sexual Abuse: Evidence from the National Reporting System for Child Abuse and Neglect. *Child Abuse and Neglect, 7*, 195-205.

Flateau, J. (1996). *The Prison Industrial Complex: Race, Crime and Justice in New York.* New York: Medger Evers College Press.

Fleck, L. (1970). *Genesis and Development of a Scientific Fact.* Chicago: University of Chicago Press.

Fogelson, F. (1970). How Social Workers Perceive Lawyers. *Social Casework, 51*(February), 95.

Gadamer, H.-G. (1989). *Truth and Method.* New York: Crossroad.

Galambos, C. (1999). Resolving Ethical Conflicts in a Managed Health Care Environment. *Health and Social Work, 24*(3), 191-1-6.

Garfinkel, H. (1975). The Origins of the Term "Ethnomethodology." In R. Turner (Ed.), *Ethnomethodology* (pp. 13-18). Baltimore, MD: Penguin Books.

Geen, R., Boots, S. W., and Tumlin, K. C. (1999). *The Cost of Protecting Vulnerable Children: Understanding Federal, State, and Local Child Welfare Spending.* Washington, DC: The Urban Institute.

Gelles, R. J. (1996). *The Book of David: How Preserving Families Can Cost Children's Lives.* New York: Basic Books.

Giddens, A. (1990). *The Consequences of Modernity.* Stanford, CA: Stanford University Press.

Giddens, A. (1991). *Modernity and Self-Identity: Self and Society in the Late Modern Age.* Stanford, CA: Stanford University Press.

Gilbert, N. (Ed.) (1997). *Combating Child Abuse: International Perspectives and Trends.* New York: Oxford University Press.

Goffman, E. (1959). *The Presentation of Self in Everyday Life.* New York: Anchor Books, Doubleday.

Goffman, E. (1961). *Asylums.* Garden City, NY: Anchor Books.

Goffman, E. (1963). *Stigma: Notes on the Management of Spoiled Identity.* Englewood Cliffs, NJ: Prentice-Hall, Inc.

Gottfredson, M. and Gottfredson, D. (1988). *Decision Making in Criminal Justice: Toward the Rational Exercise of Discretion,* Second Edition. New York: Plenum Press.

Gunnell, J. (1987). *Political Philosophy and Time.* Chicago: University of Chicago Press.

Gusfield, J. R. (1981). *Drinking, Driving and the Symbolic Order: The Culture of Public Problems.* Chicago: University of Chicago Press.

Gusfield, J. R. (1986). *Symbolic Crusade: Status Politics and the American Temperance Movement.* Urbana: University of Illinois Press.

Hagedorn, J. M. (1995). *Forsaking Our Children: Bureaucracy and Reform in the Child Welfare System.* Chicago: Lakeview Press.

Hall, H. (1984). Was Husserl a Realist or an Idealist? In H. Hall and H. Dreyfus (Eds.), *Husserl, Intentionality and Cognitive Science* (pp. 169-183). Cambridge, MA: MIT Press.

Handler, E. (1976). Social Work and Corrections: Comments on an Uneasy Partnership. *Criminology, 13*(2), 240-250.

Hartman, A. (1990). Many Ways of Knowing. *Social Work,* (January), 3-4.

Hasenfeld, Y. (1985). The Juvenile Court As a People-Processing Organization: A Political Economy. *American Journal of Sociology, 90*(4), 801-824.

Hawes, J. M. (1991). *The Children's Rights Movement: A History of Advocacy and Protection.* Boston: Twayne Publishers.

Hofstede, G. (1980). *Culture's Consequences: International Differences in Work-Related Values.* Newbury Park, CA: Sage Publications.

"Hope for the No-Hopers: Brazil's Street Children." (2000). *The Economist, 357*(8202), 43-44.

Hubner, J. and Wolfson, J. (1996). *Somebody Else's Children: The Courts, the Kids, and the Struggle to Save America's Troubled Families.* New York: Crown Publishers, Inc.

Hummel, R. P. (1982). *The Bureaucratic Experience.* New York: St. Martin's Press.

Imber-Black, E. (1998). *The Secret Life of Families: Truth-Telling, Privacy, and Reconciliation in a Tell-All Society.* New York: Bantam Books.

Inbau, F. E., Reid, J. E., and Buckley, J. P. (1986). *Criminal Interrogation and Confessions.* Baltimore, MD: Williams and Wilkins.

Irvine, J. T. (1994). *Edward Sapir: The Psychology of Culture.* Berlin, NY: Mouton de Gruyter.

Jacobs, M. D. (1986). The End of Liberalism in the Administration of Social Casework. *Administration in Social Work, 18*(May), 7-27.

Johnson, H. W. (1995). *The Social Services: An Introduction.* Itasca, IL: F.E. Peacock Publishers, Inc.

Jung, C. and Kerenyi, C. (1969). *Essays on a Science of Mythology.* Princeton, NJ: Princeton University Press.

Kadushin, A. and Martin, J. (1988). *Child Welfare Services.* New York: Macmillan Publishing Company.

Kaminsky, H. and Cosmano, R. (1990). Mediating Child Welfare Disputes: How to Focus on the Best Interest of the Child. *Mediation Quarterly, 7*(3), 229-235.

Kaplan, A. (1963). *The Conduct of Inquiry: Methodology for Behavioral Science.* New York: Harper and Row.

Karger, H. J., Midgley, J., and Brown, C. B. (2003). *Controversial Issues in Social Policy.* San Francisco: Allyn and Bacon.

Kertzer, D. I. (1988). *Ritual, Politics and Power.* New Haven, CT: Yale University Press.

Khushf, G. (1998). A Radical Rupture in the Paradigm of Modern Medicine: Conflicts of Interest, Fiduciary Obligations, and the Scientific Ideal. *Journal of Medicine and Philosophy, 23*(1), 98-122.

Krisberg, B. (1993). *Reinventing Juvenile Justice.* Newbury Park, CA: Sage Publications.

Kutchins, H. (1991). The Fiduciary Relationship: The Legal Basis for Social Workers' Responsibility to Clients. *Social Work, 36*(2), 106-113.

Kutchins, H. (1998). Does the Fiduciary Relationship Guarantee a Right to Effective Treatment? *Research on Social Work Practice, 8*(5), 615-622.

Lakoff, G. and Johnson, M. (1980). *Metaphors We Live By.* Chicago: University of Chicago Press.

Lanning, K. V. (1989a). *Child Sex Rings: A Behavioral Analysis.* Washington, DC: National Center for Missing and Exploited Children.

Lanning, K. V. (1989b). Satanic, Occult, and Ritualistic Crime: A Law Enforcement Perspective. *Police Chief, 56,* 62-83.

Lau, J. A. (1983). Lawyers vs. Social Workers: Is Cerebral Hemisphericity the Culprit? *Child Welfare, 62*(January-February), 21.

Lefebvre, H. (1968). *The Sociology of Marx.* New York: Random House.

Leung, S. and Vranica, S. (2003). Happy Meals Are No Longer Bringing Smiles at McDonald's. *Wall Street Journal,* March 31, pp. B1-B2, B4.

Lyon, K. (1998). *Witch Hunt: A True Story of Social Hysteria and Abused Justice.* New York: Avon Books.

Mathews, J. T. (1997). Power Shift. *Foreign Affairs, 76*(1), 50-66.

McLoughlin, W. (1980). *Revivals, Awakenings, and Reform.* Chicago: University of Chicago Press.

Merton, R. K. (1957). *Social Theory and Social Structure.* Glencoe, IL: The Free Press.

Meyer, J. and Rowan, B. (1977). Institutionalized Organizations: Formal Structure As Myth and Ceremony. *Journal of Sociology, 83*(2), 340-363.

Mills, C. W. (1959). *The Sociological Imagination.* New York: Oxford University Press.

Mitroff, I. I. (1983). *Stakeholders of the Organizational Mind.* San Francisco: Jossey-Bass.

Mohr, L. B. (1976). Organizations, Decisions, and Courts. *Law and Society,* Summer, 621-642.

Monk, R. (1990). *Ludwig Wittgenstein: The Duty of Genius.* New York: Penguin Books.

Morgan, G. (1996). *Images of Organization.* Newbury Park, CA: Sage Publications.

Morreim, E. H. (1995). *Balancing Act: The New Medical Ethics of Medicine's New Economics.* Washington, DC: Georgetown University Press.

Mueller, E. and Murphy, P. (1965). Communication Problems: Social Workers and Lawyers. *Social Work, 10*(April), 97.

National Association of Social Workers (1996). *Code of Ethics.* Washington, DC: Author.

Netting, F. E., Kettner, P. M., and McMurty, S. L. (1998). *Social Work Macro Practice.* Menlo Park, CA: Longman.

Netting, F. E. and O'Connor, M. K. (2003). *Organization Practice: A Social Worker's Guide to Understanding Human Services.* San Francisco: Allyn and Bacon.

Newland, C. A. (2001). Fanatical Terrorism versus Disciplines of Constitutional Democracy. *Public Administration Review, 61*(6), 643-650.

North, D. C. (1981). *Structure and Change in Economic History.* New York: W. W. Norton and Company, Inc.

North, D. C. (1990). *Institutions, Institutional Change and Economic Performance.* New York: Cambridge University Press.

Novartis Foundation for Sustainable Development (2003). Street Children in Brazil. Available at <www.foundation.novartis.com>.

Parent, M. (1996). *Turning Stones: My Days and Nights with Children at Risk.* New York: Harcourt Brace and Company.

Parsons, T. (1965). *Essays in Sociological Theory.* New York: The Free Press.

Parsons, T. (1968). *The Structure of Social Action.* New York: The Free Press.

Peirce, C. (1955). *Philosophical Writings of Peirce.* Edited by Justus Buchler. New York: Dover Publications.

Pelton, L. (1989). *For Reasons of Poverty: A Critical Analysis of the Public Child Welfare System in the United States.* New York: Praeger.

Pelton, L. H. (1990). Resolving the Crisis in Child Welfare: Simply Expanding the Present System Is Not Enough. *Public Welfare,* Fall, 19-25.

Pelton, L. (1991). Beyond Permanency Planning: Restructuring the Public Child Welfare System. *Social Work, 36*(4): 337-343.

Pelton, L. H. (1997). Child Welfare Policy and Practice: The Myth of Family Preservation. *American Journal of Orthopsychiatry, 67*(4), 545-553.

Pelzer, D. (1997). *The Lost Boy.* Deerfield Beach, FL: Health Communications, Inc.

Pfohl, S. (1977). The "Discovery" of Child Abuse. *Social Problems, 24*(3), 310-323.

Pizzini, S. (1994). The Backlash from the Perspective of a County Child Protective Services Administrator. In J. E. B. Myers (Ed.), *The Backlash: Child Protection Under Fire* (pp. 31-46). Thousand Oaks, CA: Sage Publications, Inc.

Polsky, H. and Claster, D. S. (1968). *The Dynamics of Residential Treatment: A Social System Analysis.* Durham, NC: The University of North Carolina Press.

Poole, D. A. and Lamb, M. E. (1998). *Investigative Interviews of Children.* Washington, DC: American Psychologial Association.

Popple, P. R. and Leighninger, L. (1996). *Social Work, Social Welfare and American Society.* Boston: Allyn and Bacon.

Presthus, R. (1978). *The Organizational Society.* New York: St. Martin's Press.

Purpura, P. P. (1997). *Criminal Justice: An Introduction.* Boston: Butterworth-Heinemann.

Raghavan, S. and Chatterjee, S. (2001). How Your Chocolate May Be Tainted. June 28. Knight Ridder Newspapers. Available at <http://web.realcities.com/content/rc/news/slavery/bayarea/1955535743.htm>.

Ramos, A. G. (1981). *The New Science of Organizations: A Reconceptualization of the Wealth of Nations.* Toronto: University of Toronto Press.

Rank, O. (1932). *Art and Artist.* New York: W.W. Norton and Company, Inc.

Reamer, F. G. (1983). The Concept of Paternalism in Social Work. *Social Service Review,* June, 254-271.

Reber, A. S. (1985). *Dictionary of Psychology.* New York: Penguin Books.

Ritzer, G. (1996). *The McDonaldization of Society: An Investigation into the Changing Character of Contemporary Social Life.* Thousand Oaks, CA: Pine Forge Press.

Robbins, S. P. (1997). Cults. *Encyclopedia of Social Work,* Nineteenth Edition (pp. 667-677). Washington, DC: National Association of Social Workers.

Roberts, P. C. (1999). Commentary: The Abuse of Legal Power. *The Washington Times,* p. A15.

Rogers, C. (Ed.) (1989). Do We Need "A" Reality? *The Carl Rogers Reader.* Boston: Houghton Mifflin Company.

Rohr, J. A. (1986). *To Run a Constitution: The Legitimacy of the Administrative State.* Lawrence, KS: University of Kansas Press.

Rooney, R. H. (1988). Socialization Strategies for Involuntary Clients. *Social Casework: The Journal of Contemporary Social Work,* (March), 131-140.

Rooney, R. H. (1992). *Strategies for Work with Involuntary Clients.* New York: Columbia University Press.

Russel, R. (1988). Role Perceptions of Attorneys and Caseworkers in Child Abuse Cases in Juvenile Court. *Child Welfare, 67*(3), 205-216.

Saari, C. (1991). *The Creation of Meaning in Clinical Social Work.* New York: The Guilford Press.

Saari, C. (1992). The Person-in-Environment Reconsidered: New Theoretical Bridges. *Child and Adolescent Social Work Journal, 9*(3), 205-219.

Sagatun, I. J. and Edwards, L. P. (1995). *Child Abuse and the Legal System.* Chicago: Nelson-Hall Inc.

Saleebey, D. (Ed.) (1997). *The Strengths Perspective in Social Work.* New York: Longman Publishers.

Schein, E. H. (1985). *Organizational Culture and Leadership.* San Francisco: Jossey-Bass.

Schlosser, E. (2001). *Fast Food Nation: The Dark Side of the All-American Meal.* Boston: Houghton Mifflin.

Schon, D. A. (1983). *The Reflective Practitioner: How Professionals Think in Action.* New York: Basic Books, Inc.

Schroeder, L. O. (1995). *The Legal Environment of Social Work* (Revised Edition). Washington, DC: NASW Press.

Schutz, A. (1967). *The Phenomenology of the Social World.* Chicago: Northwestern University Press.

Schwartz, W. (1974). Private Troubles and Public Issues: One Job or Two. In P. E. Weinberger (Ed.), *Perspectives on Social Welfare: An Introductory Anthology.* New York: Macmillan.

Senge, P. M. (1990). *The Fifth Discipline.* New York: Currency Doubleday.

Shils, E. A. (1982). *The Constitution of Society.* Chicago: University of Chicago Press.

Sklair, L. (1991). *A Sociology of the Global System.* Baltimore, MD: The John Hopkins University Press.

Sloan, H. W. (1967). The Relationship of Law and Social Work. *Social Work, 12*(January), 86.

Small, D. (2001). The War on Drugs Is a War on Racial Justice. *Social Research, 68*(3), 896-904.

Smalley, R. (1967). *Theory for Social Work Practice.* New York: Columbia University Press.

Smith, A. (1952). *An Inquiry into the Nature and Causes of the Wealth of Nations.* Chicago: Encyclopaedia Britannica, Inc.

Somers, M. R. and Gibson, G. D. (1996). Reclaiming the Epistemological "Other": Narrative and the Social Constitution of Identity. In C. Calhoun (Ed.), *Social Theory and the Politics of Identity* (pp. 37-99). Cambridge, MA: Blackwell.

Specht, H. and Courtney, M. E. (1994). *Unfaithful Angels: How Social Work Has Abandoned Its Mission.* New York: The Free Press.

Steele, W. W. J. (1972). Understanding the advocacy process. *Social Work, 17,* 108-109.

Stone, D. A. (1988). *Policy Paradox and Political Reason.* Glenview, IL: Scott, Foresman and Company.

Strauch, R. (1989). *The Reality Illusion: How You Make the World You Experience.* Barrytown, NY: Station Hill Press.

Sudnow, D. (1965). Normal Crimes: Sociological Features of the Penal Code in a Public Defenders Office. *Social Problems, 12,* 255-276.

Swift, K. J. (1995). *Manufacturing Bad Mothers.* Toronto: University of Toronto.

Swigert, V. and Farrell, R. (1977). Normal Homicides and the Law. *American Sociological Review, 42*(February), 16-32.

Tanveer, K. (2002). Tribal Justice Under Fire As Teen Is Ordered Gang-Raped. *The Sacramento Bee,* Sacramento, CA, July 4, p. A7. From the Associated Press.

Terkelsen, K. G. (1989). Toward a Theory of the Family Life Cycle. In E. A. Carter and M. McGoldrick (Eds.), *The Family Life Cycle: A Framework for Family Therapy* (pp. 21-52). New York: Gardner Press, Inc.

Thompson, J. D. (1967). *Organizations in Action: Social Science Bases of Administrative Theory.* New York: McGraw-Hill.

Trattner, W. I. (1976). The Federal Government and Social Welfare in Early Nineteenth-Century America. *Social Service Review,* (June), 243-255.

Trattner, W. I. (1994). *From Poor Law to Welfare State: A History of Social Welfare in America,* Fifth Edition. New York: The Free Press.

Trattner, W. I. (1999). *From Poor Law to Welfare Society: A History of Social Welfare in America,* Sixth Edition. New York: The Free Press.

Turner, T. (1977). Transformation, Hierarchy and Transcendence: A Reformulation of Van Gennep's Model of the Structure of Rites Of Passage. In S. F. Moore and B. G. Myerhoff (Eds.), *Secular Ritual* (pp. 53-70). Amsterdam, The Netherlands: Van Gorcum, Assen.

Turner, V. (1969). *The Ritual Process: Structure and Anti-Structure.* Chicago: Aldine Publishing Company.

Turner, V. (1974). *Dramas, Fields and Metaphors.* Ithaca, NY: Cornell University Press.

Turner, V. (1982). *From Ritual to Theater: The Human Seriousness of Play.* New York: PAJ Publication.

U.S. Department of Health and Human Services, Administration on Children, Youth and Families (2000). *Child Maltreatment 1998: Reports from the States to the National Child Abuse and Neglect Data System.* Washington, DC: U.S. Government Printing Office.

Veblen, T. (1977). *The Theory of the Leisure Class.* Edited by M. Lerner. New York: Penguin Books.

von Bertalanffy, L. (1968). *General Systems Theory: Foundations, Development, Applications.* New York: George Braziller.

Waldo, D. (1984). *The Administrative State.* New York: Holmes and Meier Publishers.

Walker, S. (1989). *Sense and Nonsense About Crime: A Policy Guide.* Pacific Grove, CA: Brooks/Cole Pub. Co.

Weber, M. (1978a). *Economy and Society* (Volume 1). Berkeley: University of California Press.

Weber, M. (1978b). *Economy and Society* (Volume 2). Berkeley: University of California Press.

Weil, M. (1982). Research on Issues in Collaboration Between Social Workers and Lawyers. *Social Service Review, 56*(3), 393-405.

West, C. and Zimmerman, D. H. (1991). Doing Gender. In J. Lorber and S. Farrell (Eds.), *The Social Construction of Gender* (pp. 13-37). Newbury Park, CA: Sage Publications, Inc.

White, J. D. (1986). On the Growth of Knowledge in Public Administration. *Public Administration Review, 46*(January/February), 15-24.

Whitmer, G. E. (1983). The Development of Forensic Social Work. *Social Work,* May-June, 217-223.

Wicklund, R. A. (1974). *Freedom and Reactance.* New York: John Wiley and Sons.

Wiehe, V. R. (1996). *Working with Child Abuse and Neglect: A Primer.* Thousand Oaks, CA: Sage Publications.

Wilensky, H. L. and Lebeaux, C. N. (1968). *Industrial Society and Social Welfare* (First Paperback Edition). New York: The Free Press.

Wittgenstein, L. (1966). *Lectures and Conversations on Aesthetics, Psychology and Religious Belief,* edited by C. Barrett. Berkeley: University of California Press.

Wittgenstein, L. (1970). *Zettel,* edited by G. E. M. Anscombe and translated by G. H. von Wright. Berkeley: University of California Press.

Wolff, R. (1997). Germany: A Nonpunitive Model. In N. Gilbert (Ed.), *Combatting Child Abuse: International Perspectives and Trends* (pp. 212-233). New York: Oxford University Press.

Zastrow, C. (2000). *Introduction to Social Work and Social Welfare.* Belmont, CA: Brooks/Cole, Wadsworth Publishing Company.

Index

Page numbers followed by the letter "t" indicate tables; those followed by the letter "f" indicate figures.

Order a copy of this book **with this form or online at:**
http://www.haworthpress.com/store/product.asp?sku=5109

CHILD WELFARE IN THE LEGAL SETTING
A Critical and Interpretive Perspective

_____in hardbound at $49.95 (ISBN: 0-7890-0147-0)

_____in softbound at $24.95 (ISBN: 0-7890-2351-2)

Or order online and use special offer code HEC25 in the shopping cart.

COST OF BOOKS_____

☐ **BILL ME LATER:** (Bill-me option is good on US/Canada/Mexico orders only; not good to jobbers, wholesalers, or subscription agencies.)
☐ Check here if billing address is different from shipping address and attach purchase order and billing address information.

POSTAGE & HANDLING_____
(US: $4.00 for first book & $1.50 for each additional book)
(Outside US: $5.00 for first book & $2.00 for each additional book)

Signature_____

SUBTOTAL_____

☐ **PAYMENT ENCLOSED: $_____**

IN CANADA: ADD 7% GST_____

☐ **PLEASE CHARGE TO MY CREDIT CARD.**

STATE TAX_____
(NJ, NY, OH, MN, CA, IL, IN, & SD residents, add appropriate local sales tax)

☐ Visa ☐ MasterCard ☐ AmEx ☐ Discover
☐ Diner's Club ☐ Eurocard ☐ JCB

Account # _____

FINAL TOTAL_____
(If paying in Canadian funds, convert using the current exchange rate, UNESCO coupons welcome)

Exp. Date_____

Signature_____

Prices in US dollars and subject to change without notice.

NAME_____

INSTITUTION_____

ADDRESS_____

CITY_____

STATE/ZIP_____

COUNTRY_____ COUNTY (NY residents only)_____

TEL_____ FAX_____

E-MAIL_____

May we use your e-mail address for confirmations and other types of information? ☐ Yes ☐ No
We appreciate receiving your e-mail address and fax number. Haworth would like to e-mail or fax special discount offers to you, as a preferred customer. **We will never share, rent, or exchange your e-mail address or fax number.** We regard such actions as an invasion of your privacy.

Order From Your Local Bookstore or Directly From
The Haworth Press, Inc.
10 Alice Street, Binghamton, New York 13904-1580 • USA
TELEPHONE: 1-800-HAWORTH (1-800-429-6784) / Outside US/Canada: (607) 722-5857
FAX: 1-800-895-0582 / Outside US/Canada: (607) 771-0012
E-mailto: orders@haworthpress.com

For orders outside US and Canada, you may wish to order through your local sales representative, distributor, or bookseller.
For information, see http://haworthpress.com/distributors

(Discounts are available for individual orders in US and Canada only, not booksellers/distributors.)
PLEASE PHOTOCOPY THIS FORM FOR YOUR PERSONAL USE.
http://www.HaworthPress.com

BOF04

DATE DUE